ON THE BLOODY ROAD TO
JESUS

Christ as an Apache. This painting hangs over the altar at St. Joseph's Mission on the Mescalero Apache Reservation, New Mexico.

ON THE BLOODY ROAD TO

JESUS

Christianity and the Chiricahua Apaches

H. HENRIETTA STOCKEL

UNIVERSITY OF NEW MEXICO PRESS | ALBUQUERQUE

© 2004 by the University of New Mexico Press
All rights reserved. Published 2004
10 09 08 07 06 05 04   1 2 3 4 5

Library of Congress Cataloging-in-Publication Data

Stockel, H. Henrietta, 1938–
On the bloody road to Jesus : Christianity and the Chiricahua
Apaches / H. Henrietta Stockel.— 1st ed.
    p.   cm.
Includes bibliographical references and index.
ISBN 0-8263-3208-0 (cloth : alk. paper)
    1. Chiricahua Indians—Missions.
    2. Chiricahua Indians—Religion.
    3. Chiricahua Indians—Rites and ceremonies.
    4. Indians, Treatment of—Mexico, North—History.
    5. Indians, Treatment of—United States—History.
    6. Jesuits—Missions—Mexico, North—History.
    7. Franciscans—Missions—Mexico, North—History.
    8. Protestant churches—Missions—Oklahoma—History.
    9. Christianity and culture—Mexico, North—History.
    10. Christianity and culture—United States—History.
    I. Title.
E99.C68 S86 2004
277.89'08'08997256—dc22
                                                    2003018563

Printed and bound in the U.S.A. by Edwards Brothers.
Typeset in Janson 11/14. Display type set in Serlio.
Design and composition: Robyn Mundy.
Production: Maya Allen-Gallegos.

To Louise d'Avignon Fairchild—
for everything through the years

They have assumed the names and gestures of their enemies, but have held on to their own secret souls; and in this there is a resistance and an overcoming, a long outwaiting.

N. SCOTT MOMADAY | HOUSE MADE OF DAWN

CONTENTS

ACKNOWLEDGMENTS

During the ten years this book has been on my mind, many people have heard about it and have offered helpful suggestions. I have always been thankful for their help, but a few deserve special recognition.

Charles J. Polzer, S.J., historian extraordinaire, discussed with me the activities of the Jesuits on the Spanish colonial frontier. His books and our conversations became indispensable to my research efforts. He was most congenial and supportive and opened his office files to me at the Documentary Relations of the Southwest, in the Arizona State Museum on the campus of the University of Arizona in Tucson.

Kieran McCarty, O.F.M., discussed with me the activities of the Franciscans on the Spanish colonial frontier. His books and our conversations too were absolutely necessary for my research. Father Kieran and I developed a habit of weekly interviews during which we met in his library across the courtyard from the friary at San Xavier del Bac until our sessions ended abruptly due to his illness.

Well-known author William B. Griffen volunteered to let me see the typescript of his respected work, *Apaches at War and Peace: The Janos Presidio, 1750–1858*. I am honored by his support.

A close friend, Sally Dammery, communicated regularly with me via e-mail from her home in Melbourne, Australia. I am grateful to her for introducing me to Tzvetan Todorov and European authors whose works are relevant to my topic but not well known in America. Todorov has influenced me, but Sally has guided me and influenced me more. For her, my special thanks.

Good friends in Albuquerque know who they are, but in case they forgot—thanks especially to Jane Cotter, Erika Love, and Cecile Quintal for listening and commenting through the years.

The Dietz family—Chris, Tami, and Bill—have shown true friendship in many ways, and I deeply appreciate their presence in my life.

John and Steffi Rose courted, were married, and gave birth while this book was in process. John and I share many interests about western history and get together frequently to pursue them.

Madeleine and Jack Smith periodically took me away from undivided attention to the manuscript, and their interruptions were most welcome, especially the weekend camping trip in September 2002 in Cochise's Stronghold.

A colleague, John Turcheneske, Jr., Ph.D., has been most generous in sharing information, his collection of photos, and his editing skills.

The late Eve Ball, Dan Thrapp, Mildred Cleghorn, and Ruey Darrow continue to inspire me.

Lorrie, Erika, Erik, Rachel, Justin, and Selah will someday know what was in my heart—besides them, of course.

A little white girl—Deshina—with blue eyes, brown-red spaghetti curls, and a white eyelet dress—played in the dirt in Cochise's camp until the soldiers came, long, long ago. Inseparable from her best friend, the Too-is-gah daughter, they remain that way today.

To the Chiricahua Apaches, whom I admire so much, thank you for letting me participate in your rich culture. I hope this book sheds some light on the events your ancestors encountered as they struggled so admirably and desperately to protect the responsibilities given to them by the Creator.

I tip my hat and curtsy deeply to Louise d'A. Fairchild. She has made it possible for me to devote time and energy toward my lifelong passion for the history of the Chiricahua Apaches. I am forever grateful.

AUTHOR'S NOTE

In November 1987 a major event in American Indian history took place in Seattle, Washington. A Lummi Indian, Jewell Praying Wolf James, read in public a document produced and endorsed by several local churches, all members of the Church Council of Greater Seattle. The declaration, now known as the "Bishop's Apology," asked forgiveness for the centuries-old destruction of traditional Indian ceremonies and for not assisting the Indian peoples when they were victimized by the churches acting in concert with the U.S. government. The statement, long overdue, reflected good intentions but could never undo the terrible cultural destruction imposed on Indian tribes in the name of God and country—an excellent example of blasphemy.

Christianity in colonial northern Mexico, one of the primary locations described in this book, was aided and abetted in its zeal to indoctrinate the indigenous peoples—in this case specifically the Chiricahua Apaches—into Catholicism by support first from the Spanish Empire and later from the newly independent Mexican government. Not to be outdone, from the late 1800s until 1914, successive American political administrations, having learned nothing from two centuries of failure in Mexico, entered the effort, but Protestantism was their religion of choice.

Euro-Americans strongly believed that the path to civilization for the Indians was through acceptance of Christianity and participation in its rituals. And it was most important to "civilize" the Indians, ostensibly in order to save their souls. However, one of the primary benefits of indoctrination into Christianity on the

Spanish colonial frontier was to create tax-paying citizens who would contribute—literally and figuratively—to the expansion of empire. When the United States inherited the Chiricahua Apaches from Mexico in 1848, the economic motive also loomed large; that is, their southwest homelands had to be made safe for American settlement and economic growth.

However, the Chiricahua Apaches, who had, for the most part, resisted indoctrination into Catholicism under Spanish and Mexican colonization, were a different people in the mid-1800s than they had been generations earlier. Their culture now contained adaptations that had helped them survive contact with Europeans. They were aware of how to please the outsiders' churchmen, military personnel, and political officials, all the while hiding in their hearts their beloved traditions, especially those rooted in the ancestral religion, to protect them from forced extinction. And that is one of the currents flowing through this book—a theory about cherishing beliefs so significant that all the power of empire and America could not extinguish the flame. In my opinion, the Chiricahua Apaches have never completely surrendered their traditional religion to Christianity, but they have incorporated specific dogmas that modify their ancestors' ways. It wasn't difficult, for a brief comparison of the prehistoric religion with Christianity offers tantalizing clues that may be the result of an influence from a much earlier association with Catholicism:

A major deity called *Ussen*—a corruption of the Latin word *De-us*.[1]
Ussen and Moses leading the people to a new homeland.
Lesser female deities—White Painted Woman[2] and the Virgin Mary.
Impregnation by nonmale, nonhuman sources—White Painted Woman by
    rain and lightning and the Virgin Mary by the Holy Spirit.
Sons who became saviors—Child-of-the-Water and Jesus.
The medicine cord—similar in structure to a rosary.
The puberty ceremony—a rite of passage similar to holy communion.
A great flood—told of both in Apache folklore and biblically.[3]
Snakes—evildoers in Apache folklore and the Garden of Eden.
Holy water—a vehicle of blessing as is *hoddentin*, a product of the tule.
Baptism—similar to a medicine woman's blessing of a newborn.
Afterlife—a concept of eternality present in both religions.

If the noted similarities are indeed very old adaptations to Christianity, a mystery has been created as to when and where ancestral contact with Christians occurred—an enigma that may remain forever protected behind a veil of time. Still, a history of religious syncretism would not be unusual within a dynamic community of people, such as the Chiricahua Apaches, whose culture has been characterized through time by adaptation, ethnogenesis, reinvention, varying degrees of interaction with other cultures, and cultural fluidity.

Clifford Coppersmith identifies the Apaches as one of the "Athapaskan groups descended from one of the more recent migrations across the Bering Strait. . . . Of these ancient travelers the intrepid Apachean peoples of the American Southwest . . . were the most far-flung. Linguists trace the separation of the Southern Athapaskan speakers [the Chiricahua Apaches] back to about A.D. 1000. . . . Scant evidence exists that can more completely define the paths and timing of these ever southerly migrations as these hunter-gatherers left little behind to mark their passage."[4]

This conclusion is probably not the whole story, however, as adaptations to the language were likely made as these ancestors came into contact with other peoples and adjusted. However, even if more definitive information were discovered and made available by scholars and historians, would it be sufficient to determine the one primary motive that caused the people to leave their arctic homelands and travel, over generations, southward until their Creator told them to stop? Probably not, according to Indian authors Clara Sue Kidwell, Homer Noley, and George Tinker, who recognize that "to begin to get at the complexity of Indian thought may require acknowledging that Western categories do not work for identifying, describing, naming, or explaining Indian religious realities."[5] They are certainly correct, and thus my conclusion above about the likenesses of both religions may be invalid, as then are most of the analyses and interpretations of Indian cultures compiled to date by non-Indian researchers, scholars, and historians—a daunting thought.

Setting that possibility aside for now, the Chiricahua Apaches' experience with Christianity is the focus of this book. But other components are addressed as well, for the historical Chiricahuas' spirituality entered every aspect of their lives. That is, the people perceived the sacred in all things and filled each moment with an awareness of the supernatural and respect for its powers, believing themselves to be in a personal relationship with the Creator and the cosmos. Always wary of strangers, the Chiricahua Apaches jealously guarded their religion from outsiders' eyes, as they today protect many aspects of their legacy of religious acculturation. Summing it up, the late Asa Daklugie, a highly respected leader in the middle of the twentieth century, told author Eve Ball, "My people have never liked to talk about our religion . . . because it is the only thing we possess of which the whites have not robbed us. . . . We preserve it for ourselves and our children."[6]

I share Daklugie's concerns, not only about the theft of his people's religion but, as an extension of that worry, about parts of the entire Chiricahua Apache experience being misinterpreted and thus misrepresented as they have been in many cases through the images projected on them by writers and filmmakers. Evaluation and explanation by well-meaning professional academics, after all, only perpetuates colonialism with a degree or more of credibility and really just adds outsiders' views to a unique cultural heritage that currently contains strategies developed by the Apaches to maintain tradition, culture, language, and religious rituals. So, I urge the Chiricahua Apaches to write their history as they perceive it, but until that happens, books like this one must be relied upon to describe their rich religious birthright and its inevitable collision with Christianity.

H. Henrietta Stockel
Hereford, Arizona
Apacheria

PREFACE

Words evoke images, and one of the most colorful words, *frontier*, brings to mind adventures and adventurers, challenges, opportunities, and even a "meeting point between savagery and civilization."[1] When the Spanish colonists, including the religious men, reached the end of their journey to northern Mexico in the 1600s, they were on the farthest edge of the Spanish Empire in the Americas, a "frontier" in every sense of the word. That the newcomers felt superior to the resident natives they encountered is obvious from historical accounts, but no doubt the Indians had a different interpretation.

Naming is an excellent example of Eurocentrism—the notion of cultural supremacy that characterized most colonizers in northern Mexico. According to Kidwell, Noley, and Tinker, the power to name and categorize all things constituted the "ultimate sense of domination over the environment,"[2] human beings included. For example, Father Kieran McCarty, O.F.M., a Franciscan priest/historian/author, explained, "When a Spanish expedition crossed Arizona in about 1550, they met some native women washing at a stream. The Spaniards spoke to them, asking who they were and they answered *'pianmatt'* [phonetically pronounced peem-ahtch], which means 'I don't understand.' So the Spanish called them Pimas"[3] and named their destination the *Pimeria Alta*.

Naming proceeded apace, especially with natives receiving European names. From the Indian perspective, the outsiders exhibited impressive daring and courage by eradicating names that had been theirs since the beginning of time and were, in many cases, considered sacred. Thus, through changing names and applying strange European labels, the Spaniards assumed a larger-than-life stature to the preliterate peoples, commanded the indigenes' awe and respect, and gave the impression that they were protected by their own deity. At the very least, naming wrapped them in an aura of mystery and authority so that they could capitalize on in their efforts to indoctrinate.

Today the popular subject of naming concerns how contemporary Indian peoples wish to be generally known—as Native Americans, as American Indians, or by other names.[4] When consensus is reached, it will no doubt satisfy some and displease others. And so it is with my selection of words in this book.

I have deliberately chosen to use the terms *indigenes, indigenous, Indian,* and *native* instead of the other label in current usage, Native American. In any case, all of these umbrella terms "homogenize one of the most linguistically and culturally plural areas the world has ever known," according to Nancy Shoemaker.[5]

As is clear, I disagree with those who state that use of the noun *Indian* is confusing and may refer to the people who live on the subcontinent of India. This point of view is invalid, simply because context matters. If I am discussing the Chiricahua Apaches, no one reading or listening to me would ever confuse my references with residents of Bombay. Also, I have been scolded for calling the Indians "natives," which evoked the image of Africans in one critic. This individual was unaware that many respected authors use the term "native" when referring to the first Americans without objection. And so will I, but it will be interchangeable with other references in a manner that causes no confusion of terms.

My use of *culture* is widespread and should be understood to mean the cumulative experiences of a people that are transmitted, verbally and by example, to subsequent generations. As such, a culture is alive and active, always adding or deleting, adapting, adopting, accommodating, incorporating, resisting, rejecting; culture is a moving target for change.

In previous writings I have always used the terms *Chiricahua Apaches* and *Apaches* synonymously. I will again. While I acknowledge and have regard for the other major Apache groups, consistent use of the full designation *Chiricahua Apaches* became cumbersome to me, and I thought readers would have the same reaction. Whenever the other Apache groups are cited in this book, I refer to them by their proper full names, so readers may trust that the single word *Apache* always means *Chiricahua Apaches.*

I follow noted anthropologist Morris Opler's lead in identifying the four bands of the nineteenth-century Chiricahua Apaches. The easternmost group was known variously as the Mimbres, Coppermine, Warm Springs, Mogollons, and Gilas. The southern Chiricahuas were called the Janeros, Carrizaleños, Pinery Apaches, and Nednhis. The Bedonkohes were the smallest in number and merged with another band in the 1860s. Cochise's band was designated as the Central Chiricahuas. In early years there was no Chiricahua Apache tribe that was united by a centralized political framework. In time, other Apache groups' losses due to disease and warfare reduced their populations, and consolidation occurred for protection and, not incidentally, reproduction. In 1886, at the time of their final surrender, the combined Chiricahua Apaches numbered more than five hundred men, women, and children.

Throughout their history as a free people, the Apaches were primarily hunter-gatherers with a well-developed raiding complex that became refined in the seventeenth or eighteenth century and continued on until Geronimo's capitulation in September 1886. In the eighteenth and nineteenth centuries, as most of the Chiricahuas fought to maintain their way of life, legends grew about their prowess and incomparable ability to resist the newcomers' forced changes. Many of the myths glorified battles and ignored the fact that the Apaches were also human beings who loved, laughed, wept, gave birth, hunted, cooked, sewed, bled, were hungry and sick, healthy and satisfied. Importantly, they were a proud and strong people who passed on a rich, complex cultural heritage to their descendants.

In discussing the religious segment of their lifeways, I will seldom use the term *convert* or its derivatives, but when I do, the words will either be placed within quotation marks or will be direct quotes from sources. I have a good reason. On the colonial frontier there was no exact way of determining an individual's honest acceptance of Christianity—no yardstick with uniform, standard benchmarks, for example, or criteria that measured how far along a specific Indian was toward a fully informed understanding of Christianity prior to the total acceptance of its principles and practices. In other words, determining someone's progress along the road to Christianity, that is, "conversion," was subjective and varied from missionary to missionary in terms of evaluation and from mission to mission. Consequently, in bringing to life the Chiricahua Apaches' individual and tribal relationships with Christianity and its agents, I prefer the word *indoctrination*, which is synonymous with *instructing*, in the sense of *teaching*.

The distinction between *conversion* and *indoctrination* serves to illustrate the fact that many Chiricahuas who voluntarily lived at the missions, or were captives there, had incorporated certain Christian tenets. In spite of appearances, gradations of beliefs in Christianity among many of the mission Indians flew in the face of the priests' often glossy reports of success in convincing the Indians to accept Jesus as their savior and become Christians in thought, word, and deed. Or, according to Kidwell, Noley, and Tinker, "Any two cultures which live side by side will develop some intimacy that results in borrowing . . . from each other . . . especially where one culture is dominated by the other. The continuity of [traditional religious] practice is, however, greater than has generally been conceded by scholars."[6]

Deculturation was the colonial frontier priests' intent—erasing culture and replacing most, if not all, of it with the colonizers' culture.[7] In that regard, it was clearly in the best interests of the Europeans to keep members of the northern Mexico tribes alive and in a contained mission setting in order to continue to proselytize, indoctrinate, and acculturate them—a goal that must have frequently been seen as elusive, given the devastating and deadly impact of warfare, slavery, deportation, and European diseases on the native population. With the power and authority of the Spanish Empire behind them, it is not difficult to imagine that the missionaries believed that all native religio-cultural customs could be replaced by a set of European values. Occasionally, it could have appeared to individual Jesuits and Franciscans that they were incorrect, but, nonetheless, maintaining the unbalanced power equation through deculturation was absolutely necessary if they were to fulfill their religious and secular obligations—creating tax-paying citizens of the Christian Indians.

Other frequently used expressions also merit brief explanations. *Accommodation/resistance* as concerns the Indians' contact with other cultures is self-evident. *Syncretism* means the blending of dissimilar symbols, acts, and beliefs to produce a new form. From the missionaries' perspective, syncretism probably was a contamination of the universal truth as they saw, acknowledged, and represented it, but from the Indian point of view, along with being a form of cultural change, syncretism was often more similar to accommodation than to acculturation and assimilation. The twin terms *acculturation* and *assimilation* are used in their sociological sense, that is, the process of and ultimate merging of cultural traits from previously distinct cultural groups. Readers may consider the two terms to be synonymous as they are used in the book, although my learned Australian friend and colleague Sally Dammery insists that indigenous peoples were "integrated" rather than "assimilated" in the surrounding dominant cultures. She believes that through assimilation, all traces of the original culture are lost, whereas integration permits selected characteristics to remain. Similarly, she contends that oral history is not really "history" in the purist sense of the word but is really "testimony."

Be that as it may, while the Chiricahua Apaches adopted social aspects of the Spanish culture that enhanced their own lifeways, such as acquiring horses and learning to speak Spanish, in many instances adaptation supplemented and modified rather than supplanted their religious customs. The word *worship*, which is a deliberate description, appears frequently, but readers should know that Indian writers Kidwell, Noley, and Tinker object to the word because it implies "praise," which is missing in many Indian religious ceremonies. Kidwell asserts that because Indian people see themselves as "participating in an ongoing relationship with the spirits, praise is inappropriate because it implies a sense of individual ego that does not exist in Native beliefs."[8] It is difficult to know exactly what Kidwell means about the "sense of individual ego," but I interpret it as meaning that natives assume a humble position that precludes praising the spirits; to praise would assume an equal status.

It is most important for readers to keep in mind the times in which the events written about happened. Initially, it was a moment in world history when the greatness of the Spanish Empire was supreme, when Indians were looked upon as pagans in need of spiritual redemption, and when the religious men of the Jesuit and Franciscan orders, and other dedicated men and women, risked their lives every day to carry the Word of God. The colonial frontier priests were totally committed and dedicated, a situation guaranteed to cause conflict with the Chiricahua Apaches, who were equally pious in their ancestral religious beliefs and understood without question that Ussen and spiritual forces had placed them in a particular place with a responsibility for the area and a filial obligation to their friends and relatives who also lived there. In fairness, one must try to understand and appreciate both perspectives.

Later, when the Apaches were exposed to American Protestantism, a similar tolerant comprehension is needed. As prisoners of war at Fort Sill, Oklahoma, the Apaches encountered a concentrated number of determined Dutch Reformed Church missionaries and workers. Confined to a military reserve and physically unable to flee indoctrination at that time, they experienced a religious event so unique and so personally significant that it changed their lives forever.

A caveat: Kidwell and her colleagues believe that "American Indian peoples are being co-opted into a cultural frame of reference that necessitates . . . assimilation to the language and social structures of the conqueror."[9] I agree, but until the dream of an appropriate language is realized, I have no choice but to write in the words of the colonizer.

INTRODUCTION

The first Spaniard to step into northern Mexico in the mid-1500s probably was Álvar Núñez Cabeza de Vaca, a sailor who, with three companions, survived a shipwreck off the coast of Texas. The four men walked westward for years until they met colleagues on Mexico's west coast. In his later writings Cabeza de Vaca did not specifically identify by name the many Indian groups he encountered, but it is likely the Chiricahua Apaches were living somewhere along his route.[1]

Having left a region just below the Arctic Circle, probably in the 1400s, the Apaches' migratory route southward stopped in northern Mexico, which then included southeastern Arizona. Puzzling to many researchers, historians, and anthropologists is why the trek ended there. The Apaches don't find this bewildering at all. From a statement made by Cochise—"I came here because God told me to do so"[2]—to a remark about the land by contemporary leader Berle Kanseah—"It's ours, and it's sacred, and it's how we were intended to be, placed here in the Southwest"[3]—the cause is clear. The Creator, Ussen,[4] selected the site that would become the Apaches' new homelands and through this process spiritually and physically anchored the people and their culture in the high desert hills, mountains, valleys, rivers, trees, and stones of northern Mexico. The land and the entire environment thus became sacred to the Apaches as the manifestation of Ussen's wishes, omniscience, and omnipresence.

The dramatic change in physical location from the arctic tundra to the desert necessitated an overarching cultural shift that, in turn, demanded adaptation. For example, caribou meat, previously a main staple, didn't exist in northern Mexico, where venison and other wild game abounded. Introducing a new meat source would have initially caused physiological consequences, so a pharmacological formulary of desert plants to treat various ailments had to be developed, as did a discriminating menu consisting also of unfamiliar edible vegetation. Clothing too had to be changed. Heavy hides were no longer needed; the lighter skins of desert-dwelling animals had to be gently tanned and sewn with sinew from an animal or a cactus. Apache women built cooling shelters out of branches and boughs, and they studied which natural plant products were useful, such as aloe vera, in protecting everyone from the blazing desert sun. Significantly, complex ways of relating to their Indian neighbors, most of whom were sedentary farmers, had to be created through trial and error.

These changeovers, especially coexistence with other tribes, constituted a fluid pattern of continuing cultural reinvention through adaptation that ensured the group's comfort and security in its newest surroundings. But when the Europeans appeared, especially the religious men, no longer were the Chiricahuas willing to accommodate another's presence. No longer were they tolerant of another's religion. No longer were they able to live at peace with these neighbors; they now preferred raiding and fighting. What had happened? Despite certain similarities, the religious threat posed by the Europeans in the form of *forceful* substitution of the culturally strange and alienating concepts of Christianity for the sacred Apache religious heritage presented a menace they had never before experienced. Force, as exercised by the newcomers, was a concept alien to the Apache culture of old, in which agreement and acquiescence were voluntary. Additionally, the religious beliefs developed by the revered ancients, and modified through the ages when appropriate, had been most satisfactory and had provided meaning and support for generations. Now the outsiders insisted that the people observe a new set of symbols and that their religion must replace ancestral spirituality. To the Apaches, the entire situation was ominous, particularly since the whole of life to them was a religious act that continued from the distant past to the present.

Without exception, Apache religio-cultural customs and daily routines had tautly held the tribe together for millennia, from the day when White Painted Woman gave birth to Child-of-the-Water[5] down through their rich history to the journey's end. As only one example, preparing food was

Fig. 1. Apache wickiup (traditional dwelling). Postcard photo, n.d.

a religious act during which the women gave thanks to the Creator for the animal, for the hunter and his skill, for the hunter's safe journey to and from the killing ground, for the fire and wood necessary to cook the meat, for the woman's skill in butchering, for the nourishment the animal provided to her husband, children, and herself, for the dogs who would eat the leavings and become strong enough to serve as pack animals, for the family's health, and for her community of relatives and friends who would directly and indirectly benefit from the family's well-being. Individuals and families were seen culturally as part of the whole. Each member of the group was important to the smooth functioning of the entire tribe; conversely, when one member failed, the impact was felt among all.[6]

Tolerance of other ways of worship had also been a proud trait of Chiricahua society because other tribes' religions were understood as having been given to them by the Creator with deliberate instructions that would not meet another tribe's needs. "One group sees no need to convert another to its religious system," wrote Jace Weaver,[7] a view quite different from that held by the Jesuit, Franciscan, and Dutch Reformed missionaries, whose goal was "to remove the Indian person from . . . the tribal group in order to associate him or her with the artificial community of Christ," according to Kidwell, Noley, and Tinker.[8] To understand the new situation, the people looked to long-standing cultural customs.

Unfortunately, although ancient tribal memories had provided solutions to most problems, no actual remedies existed to counter this perceived religious peril. Compounding the situation, the strangers had brought wine, horses, mules, cattle, and other livestock—providing easy access to liquor, food, and transportation—and so certain tribal members were seduced into believing that accepting the Spaniards' religion was bearable in light of these and other benefits. And so, for the first time in memory, cultural allegiances began to weaken.

As time went on, more and more Chiricahuas succumbed to the benefits of friendship with the Spaniards. Many moved into the missions and quickly recognized that taking advantage of what was offered only required simple trade-offs that they could easily manage—labor, learning, and listening to what the outsiders called "the Word of God." For some, acquiescence to the European ways was "merely an outward appearance . . . a parallel universe. . . . The outward commitment allows for a layer of protection for traditional cultural values and the ceremonial forms that accompany those values."[9] Others were quite sincere and saw only a little difference between the ancestral religion and Catholicism.

However, when life at the missions became intolerable, many freedom-loving Apaches walked away and returned to their groups with the skills they had acquired. A few had become semiliterate in the Spanish language, and that ability helped their group during trade negotiations with friendly ranchers and settlers. Other returnees brought back valuable information such as future dates when several supply caravans were due. Profitable raids could then be planned.

Some of the homeward-bound Chiricahuas had tales to tell about the Jesuits and Franciscans, whose actions were worrisome in that they reflected one or more of the traits identified by the ancestral culture as defining witches. But a few Apaches believed differently—that the priests' attire indicated a closeness to the bearded, dark men's God and that their association with these men could possibly give them access to the Spaniards' power. Several others may also have concluded that the missionaries were like medicine men in that they dressed in ceremonial clothing when conducting rituals.[10] It may be said that individual reactions to the newcomers varied so widely that they created a situation in Chiricahua Apache cultural history when consensus could not be reached, further evidence of a cultural shift.

Returnees told about having seen babies from other tribes blessed by the priests with water from the streams made sacred with their prayers. Nothing wrong with that, they said, for it was like what the medicine woman did during the Apache newborns' ceremonies,[11] but the difference was that now many infants who had felt the water had sickened and died. It is reasonable to suspect that the Apaches could have connected the deaths to ceremonial holy water, especially since dozens of roaming livestock freely deposited urine and excrement everywhere, including in the watercourses.[12] Tribal knowledge gained through experience had created a strict code of behavior regarding personal habits. For example, when encamped for a length of time at a certain place, the Chiricahuas relied on a medicine woman to identify distant locations to be used for human waste disposal. Far from camp and the water supply, when those areas became unhealthy, the medicine woman either recommended that the group move on, or she located other sites.[13] In the more restrictive mission setting, the same freedom to avoid contaminated locations could not be practiced, and while the Apaches surely were revolted by what they had to endure, the circumstances made for vivid gossip and storytelling.

The missions were one of three institutions that characterized northern Mexico in the seventeenth, eighteenth, and nineteenth centuries, the other two being presidios and civilian settlements.[14] All three were expected to work together harmoniously to civilize, Hispanicize, and Christianize the Indians. David Weber concludes, "The Spanish struggle to control the New World and its peoples became . . . a moral crusade to spread Spanish culture and Catholicism to pagans in all parts of the Americas."[15] Not to be overlooked are Spain's material and political motives as well: gold and silver, as the acquisition of wealth was an end in itself; Christianized ("civilized") Indians were expected to contribute to the largesse by paying taxes to the empire.

The religious intent for the frontier, however, avoided any overt reference to mammon: priests were to gather the Indians in settlements around the missions; civilian villages, peopled by the families of farmers, ranchers, merchants, and soldiers, would be located nearby; and for everyone's protection, soldiers would be garrisoned in area presidios to provide the physical presence necessary to deter or respond to any problems. This deliberate approach was designed to eventually bring the land and its varied native populations under complete Spanish dominion. Or so it was expected.[16]

The Jesuits, Franciscans, and other Europeans who relocated to northern Mexico in pursuit of this goal or for personal reasons moved into a desert environment where the earth is soft, dry, and sandy underfoot and dust flies sideways from a hurrying footstep or from an animal's heavy gait. In the mountain ranges, huge boulders, higher than a man, served as shields behind which, during conflicts, foes could become invulnerable to each other. Breastworks, built by piling high one ancient rock at a time, safeguarded a shooter as he lay on uncomfortable, pebbled ground, or bare dirt, or native grass patches and aimed his weapon. He'd best be wary of his surroundings, though, for not only humans were the enemy. Anyone lying low could find himself close to a snake, scorpion, tarantula, giant centipede, or any one of the multitudinous creatures that call the desert home. Above him, another dangerous foe: the sun, blazing mercilessly for ten months of the year.

Wildlife such as coyotes and game such as deer, antelopes, and javelinas didn't seem to mind the hot winds that swept the land every afternoon and could raise the dirt as high as a person's face. Water was scarce in the often arid valleys below the mountains, hard to find except for three to four summer months a year, when driving sheets of rain fleetingly filled the open, gaping arroyos that crosscut the land. All activity halted for a time when the yearly monsoons drenched and turned the earth into a cement-like, sucking mud.

Low-growing stands of mesquite trees here and there across the land beckoned and promised shade and solace, but their long thorns were sharp and could tear clothing and skin to shreds. Prickly cacti popped up everywhere and, in particular, thickets of tall ocotillo, standing side by side like armed guards, frequently permitted no passage. Live and scrub oaks grew in the mountains, their leafy branches breaking the heat somewhat, but annoying swarms of buzzing and biting flies hovered around, making it difficult if not impossible to enjoy the trees' shelter.

When the sun dropped below the horizon, everyone and everything breathed a sigh of relief. The air cooled quickly, but life remained somewhat treacherous. Snakes loved that time and squirmed and slithered toward the surface of a downed dead tree limb or warm rock, there to absorb the day's last warmth. Tarantulas scratched out from their nests. Coyotes awakened hungry, so jackrabbits hopped a little faster. Roadrunners with pointed beaks darted among the shrubs, seeking a tasty supper of insects. Families of quail with more than a dozen offspring scurried low to the ground, trying get out of everything's way. Groups of turkey vultures circled high in the sky for one last time before nightfall, scouring the terrain below for an evening meal.

To the Apaches, this sacred land was not as the Spaniards named it, the Pimeria Alta. It was their homelands, a site Dan L. Thrapp described as "being enormous in extent" and stretching "from the willow thickets along the Colorado into the broken mountains beyond the Rio Grande, and from the great canyons of the north southward for a thousand miles into Mexico." Thrapp eloquently portrayed the geography of the land from its beginning, when geological changes caused the upswelling that became the plateaus and the mountains, to the great rivers such as the Colorado and the Rio Grande in the United States and the Bavispe and Rio Yaqui in Mexico, to the great deserts of the Southwest, "a land of almost infinite extent."[17] Like Thrapp, we will call it *Apacheria* and will note the conflicts and differing points of view about the high desert. For example, the Spaniards immediately began to "modify and commodify" the land[18] to suit their needs, while the Apaches valued the repetition of seasonal events, especially as they related to their spirituality; a personal relationship with the land sustained their spirituality.

To become familiar with the Chiricahuas' background, the first chapter introduces certain of the historical people's religious beliefs and ceremonies. It is important to recognize that in all aspects of Chiricahua life, a highly private connection existed with Ussen and was as natural to the people as breathing.

The second chapter describes some of the circumstances extant on the Spanish colonial frontier at the moment of contact and then beyond. This book only partially summarizes the situation at that time. Future descriptions and discussions are necessary to fully lay out the many European externalities that impacted all the Indians' lifeways but are beyond the scope of this book.

Subsequent chapters lead the readers through the events that culminated in the 1886 surrender, then the twenty-seven years of incarceration as American prisoners of war that followed and the life-changing consequences of the children's education. Among these experiences were the complexities of religious indoctrination and the participation by the Chiricahua Apaches in their own destiny, not as victims but, in many ways, as willing contributors to their fate, despite the devastating effect of Euro-American religious, cultural, and economic imperialism.

CHAPTER ONE

Creation Myths, Sacred Stories, and Rituals

Most societies around the world call upon legends to explain their origins. These tales form the living core of a belief system, and as such they clarify customs, satisfy curiosity, and interpret history. The examples these creation myths and cultural stories present often demonstrate the worth of living a moral life, but they don't have to be ethical. Most require no proof, but all continue to thrive inside the culture. Importantly, the stories need not coincide with any anthropological, geological, archeological, or historical data. They must, however, have been handed down through the generations. In other words, they are not scientific and can exist even as fantasy, adding multidimensions to the tasks of interpretive anthropologists and historians.

Christianity's creation myth favors one almighty Being called God and two once perfect people, Adam and Eve. In the King James version of the Bible, Genesis 1:26–28, on the fifth day God talks about creating males and females in His own image and giving them dominion "over all the earth, and over every creeping thing that creepeth upon the earth." As described in Genesis 2:7, 22, Adam and Eve were made from the dust of the ground and she from Adam's rib. Then God placed them together, Adam first, in a lush utopian setting, the Garden of Eden, and expected them to behave well. You know the rest.

The actions of these first people, along with the dramatic occurrences in that lush paradise, have resounded for millennia all across the planet. The meaning of this Christian legend has inspired millions of people to believe in a particular theology and has had such enormous appeal that Christianity has grown from its beginning as an obscure Jewish sect to become one of the world's major religions today. No one can deny that Christianity has been so compelling and so powerful that it has influenced the course of human history on earth.

Most contemporary Chiricahua Apaches practice Christianity in one form or another and simultaneously have no conflict in looking to ancient stories that explain their origins and guide their behavior. It is as if Christianity perches on one side of an invisible line while on the other side certain aspects of the ancestral lifeway remain intact. Clearly, both ways of worship support each other in a syncretic relationship.[1] One of the best examples of the combined religions occurred several years ago at an annual puberty ceremony. The late Wendell Chino, then chairman of the Mescalero Apache Tribe and an ordained Reformed Church of America minister, opened the traditional ceremony—a traditional puberty rite—with a Christian prayer spoken in the Apache language.

Traditional Apache Beliefs

Yastasitasitan-tan-ne is the Apache name for the Creator, but through custom the name is not spoken.[2] "The Apaches have always believed in one God," Asa Daklugie told author Eve Ball more than half a century ago, saying,

> The word Ussen means Creator of Life. He put the Apache on the land which He had created for us, and He laid down certain laws which we were to obey. These are very much your Ten Commandments, with the exception of our not being required to observe the Sabbath. Of that we knew nothing.
>
> That part of your religion as told in the Old Testament I think I understand. It seems to me much like what I was taught as a child. But there are some things in the New Testament that I doubt many Apaches understand—like your queer three-

headed God. And we make no pretense of loving our enemies as you say you do. Have you ever known anybody who really did that? I have not. Ussen did not command that of the Apaches. He did tell them that they were not to fight unless attacked, but if that should happen He did not forbid them to defend themselves.

Your keeping your God locked up in a trap all week and letting Him out an hour or two on Sunday is also strange. To us, instead of being our prisoner, Ussen is free and everywhere, always with us. We obey Him. You say you do, but your people use profane language. We have too much respect to use it; in our language there is not any profanity. . . .

With us religion is a personal thing; we have neither an organization or a minister to intercede for us with Ussen, but we pray directly to Him and He answers us. Not always; sometimes we ask for things He does not think best for us.[3]

Daklugie also repeated a creation myth, saying, "In the beginning, the Chiricahuas were born from a cloud. It was hanging in the sky when Lightning struck it. The Apache came to earth like a flock of birds. . . . Fire came from lightning too. . . . It belonged to Ussen, Creator of Life."[4]

A story about the Bible, different from a creation myth, told by an anonymous individual and handed down as a legend, begins when Ussen gave a certain Indian a special, unidentified book. As long as that book was kept, according to the tale, the Indians would prosper. If it was destroyed or neglected in any way, the Indians would be beset by troubles, such as a decrease in population. When the owner of the book died, the Indians burned all his property, as was the custom. Unfortunately, the book also went into the fire, and bad luck descended quickly.[5]

After hearing the tale, respected anthropologist Morris E. Opler commented, "I think such stories as these were made up by missionaries long ago and told to the Indians to illustrate certain things and to make things easier for the Indian to understand. These stories have been taken over by the Indian and mixed with Indian ideas as they are retold. The book is probably the Bible, and the reason the story was told was to get the Indians to hang on to the Bible."[6]

Opler was nonspecific about which group of missionaries he thought responsible for the tale, but the admonition itself is so general and so transparent in its desire to convey the value of the Bible that the missionaries could have been either Catholic or Protestant. The effort was obviously successful or the story could not have existed long enough to be repeated.

As a basic ingredient in the transmission of cultural knowledge, storytelling was important to all generations of Apaches. Geronimo liked to tell sacred stories, but the ones he favored most appear on the surface to be related to the ancestral ways and to have nothing to do with Christianity. A popular creation story was included in his autobiography:

> Long ago when the world was covered with darkness, all manner of beasts, including serpents, roamed the earth. Another tribe of creatures also lived: the birds, who were a tightly organized group under an eagle chief. Disagreements between the two groups grew heated. The birds wanted light and the beasts, naturally, preferred the opposite. Finally the only solution was to fight it out. The beasts were armed with clubs, the birds with bows and arrows. The serpents, on the other hand, were so wise that they could not be killed and took refuge in an Arizona cliff overhang. The battle raged for many days, but at last the birds were victorious and light filled the earth. The stage was then set for humans to safely appear.
>
> One woman was alive. She had been blessed in the past with many children, but they all had been destroyed by the beasts. After many years of living in the light she became pregnant by a rainstorm and gave birth to a son.[7] When the child was older, he wandered from their home in a cave and met a serpent in the form of a dragon. The boy and the dragon fought over a piece of meat, each using arrows. The dragon's weapons missed the youngster, but the boy's arrows struck the dragon right over his heart. He was killed and the world was made safe. This boy's name was Apache. He was the first chief of the Indians and wore the eagle's feathers as the sign of justice, wisdom, and power.[8]

The woman in the story who was alive, and whose name Geronimo did not mention, is White Painted Woman; it is she who was fertilized by rain.[9] A Mescalero Apache medicine man told Claire Farrer who she was:

> They say [she] first came to us from the East. Oh! She was beautiful, a beautiful young woman. She lived with us. She showed us many things. She grew to full adulthood and lived down there. [He gestured with his lips to the south.] She had children there. Then she became old, very old. Soon she would begin her westward journey. But first she became even older with thinned skin and white, white hair, like the snow in the north country where our people used to live.
>
> She walked on three; she walked with gish/cane. Then one day she died. The People were so sad; we were sad, for we loved her dearly. But, we were surprised, too. All of us were surprised, for the next morning, the next sunrise, she appeared to us in the east again, a young woman again.
>
> That's what my grandparents told me.[10]

In this example, White Painted Woman personifies the concept of eternal life and, some would conclude, reincarnation. Interestingly, this female cultural icon, similar to the Virgin Mary, could have been the result of earliest contact with Christianity.

More than a few Apache creation myths and sacred stories are intriguing due to their resemblance to Christianity. In particular, both God and Ussen created the world and everything in it before they placed people in the setting. God worked for six days and rested on the seventh. Ussen, according to traditional belief, created the universe in three days and made humankind on the fourth. He never rested.[11]

A major contrast, however, between Apache and Christian belief is the status of human beings vis-à-vis the rest of creation. God's wish, as expressed in Genesis, was for people to have dominion over all the creatures of the earth, to be at the zenith of existence. On the other hand, Ussen created people to rely on all things in the natural world, so he relegated Apaches to the lowest rung of the ladder, so to speak. In that position, Ussen expected Apaches to be respectful and considerate of all of creation because they were dependent on the world around them.[12]

The marked difference leads directly to an individual's

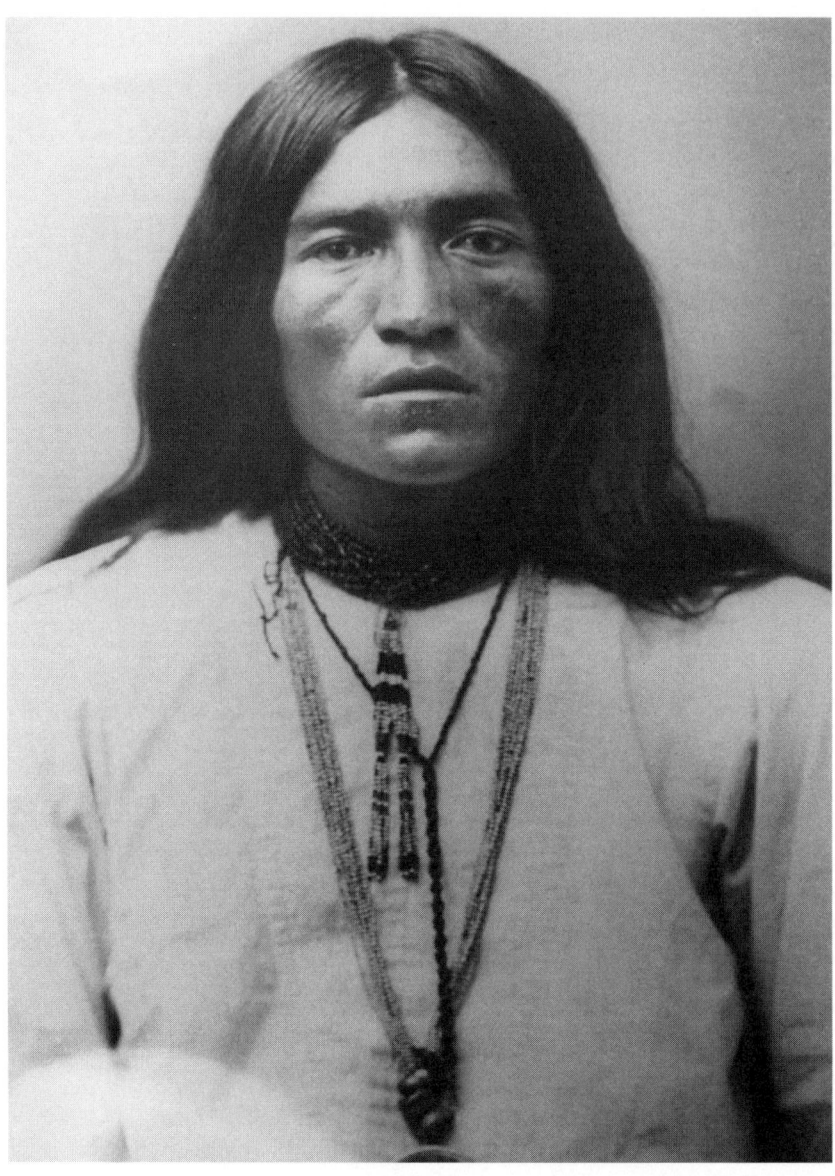

Fig. 2. Chiricahua Apache warrior Notalq, a member of Chato's delegation to Washington, D.C., in 1886. Courtesy of Frisco Native American Museum, Frisco, North Carolina.

Fig. 3. Chiricahua Apache Siki Toclanny, wife of Rogers Toclanny. Courtesy of Fort Sill National Historic Landmark collections, photo #P3605.

Fig. 4. Chiricahua Apache Marianetta (possibly known as Zi-yeh), wife of Geronimo. Courtesy of the Smithsonian Institution.

Fig. 5. Chiricahua Apache family, possibly Kaytennae and Gouyen. Children's identity is unknown. Courtesy of U.S. Army Military Institution.

Fig. 6. Chiricahua Apache Ha-o-zinne, third wife of Chief Naiche. Courtesy of Fort Sill National Historic Landmark collections, photo #3602.

perception of himself, his society, and his place in the universe. As I see it, throughout history the Euro-American mind has been saturated with the self-importance that illustrates the biblical reference to "dominion." Examples of this attitude of superiority date all the way from the apple in the Garden of Eden to the irony of creating contemporary weapons capable of destroying the planet in the name of bringing peace to the world.

Apaches, reflecting Ussen's wish for them to be dependent on their environment, are not audacious enough to identify a specific site in which their religion began, such as the Garden of Eden, but they are more explicit than Christianity regarding nature, the cosmos, and the creatures of the earth. For example, in traditional belief, the sun is Ussen's representative on earth, the moon is meant to be the Apaches' eyesight at night, the stars were made to guide the night travelers, the wind was to carry the people's words, and the rainbow was to remind the people of Ussen's beauty. Eagles, buffalo, elk, deer, and antelope were named by Ussen to contribute to ceremonies and to provide food, clothing, and shelter. The coyote was created for amusement and to reflect the foolishness of people.[13]

Contact with snakes is an Apache cultural taboo with near fatal clinical consequences for noncompliance, similar to what occurred in Eden. Traditional belief warns that if it is impossible to evade a snake because of an accidental meeting while walking, for example, illness is understood to be a likely result. An action as innocent as stepping on a snake's slithery impressions in the desert dust may cause a malady to appear in the form of "loathsome sores that attack the face," according to Opler,[14] or cause one's skin to peel, similar to a snake shedding its skin. Aches and pains and crawling sensations all over the body may accompany the process. Preventing these clinical consequences requires an immediate prayer after throwing sacred pollen on the snake's trail and then, when back at camp, enlisting the healing arts of a shaman who specializes in curing the effects of the affliction. Prayer is a necessary part of the ceremony and is spoken aloud: "Be good, O! Snake! Be good, Get away from here! Go not here where children and women go. Stay in your cave (or hole). Don't go about here."[15] If a shaman with the power to cure snake sickness cannot be found, traditional Apaches believed the crawling sensation could reach the victim's heart and he would perish.

In a modern example, several episodes of bad luck occurred after a rattlesnake entered an Apache woman's home in Oklahoma. She quickly had the serpent removed by a local herpetologist and didn't become ill with the dreaded "loathsome sores," but soon afterward she had car trouble and broke her glasses and a beloved relative became quite ill. Perhaps the snake was an omen heralding trouble. Many Chiricahuas only nod when this situation is discussed but will not offer an opinion about what non-Indians might conclude is nothing more than a coincidence.

Another parallel between Christian thought and traditional Apache beliefs occurs in the example of a woman's impregnation by nonmale, nonhuman sources. Geronimo named rain as the father of White Painted Woman's son, Child-of-the-Water. Somewhat similarly, Christianity identifies the Holy Spirit as the begetter of the Virgin Mary's son, Jesus. In these two situations, a male child is born and his role becomes that of a savior. Both putative sources of fatherhood are not identified by gender, an enigma discussed by the Reverend Robert S. Ove, a retired Lutheran minister who lived among the Chiricahua Apaches during the years 1948 through 1950.

"The Holy Spirit is always a mystery," he said. "There are some in the church who attribute femaleness to the Holy Spirit. In a trinity composed of a Father and Son, it would make sense, except that whenever Jesus refers to the Holy Spirit, it is always 'he.'[16] Not even the scholars agree unless they are conservative, in which case it is always a male Holy Spirit. The fact that 'he' impregnates Mary is a hint of maleness although the Holy Spirit may be androgynous or totally sexless. That the Holy Spirit is a mystery leaves it in limbo. I see no problem of equating him-it with the White Painted Lady."[17]

A third resemblance of the two cultures' beliefs occurs in the Apache story about a young person taking on a huge, powerful force and becoming victorious. In chapter 17 of the biblical book 1 Samuel, a youthful David has already killed a lion and a bear when he defeats the huge Philistine named Goliath with a single stone to the forehead. Child-of-the-Water also killed a giant as described in the following legend:

Child-of-the-Water . . . was strong in spirit and could do away with evil. He was challenged by a giant creature who lived in the same area of the earth as did he and his mother. One day the giant came around soon after White Painted Woman had finished nursing and washing her baby.

The giant pestered her with questions and accusations until she sent him on his way. He returned to harass the mother from time to time until the boy grew big and strong and told the giant he had been sent to kill all the monsters. A fight ensued during which Child-of-the-Water killed the giant with four arrows and by so doing made the earth safe.[18]

Another sacred story tells of a meeting between the boy and his father, Lightning. One day the boy asked to meet his father, but White Painted Woman denied him permission to go outside because of a terrible rainstorm. The boy insisted, saying, "I can go. I am the son of Lightning." Then White Painted Woman said to Lightning, "This is your son." Lightning said, "I do not believe he is my son, but I will test him." So Lightning tested him. Child-of-the-Water stood to the east and black lightning struck him. But it did not harm him. Then he stood to the south and blue lightning struck him. Then he stood to the west and yellow lightning struck him. Finally he stood to the north, where white lightning struck him. He was not injured at all. The Lightning said, "Now I know he is my son."[19]

References to testing a son are similar to God's propensity for testing his loved ones, but this particular Apache tale introduces another aspect of Chiricahua spiritual thought: the sacred concept of the four directions. The sun, Ussen's representative on earth, rises in the east, and so that direction is the most honored; the sun reinforces, on a daily basis, the omniscience and omnipresence of Ussen; many entryways to Apache houses, wickiups, and tipis face the east. The south is thought of as being warm, as women are, and its soft rains encourage seeds to grow into food, fill watercourses with water for the people and the animals to drink, and cleanse the desert air of its choking dust. The west has strength, the kind of power warriors need when fighting for their beliefs or to protect their women and children, or the west provides the skill hunters need to return with food for their families and the tribe. The north

Fig. 7. Geronimo at Fort Sill, ca. 1900. Courtesy of the Campbell Collection, Western History Collections, University of Oklahoma Library, photo #158.

ONE

Fig. 8. Apache wickiup (traditional dwelling), ca. 1883. Courtesy of Frisco Native American Museum, Frisco, North Carolina.

Fig. 9. Lenna Geronimo wearing her puberty dress. Courtesy of the Smithsonian Institution.

Fig. 10. Unidentified Chiricahua Apache bride wearing traditional bridal dress. Courtesy of Frisco Native American Museum, Frisco, North Carolina.

Fig. 11. Chiricahua Apache warrior Be-da-zis-shu. Courtesy of Frisco Native American Museum, Frisco, North Carolina.

brings cold, allowing roots, plants, animals, and people to rest and revitalize for the coming fertile spring season when the sun will rise higher in the east, the rains will again nourish, and the men will become strong once more. In Apache belief, each season continuously plays into the other, providing year-round balance for the earth and all its inhabitants.[20]

The physical symbol of the four directions—a vertical bar with a horizontal crossbar—may be likened to the Christian symbol of the cross. It is probable that the Apaches accepted the symbol long before their contact with the Europeans, as did many Indian tribes, although this may never be known. If, however, the symbol of the cross was adopted postcontact, it is a clear example of syncretism.[21]

Writing his classic work, *The Medicine Men of the Apache*, in the late 1800s, John Gregory Bourke stated that the image of a cross had appeared in many places in Apache symbolism, including a place as unlikely as the tops of warriors' moccasins. When planning to go into an unfamiliar area, Bourke wrote, the men hoped that painting a cross on their footwear with *hoddentin*—tule pollen—would keep them from following a wrong trail. He stated that in so doing, they expressed the belief that the cross represented the sacred four directions.[22]

A fourth similarity exists in siblings. Jesus is said to have had four brothers and at least two sisters; the eldest brother was named James.[23] Child-of-the-Water's brother, called Killer-of-Enemies, is most often portrayed as older, already grown when the younger son of White Painted Woman is born.[24] But as is characteristic of the flexibility of Apache myths, he has also variously been described as White Painted Woman's brother, her husband, or a twin brother to Child-of-the-Water. In some Chiricahua tales, Killer-of-Enemies is the less heroic of both boys but has also accomplished various admirable feats, such as freeing animals from underground, where they had been held captive by a crow.[25]

One story describes how, with the assistance of Coyote, Killer-of-Enemies brought cattle up from their underground prison by turning himself into a puppy, entering the crows' camp, and playing with the crows' children. The puppy grew into a good-sized dog in time. Every day the crows mounted their horses and rode out to a stump that covered a hole where cattle were hidden. A large buffalo bull guarded the stump each day. Once, when the crows rode off in the opposite direction, Coyote and the dog went to the stump, asked the buffalo for permission to go underground, and were refused. The dog had no choice: he turned himself into his human form as Killer-of-Enemies, kicked the stump four times, and he and Coyote entered an underground vault full of monsters. They bribed the monsters' leader with tobacco, and he let them through to where the cattle lived. Killer-of-Enemies herded all the cattle out of the underground, but Coyote ran around killing them. Finally Coyote jumped onto the chest of the buffalo and rode away. Still, the cattle weren't free from the crows that saw Killer-of-Enemies herding them away. The crows flew after the cows but couldn't drive them back, even though they made their cawing sound.[26]

This particular story is newer than many others and probably came into being postcontact after the Spanish brought livestock to the Apache homelands; before then, cattle might have been unknown in Apacheria. As with many tales, this one also lends guidance to the people by informing them that Ussen expects them to be inventive and to manipulate adverse conditions so they evolve to the Apaches' benefit.

Highlighted in quite a few Apache stories, the mischievous Coyote can wear many different hats. He has been known to be a trickster, a valued bringer of warmth through fire, and a bumbler who couldn't do anything right. Many of the lighthearted tales connect in some way to sacred stories and modify the more serious accounts. For example, the version of the way darkness arrived—Coyote accidentally let it out of a sack and it quickly covered the earth—supplements the creation myths that describe Ussen's work and identifies the trickster as an antihero, thus not to be imitated.[27]

Coyote can also be responsible for causing strange illnesses that only a skilled medicine man with impressive supernatural power, someone like Geronimo, could heal. To begin the ancient rituals that would help him diagnose a mysterious ailment, Geronimo rolled a cigarette and puffed to the four directions, starting with the east. After he threw the cigarette away, he carefully rubbed the ailing parts of the patient's body with yellow pollen from the tule. As he did so, he prayed and sang songs about Coyote in which he shamelessly flattered Coyote's ability as a trickster. Still singing much later, Geronimo also acknowledged Coyote's occasional invisibility.[28] Interspersed among these compliments, Geronimo asked Coyote to help him cure the patient, and then, at the close of each song, Geronimo imitated the Coyote's howl. Given Geronimo's reputation, his power, and divine intervention, the patient believed he had an excellent chance at recovery.

Water is especially important to desert dwellers, as is shown in Chiricahua mythology through Child-of-the-Water's origin in rain. Oral testimonies and oral traditions are replete with accounts of relationships between Apaches and water, including a story that, similar to the biblical tale, recounts a great flood.[29]

In Apache legend, there were people on earth who did not know Ussen, and their ignorant behavior caused the ocean to rise until it covered the earth. All but a few people, animals, and birds were drowned, and these were saved because they raced up to the top of a mountain. When the water receded, a gun and a bow and arrow were put in front of the survivors. The first man took the gun; the second man took the bow and arrow. The first became the white man; the second became the Indian.[30]

When the torrential rains, described in Genesis, came to Noah, they surely must have been accompanied by tremendous thunder and lightning, natural elements that, in Christianity, are not anthropomorphized. In Apache lore, however, Thunder people exist. Some are good, some are evil, and all their arrows are lightning. When the good express themselves and pass over the earth in a soft, gentle way, their rains bring relief from heat for all and fertilize the earth. When the bad are angry, their storms tear up trees and cause terrible trouble for animals and people alike. Any one of these evil Thunder people may cause someone to be struck by a lightning arrow. So, it is very important for human beings to act respectfully toward the Thunder people to avoid incurring their wrath.[31] One tried-and-true way to behave during a heavy rainstorm is to imitate the call of a speckled bird. In pretending he is a bird capable of darting around, the Apache believes he is symbolically able to avoid being struck by a lightning bolt.[32]

Another means of protection from harm during storms is a desert plant called sage (*Salvia*, not to be confused with the medicinally potent sagebrush *Artemisia tridentata*).[33] A sprig of sage, molded into the form of a cross, is usually pinned onto clothing for safety, and a larger display of sage in the same shape can occupy a space on the wall of a house or be placed over the entryway to keep malevolence away. A small piece of bark, broken off the east face of a tree that had been struck by lightning, also provides a defense against trouble from rainstorms and is ordinarily carried in a pouch with other safeguards. A very thin slat of pine, cedar, or fir may be carved into the shape of a human body and attached to children's cradleboards to keep them safe from harm.

Along with carrying charms such as sage and bark, an Apache prays aloud for safety during a rainstorm. And when thunderclaps and lightning flashes are very close, the Chiricahua greets them as if they were his grandfather, saying:

> *"Continue in a good way;*
> *Be kind as you go through;*
> *Do not frighten these poor people;*
> *My grandfather, let it be well;*
> *Don't frighten us poor people."*[34]

The Chiricahua Apaches of old prayed for, and counted on, cooperation among the natural elements and earthly people for survival. If disruption in a normal cycle occurred, such as a drought, Apache prayers intensified, not only because of the immediate circumstances but because of the omen that every unusual climatic condition represented.[35]

Under ordinary conditions, Apaches could and often did pray many times a day, wherever they were. It was routine to see an Apache at a campsite moving his lips in prayer as he tended to his horses or to hear a woman praying as she laid kindling wood on the ground to build a fire. These prayers were often accompanied by respectful actions. For example, before mounting their horses and riding off in search of game, Apache hunters scattered hoddentin for a blessing and then attached a small buckskin pouch full of hoddentin to their belts.

HODDENTIN

Considered to be one of the most sacred items in the Apache religion, hoddentin (pronounced "ho-den-teen") hides inside the thick brown covering at the top of a cat tule stalk, which grows in many of the little ponds and marshes of Apacheria.[36] To prepare hoddentin for ceremonial purposes, medicine men harvest the plant when it is at a certain level of maturity. Back at camp, they spread the bundle of collected tules onto a hide and let them dry in the sun. Next they scrape off the brown covering and allow the sacred yellow dustlike interior to fall onto the hide, where it continues to dry to a certain consistency before being gathered up and stored. Through prayers and incantations at each step in the drying process, the pollen is blessed and then saved for use in sacred rituals.

In former years, each warrior leaving camp for a battle placed a pouch full of hoddentin somewhere on his person, often tucked into his ammunition belt, thus guaranteeing protection and success. Before mounting his horse, the fighter took a pinch of hoddentin, threw it to the sun, and put some in his mouth and on the crown of his head. If he became tired during a march or after combat, a bit of hoddentin on his tongue revitalized him. When the men returned safely to camp, they threw pollen to the sun and to the directions as a gesture of thankfulness. If someone was wounded in battle and a medicine man accompanied the war party, the healer prayed aloud as he walked in front of the injured person and his horse from the site of the conflict back to camp. While praying for the warrior's recovery, the holy man sprinkled pinches of hoddentin at intervals to ensure that their path to the safety of the camp would be made easy.

Bourke reported a conversation with an Apache in the late 1800s about hoddentin. The man told him, "When we Apache go on the warpath, hunt, or plant, we always throw a pinch of hoddentin to the sun, saying, 'with the favor of the sun, or permission of the sun, I am going out to fight, hunt, or plant,' as the case may be, 'and I want the sun to help me.'"[37]

Bourke's informant indicated that the pollen acted as an intercessor between the Chiricahua Apaches and the deities, much as Roman Catholics call upon the saints and the Virgin Mary to help them with their petitions. Employing hoddentin in this manner may have been a syncretic adaptation from Catholicism to which Apache ancestors had been exposed centuries earlier, or the Chiricahuas may simply have believed in the efficacy of interveners.

Bourke also wrote that the pollen "is thrown to the sun in the early morning, is cast upon the trail of snakes, fills the air in war-dances of unusual solemnity, and is used most freely around the couch of the dying." Elaborating, Bourke described a ceremony performed at the bed of an Apache man who was seriously ill and close to death from an ailment in his head and chest.

> The singing consisted of a recitation by a trio of "medicine-men" and a choral refrain from the united voices of all present.
>
> At intervals an old squaw, seated at the head of the sick man, and near the drummer and "medicine-men" would arise, and, with much mumbling and mystic manipulation, sprinkle *Hoddentin* over the heads of the "medicine-men," then of the choristers, and lastly over and around the couch of the sick man.
>
> The *Hoddentin* . . . was sprinkled around the sick man's couch and, in the form of a cross, upon his breast and abdomen. While so doing, the sprinkler mumbled the following prayer . . . put into English it would mean, "Be good, we beg, and grant favour to the people (Apaches) here."

Note the similarity between this ceremony and the Catholic rite of extreme unction, another possible example of syncretism.

Bourke convinced a former Mexican captive of the Chiricahuas to explain the philosophy behind praying in the Apache way. The man said, "We ask the favour of God. By His favour we exist always. The word of God is good. Although God has not put water on our heads (that is, baptized us), God will always be kind to us. When God wills a man shall die, he dies. If God wants a man to live to be old, he will live. I am very glad. I think that bad people will not go up above, but down below. There are saints whose prayers will send rain to water the little spears of grass shooting out of the ground. Perhaps this man will die, if God so will. God sees all: He hears all."[38]

The strong Christian influence caught Bourke's attention, and he noted that Apaches boldly adopted or took whatever they liked from the religion of those around them when that special something captured their fancy. Bourke noted that the Apaches often decorated themselves with crosses, medals, and pictures of saints taken on the spot from corpses of murdered Mexicans. Then they walked away, leaving the bodies for predators.

BURIAL CUSTOMS

A tribal member's death in camp activated historical Chiricahua mortuary practices that were an essential component of traditional religion.[39] Readying a body for burial was ordinarily done by a female relative of the deceased but not with any willingness, for Apaches were reluctant to touch their dead. Still, someone always stepped forward to do it. One practice called for bathing the body, combing the hair, and placing red paint on the dead person's face. Then the tribe's mortician in this case dressed the deceased in attractive clothing. A male relative mounted him on his horse, sat behind him to hold him up, and rode the horse to the burial site where the body would be interred, probably on the same day as the death occurred.

If an aboveground burial was planned, members of the burial party wrapped the body in a blanket, canvas, or hide, put brush under and over it, and placed a few rocks on top of it if they were handy. Or they laid the body on a layer of rocks, piled brush on top, dropped leaves and dirt above that, and carefully set more rocks over all, forming a mound that, with a little luck, would not attract wildlife.[40]

Depending on the character and quality of the terrain and the types and preponderance of wildlife, it could have been reckless to bury a body aboveground. On those occasions, nearby caves and crevices were used and then sealed with boulders. For example, Cochise was buried in Arizona's Dragoon Mountains in a secret place unknown even to his contemporary descendants. Due to the difficulty in opening an in-ground grave in that mountain range's extremely rocky ground, knotted with tough, gnarled roots, Cochise was lowered into a breach between boulders with his head facing west, as tradition dictated. Various legends about this major event in Chiricahua Apache history tell of Cochise's dog and horse being killed at the site and buried with him. The animals' deaths too would have been dictated by custom, for if allowed to live, they would remind survivors of Cochise, not a good idea, for once an Apache was dead, custom prohibited anyone from publicly remembering him. Even the deceased's personal items were burned or destroyed, and on occasion the entire campsite was moved shortly after the death because the relatives preferred to get away.[41]

A period of mourning lasting about a year was observed in historic times and still is honored by some families today. Opler's informant said that "for some time after the death of his wife, a man will not dress in fine clothes and won't go to social dances. A woman will not attend the social dancing at a puberty rite . . . [and] will wait about a year before she will go to such affairs."[42]

Modifications to the original burial customs have been made through the years. For example, a few minutes after death occurs, a close relative may go outside and shoot a good many cartridges into the air. The practice could have begun when the Chiricahuas saw soldiers shooting over the graves of their dead comrades, for it had not been done with arrows before the Europeans brought guns into Apacheria; arrows were too precious.

A few Apaches today are still influenced by the ancient customs, especially the one that prohibits mentioning the deceased's name. Elbys Naiche Hugar, a great-granddaughter of Cochise, has her own thoughts about it. "Your dead relative may be very busy doing something important where he is and when he hears you speak his name, he'll be interrupted. He might not like that."[43]

Hugar's explanation reveals the Apache belief in life after death, a certainty that might have existed within the culture long before the Spaniards brought the Christian tenet of eternal life to the colonial frontier. Chiricahua Apache oral testimony tells of a person, immediately after death, going through an opening in the ground. Underneath the earth is a great pile of sand, shaped somewhat like a tipi, that the person enters and is then closed off. The surroundings are idyllic with lush grasses, cool water running in streams, warm sunshine, and bountiful rains. The tule grows abundantly, providing more than enough hoddentin for ceremonies. Everyone has plenty to eat, all the people are pleasant, and there is no sickness, no pain, and no sorrow. The puberty ceremony and the dance of the Mountain Spirits still occur. Best of all, each person is with his own group and does the same things he enjoyed when he was alive on earth. But since no one would wish to be disturbed or called from that environment, it is imperative that the survivors, friends, and relatives do not speak the name of the deceased.

It is curious that this sacred story speaks of a utopia underneath the earth. In Christian thought, the same utopia would be considered to be "heaven," a location above, not below, the earth.

ONE

Another constraint against speaking the dead person's name is a fear of ghost sickness, an ailment thought to be caused by annoying dead relatives and friends and not letting them rest in peace.[44] The clinical symptoms of this malady are similar to those of extreme fright: tachycardia, choking, weakness, vomiting, irrational fears, crying, and headaches. Although long ago there were healers who specialized in curing ghost sickness through specific prayers and ceremonies, routine precautions were taken by almost everyone to avoid becoming ill with this affliction, but particularly by everyone who was involved in preparing the deceased's body for burial. Along with never mentioning the person's name again, members of the family who were even around the dead body burned all the clothes they wore while performing any preburial task. They bathed their bodies in the smoke of the sage plant and protected themselves while asleep by placing ashes near their beds. At the grave, they brushed their bodies with green grass and then left the grass on the ground in the shape of a cross.[45]

Becoming more lighthearted, oral testimony also warns against speaking a deceased's name because he could be playing cards and holding a winning hand. When his name is spoken, he would respond and possibly then lose the card game, which would make him very angry. And one risks peril when one angers the dead.

WITCHCRAFT

The historical Chiricahua culture contained what today would be called "guidelines" for determining that an individual was a witch. Many descriptions have been passed down generation to generation: witches are friendly with ghosts; they never need to take any precautions as they handle the dead, for becoming involved with corpses in any way is not dangerous to them; they usually have amulets to work with; they spread sickness; they are troublemakers in that they cause personal misfortune and public disasters; their habits are strange; they act peculiarly; they wear beads openly; their manner of dress is different; they are chronic braggarts or misers; and they are sexually aberrant in some ways.[46]

Guilty individuals were also identified through exhibiting unmistakable characteristics such as pointing with fingers, demonstrating a preference for sleeping alone outdoors, refusing to eat foods cooked by others, dancing naked in the woods, or talking about someone else in a cruel manner; gossiping was permitted, provided it didn't become too ugly.

Admittedly, most of these descriptions are so vague that one or more might apply to anyone at any time, and it is easy to be deceived by their superficiality. However, the apparent generality of the characterizations is a clue to frightening threats that witches and witchcraft presented to the historic Chiricahuas. Had the definition been more specific than general, the numbers of identified witches would have been less, but in that case, in the Apache way of thinking, more might have escaped detection. Thus, it was necessary for the "net" to catch more, just so no one slipped through. By way of further explanation, Apaches saw danger lurking everywhere and had learned to survive in the harsh environment by their wits, imagination, and reliance on cultural memories.

An accusation of practicing witchcraft made against another tribal member was so serious that it was never made frivolously, and fortunately, culturally prescribed relief was available. Following customs, the accusing individual would call a council meeting during which he presented his case. Then the influential men of the tribe would decide on the type of punishment appropriate to the offense. Once identified, an Apache witch's life was ordinarily at an end, for a family member related to a bewitched individual was honor bound to take revenge.[47]

MEDICINE MEN AND WOMEN

Chiricahua Apaches of old believed medicine men and medicine women were blessed with a talent that was different from that of all others in the tribe.[48] They are viewed as historians in that they are knowledgeable about the tribe's evolution. They are philosophers in that they have reasons and explanations for the processes and existence of Apache life. They are priests and physicians in that they provide the means of curing illnesses. They are counselors in that they provide culturally relevant social consultation; they are leaders as they have wisdom, knowledge, and community respect. While all individual traits were necessary for the survival of the group, the healers were the first among equals because of their intimate relationship with the Creator and the cultural belief that the Creator supported and sustained the connection.

Healing ceremonies were designed with two specific goals: to restore the ailing individual to good health and to convince him of the medicine person's great powers. Half of that belief was already in place when the patient was motivated to seek a healer's help, and part of the ritual consisted of the healer enumerating certain events in the victim's life, all of which were well known because of the closeness of the group within this affiliation-oriented culture. When the healer reminded the patient of certain details of his life, it verified the medicine person's great powers in the eyes of the patient. After the diagnosis, the medicine man or medicine woman invoked his power's help to cure the ailment. Often he sang ceremonial songs and prayed aloud with great fanfare to communicate supernaturally and gain his power's aid. Then, in a dramatic demonstration of might, the healer did battle with the evil that was at the root of the trouble; he usually won.

Occasionally the medicine man "threw" the patient's ailment onto a nearby boulder and then painted or pecked around it, creating what has come to be known as "rock art," which often today has been seen as something else by those who study pictographs. But before the patient was allowed to leave the site, the medicine man imposed some restrictions, such as limiting the foods he might eat and naming the items he must neither have in his home nor carry on his person; such a prohibition could be a stone of a certain color.[49]

Every Chiricahua Apache was considered to have a unique gift of some type of power from the first day of life.[50] To the people, power of all kinds pervaded the universe, was alive, patient, and waited and watched until the individual was ready to receive it, possibly through a word, some clear sign, or in a dream. The power itself determined the means of communication and the time and place an individual would be contacted, such as through animals, plants, natural forces, or inanimate objects.

As an example, a person of any age could be out for a walk in the desert or mountain homelands when a sudden rainstorm came up. As the sky grew dark and ominous, the Apache looked around for some sort of shelter. Lightning bolts illuminated an empty shack nearby that afforded temporary refuge. Back home after the storm, in a dream that night the voice of lightning spoke to the Apache, woke him up, and revealed the details of the ceremony he was being given. Lightning taught the person the appropriate prayers and songs, the ritual motions necessary, the restrictions, and the ceremonial paraphernalia and named the natural substances, such as pollen or rocks, that he would need to conduct a healing ritual. Since the power derived from lightning is extremely strong, this Apache, if he has a good relationship with his power and doesn't antagonize it, will be able to cure resistant ailments that other medicine men and medicine women have been unable to heal. If he angers his power in any way, possibly by failing to live up to the power's expectations, his successes may be few, his reputation suffers, and he will lose face within his tribe—a terrible experience for an Apache.[51]

Power has no preference insofar as gender is concerned. Apache women receive power in the same way as men do; the ancestral society viewed medicine women on a par with medicine men. Many women, however, excelled at midwifery, curing children's cuts and scrapes, and other extensions of motherhood. By no means was this ability thought to be inferior to that of other healers, with the exception of a medicine man whose power came from lightning, so they were highly respected as healers and had younger people apprenticed to them, as did medicine men.

Some years ago, researcher Teresa Pijoan, a native of San Juan Pueblo in New Mexico, interviewed a Mescalero Apache woman to record her comments about traditional healers. Although the elder insisted on anonymity, her comments were so descriptive that they are included here without any specific attribution. In a discussion, she said,

> Medicine men and medicine women hold great power. The White Eyes [Anglo] people never understood nor respected them. Medicine people brought healing, held power, helped make decisions in the group. The Apache got *viruelos* [smallpox] because it could not be fought. It came, killed, and left dead. Medicine people knew that [the cause] was Mexican people's blankets and shirts.
>
> Our people did not have pain with teeth and we did not get bone swellings like the Plains people and the grinders of the

Pueblos. We did not get pain or hurts from the spirits until the spots came.

Medicine people taught children how to heal with herbs, how to use plants and teas for cures. Medicine people were rewarded with presents—valuable presents.

Medicine people work with plants, herbs, songs, chants, heat, cold, and spirit. A person may be sick but their body shows no wound.

Medicine people know it is spirit that is hurt or being evil. They work on this. They heal this. Ussen helped medicine people know what was wrong. Ussen gives the power to heal.

Long ago a man went into a cave near El Paso. He was a healer. He knew where there was a place of puberty rites. He did not disturb the ceremony, but took herbs that grew there. It was medicine that could cure anything. It was all used and now there is no more.[52]

COMPARISONS

In the historical Apache religion, no particular individual leads a group in an organized fashion within a church as does a Christian priest or a minister, but there definitely are similarities in the clothing.[53] For example, while conducting services, Catholic priests and some Protestant ministers wear specifically designed religious apparel; an Apache spiritual leader wears a medicine cord of from one to four thin strands of rope woven or braided together.[54] These holy cords were once considered so sacred that strangers were not permitted to see or handle them or even talk about them. Decorated with beads or shells and sacred stones tied onto the cord, some also hold petrified wood, crystals, eagle down, hawk or eaglet claws, rattlesnake rattles, small hide bags of hoddentin, twigs, pieces of trees that had been struck by lightning, and abalone shell. If a cross is also attached, the medicine cord takes on a faint resemblance to a rosary.

Bourke likened the Apache medicine cord to the rope belt worn around the waists of St. Francis and his followers. Quoting French writer Bernard Picart, Bourke writes (in French) that St. Francis's cord often cured illnesses and strengthened one's health. Clearly taking license in depicting the likeness, Bourke noted that

St. Monica's girdle had five knots and the monks of the Levant used a girdle with twelve knots to show that they were followers of the twelve apostles.[55] Religious hats were also part of Apache sacred wear, much as a bishop's miter proclaims his status. Medicine men usually donned buckskin caps that were thought to give life and strength to the owner, help him predict the future, aid in seeing an enemy approach, and help cure the sick. Symbols of natural elements such as clouds, rainbows, and stars were painted on the hat, and it ordinarily had a long "tail," which Bourke believed represented a centipede, a common desert insect familiar to the Apaches.[56]

THE PUBERTY CEREMONY

The ancient puberty ceremony is the best example of a traditional ritual that combines all three sacred elements of prayers, songs, and blessings. The rite antedates any known contact at all with Europeans, having been given to the Chiricahua Apaches in the time before time by White Painted Woman.

In her instructions to the Chiricahua Apaches, White Painted Woman's exact words were, "We will have the girls' puberty rite. When the girls first menstruate, you shall have a feast. There shall be songs for the girls. During this feast, the *Gah'e* [Mountain Spirit dancers] shall dance in front. After that there shall be round dancing and face to face dancing."[57]

Puberty ceremonies were (and still are) a joyful, essential, and spiritual part of becoming an adult female in the tribe.[58] Since that earliest of times when White Painted Woman presented the ritual, the Apaches have continued it, regardless of where they were or of what was happening—warring with the Spanish, Mexican, or American armies, in captivity as American prisoners of war, or on a reservation. Only in Oklahoma, in more recent times, did the ceremony almost fade into obscurity among the descendants. However, in the last several years it has struggled to return, proving its ageless viability and vitality.

In keeping with the Chiricahua custom of more than one story describing the same event, another sacred tale about the puberty ceremony, different from the mandate by White Painted Woman, begins with the grandfather of the gods giving Old Woman a message for the Apaches. According to the tale, Old Woman found it difficult to keep up with other members of the tribe as they followed the buffalo and other sources of food. Exhausted, she fell by the wayside and others moved on without her. She slept and fell into a coma. Suddenly a constant jingling penetrated her deathlike state and caused her to become instantly alert. She heard a spirit voice that described the process of the puberty ceremony and urged her to hurry and rejoin her tribe so she could instruct them. Revivified, Old Woman followed the directions.[59]

Dan Nicholas, a full-blooded Chiricahua Apache living at Mescalero in 1939, wrote an article about a puberty ceremony that is again different from the others. Nicholas reported that the rite was given to the people not by White Painted Woman but by Ussen, the Giver of Life, through a lesser deity named Esdzanadeha—another name for White Painted Woman.[60] Beautiful Esdzanadeha reared her son, Killer-of-Enemies, in spite of several monsters who were depopulating the earth at that time. Her son killed the monsters to make the world safe for the Apache people, and because of this, Esdzanadeha is revered.[61]

To honor White Painted Woman during the puberty ceremony, the maidens wear an elaborate buckskin dress similar to the one she wore at the beginning of the Apache people. Grandmothers bead or paint symbols onto the top of the dress well in advance of the expected date of the ceremony. Also in good time, the family selects the girl's sponsor—a woman carefully chosen to instruct and accompany the girl through the sacred rite and to paint her body yellow with pollen, considered to be a fertilizing color, and red to symbolize blood and life.[62]

In historical days the puberty dress was made from doeskins or buckskins starting with a large hide that was hand-tanned with an animal's brains and cut into two pieces, an upper blouse and a lower skirt. The tail of a black-tailed doe was suspended from the back hem of the blouse. Usually the girl's mother, grandmother, or another female relative fringed the hide, sewed a tiny jingle to each fringe, and decorated the dress. Some dresses kept the natural color, and some were painted with strips of green or yellow; the maiden's wishes determined the color. The dress was blessed by having someone sing for it, usually an older woman who began her songs as long as two months in advance of the scheduled ceremony and was paid in commodities for her services.

Also in olden times, for about a year prior to the actual ceremony, the girl's parents and relatives stored various foods such as piñon nuts, mesquite beans, yucca, and fruit—all to be eventually prepared and served at the ceremony by family members according to tradition.[63]

The actual ceremony began at dawn of the first day when a girl's sponsor bathed her and instructed her in the words that were necessary to start the celebration of her womanhood. The sponsor then dressed the girl, who faced the east, starting from the right foot, and the older woman prayed as she placed each item of clothing on the maiden's body. She draped pieces of shells and necklaces of beads around the girl's neck, inserted earrings in her earlobes, and pinned two black feathers from the tail of the female eagle into her hair.

To ensure that the girl would have a good appetite throughout her life, a medicine man or medicine woman fed the young woman a piece of wild fruit marked with a cross of pollen while she was preparing to leave her wickiup for the ceremonial grounds. The sponsor had already attached a reed and a scratcher to her dress so that her lips would not touch water for four days, nor would her fingernails become dirty by scratching an itch. If the girl made a mistake and drank water from a cup rather than the reed, the belief was that she would invite rain, which in turn would impede the progress of the ceremony. Also, the sponsor told the girl she could not look at the sky or be disobedient for that would also cause rain clouds to gather. The sponsor warned the girl against laughing excessively, for such behavior would cause her to have a prematurely wrinkled face, and any character traits a girl showed during the ceremony would distinguish her for the rest of her life. So she couldn't lose her temper, make fun of anyone, or swear. But she could talk a little, heed what she was told, and maintain grave, dignified manners.

After the medicine men erected a tipi on the ceremonial grounds early on the first morning of the ritual, a girl and her sponsor came forward. The attendant placed a tanned hide on the ground and the maiden knelt on it. Her sponsor marked her face and body with the pollen, after which the girl did the same to the older woman. When the painting was done, the maiden lay down on the hide and was rubbed from foot to head, from the right side to the left, by the attendant, who simultaneously prayed for the girl to have a good disposition, good morals, good health, and a long life.

The younger woman then ran around a woven basket, placed on the ground about thirty paces from the medicine tipi, four times to symbolize a woman's stages of life—infancy, childhood, adulthood, and old age. The runs also marked White Painted Woman's journey from the east, where she initially emerged as a beautiful young woman, across the spectrum of time to the west, where she disappeared when elderly, before she reappeared again as a youth in the east. Inside the basket were sacred items, including pollen, a deer or elk hoof rattle, and a bundle of grass and feathers. All represent each of the four days the Creator used to make the world and its occupants.

After each single run, the basket was moved closer to the sacred tipi so that after the last run the girl picked up the basket and held it to each direction in clockwise order, starting with the south. This gesture ensured that any sickness or ailment that might harm her was chased away. The run itself demonstrated the maiden's physical fitness, so important to the girl and to the future of the tribe.

(Elders who watch the ceremony can tell whether a girl will be a "good Apache woman," meaning that she will live up to the community's general expectations, by the way she runs. During one recent ceremony, a girl fell and an audible gasp arose from the spectators. Prayers were immediately offered for her future well-being even though, when she picked herself up and continued her run, she acted as if nothing untoward had happened.)

After nightfall on each of the four nights, the maiden knelt in the rear of the medicine tipi in front of a low fire burning in a central fire pit. Medicine men sang sotto voce in accompaniment to the sounds made by shaking deer hoof rattles. At a designated point in the service the girl began to dance and continued for hours with little relief except for an occasional rest period. This exhausting activity demonstrated her endurance, a quality much desired in an Apache woman, then and now.

About ten minutes before sunrise on the fifth morning, one of the medicine men began the closing ceremony by painting an outline of the sun on the palm of his left hand just as the sun approached the medicine tipi's entryway. At that exact moment, he rubbed his hand over the head and face of the girl—who had spent the previous night in the tipi—before using a brush of gramma grass into which an eagle feather had been inserted to paint the girl's face, arms, and legs with white clay. On the right side of her face he also painted stripes of red and white, representing the rainbow. As the girl left the sacred tipi, Apache women carried baskets of food onto the ceremonial grounds and placed them in a single line running eastward from the fire pit. The observers gathered around and the food was distributed. The final closure of the ceremony was marked by the medicine men dismantling the sacred tipi.

Theoretically and practically, the puberty ceremony showed Apache girls the way toward a good life by its emphasis on four all-important life objectives: physical strength, a good disposition, prosperity, and a sound and healthy, uncrippled old age. The phases of the ritual associated with massage and running symbolically provide the young woman with the physical strength needed for her life ahead, a pleasant attitude promised that the girl will always have the support and assistance of her relatives, prosperity was measured in freedom from hunger and an adequate supply of meat for her family despite ever present environmental dangers, and living to an old age was viewed as evidence of victory over all the dark forces in the universe designed to do harm.

Ten years ago, the cost for the entire ceremony was estimated at $8,000 to $10,000 when one tallied all the expenses, including the cost of feeding many family members, guests, and outside visitors for four days.[64] The cost has probably doubled by now.

This expense is a far cry from when Chiricahua Apache woman Blossom Haozous saw her first puberty ceremony while still a child prisoner of war at Fort Sill. She spoke about it with interviewer Pat O'Brien in 1976, when Mrs. Haozous was eighty-three years old. "They gave a feast and dance," she said. "I was so little, I don't remember much about it. I was a little bit frightened of the fire dancers [Mountain Spirit dancers] when I first saw them. I never saw anything like that before. The whole tribe would come to the feasts. There were a few hundred of us. There was enough meat for a little piece for everybody. Most of the time they had a big place there where they did the cooking. They usually boiled the meat or broiled it over the hot coals. They also had dried corn. They'd boil it with the beef bones."

Mrs. Haozous next remembered her own puberty ceremony, held about seventy years earlier, saying,

> They sing to you and spread a big buckskin on the ground and then they place you on there on your stomach and then they massage you. They do all kinds of things to you and then they pray for you. Then they let you get up. Then they put a basket of feathers and some kind of grass—it's eagle feathers and something that's supposed to be sacred. They put it in this woven Indian basket out toward the east and then they stand the girl up after they massaged her and they give her a little shove. On the fourth time, she gets a big shove. She runs around the basket and then comes back. They'd do that over and over four times. During those days when they're giving you your dance, they put on your buckskin dress and you wear it the full four days. You're not allowed to drink water out of a cup; they used to give you a bamboo tube that they would tie onto your dress and you'd drink with that. They said you weren't supposed to wash your face for four days. Nothing different happened on any of the other days but on the last. On the last day is when they throw out all that food for people to pick up. That was the give-away to the crowd.[65]

Mrs. Haozous's puberty ceremony was held at Fort Sill, Oklahoma, when she was still a child prisoner of war. Her testimony supports the fact that the U.S. Army permitted certain traditional ceremonies to continue. The exact date of the ritual could not be determined, but if it was in 1906, for example, the Protestant missionaries were already active among the Chiricahua Apaches and would have objected strongly. As an adult, Mrs. Haozous became quite involved with the Dutch Reformed Church.

THE MOUNTAIN SPIRIT DANCERS

As an integral part of the entire puberty ceremony, the Mountain Spirit dancers assist the maiden to become a woman in the eyes of the tribe.[66] The origin of these legendary holy people reaches back to a time before time. One sacred story describes two young Apache men who were physically disabled—one blind and the other lame. Because of their handicaps, they couldn't keep up with the tribe during warfare, and so they had to be left behind after one particular battle. Warriors placed them together in a hillside cave with enough food and water to keep them well supplied until someone would return for them.

The two sat closely together in the dark cave, fearing that they would be taken captive at any moment by their enemies. Many days and weeks passed, and they slowly lost hope of ever being reconciled with their families. One evening, shortly after dusk, the men heard strange noises and worried that their hiding place had been discovered. The unfamiliar sound came closer and closer until it suddenly stopped right at the entrance to the cave, where five figures of men who seemed unreal were strangely clad in exotic outfits composed of kilts made of deerskin, belts of hide, and high-legged buckskin moccasins. Over their faces they wore black masks. Their bodies were individually decorated with symbols representing corn, wind, and rain. No two looked alike. They wore great headdresses of wooden slats painted with symbolic figures. In each hand they held jagged staves; the right one had a cross painted on it, representing the four directions. Standing between the figures of the gods was a small form, masked but without headdress, his body painted white. He spoke to the men and urged them not to be afraid, for they all had come from the four directions to relieve them of their suffering and deliver them safely to their people.

The five began to dance around a fire that had suddenly come up, as had the winds and the rain, bringing food and life. At regular intervals the figures uttered a soft cooing sound, like the voice of a woman. The dancers chanted continuously and waved their staves to drive away the evil spirit that had made one man blind and another lame. When the dance ended, the holy people led the two handicapped men through the entrance out onto a trail toward a huge rock that overlooked the cave. The dancer who was painted white hit the rock with his stave and it split, opening a passageway through which all entered. While walking this path, the blind man regained his vision and the lame man was once again able to walk normally. To their astonishment, they also were beautifully clothed in buckskins and held the finest curved bows and arrows in their hands. When they turned to thank the dancers, no one was in sight.

ONE

Looking to the east they saw an encampment of tipis and found their people.

Shortly after the men were reunited with their tribe, the dance of the Mountain Spirits was performed for the first time outside of the cave. Each step of the dance, as described by the two men, was carefully followed. Groups of dancers eventually formed, headed by leaders who were chosen by the two men.[67]

These ancient beliefs are alive today in the persons of the Mescalero, Lipan, and Chiricahua Apache dancers who perform the sacred steps at puberty ceremonies in New Mexico and on special occasions in Oklahoma. These days it is not unusual to see female clergy participating in this ancient ritual, dancing around the bonfire while the Mountain Spirit dancers imitate and repeat, by their dance steps, the sacredness of the very first dance. It is a moving and awesome sight.

Comments of Paul Ortega, Mescalero Apache Medicine Man

A noted healer, Paul Ortega consented to talk about himself, his abilities, and the connection Apache healing has to religion in an interview with him for the Oral History Project at the University of New Mexico's Health Sciences Center Library.

Ortega believes that people heal themselves and that the task of medicine men and medicine women is to "just abide by what [people] want. . . . We only work with people who want to be helped." Years ago Ortega's grandmother helped his grandfather through massage. "She used to sing or hum to herself as she rubbed him," Ortega said. He quoted her telling her husband, "I'm bringing all this problem that you have got here and then I'm taking it out to the fingers and I'm pulling it out and I'm throwing it away now. . . . I'm making his mind work. . . . I'm doing it until I get the pain out of him. He has to get it out, not me.

"I never pray for myself. I always pray for everybody else, hoping that somebody will pray for me. When you pray in the Apache way, you thank the Creator for giving you all things. It's not praying for yourself. You see, when most people learn prayers, they think it's a special thing. It's not. Prayers belong to everybody.

There are no hidden agendas in prayers. I think once you learn to respect things, you give thanks. When somebody teaches you a prayer, you have to learn to pray for everybody else except yourself."

Ortega concluded by saying, "A medicine man is a person who felt comfortable anywhere he went, whether it was out on the mountains or out on the plains or out on the desert." He believed that medicine men and medicine women were part of everything in the natural world but were different because they had a special gift of healing, and in showing their appreciation for this gift, they should pray by saying, "Thank you for giving me the ways of life to be able to see and feel and taste and talk about things."[68]

A Few Words . . .

Chiricahua Apache creation myths, sacred stories, and rituals sustained the people both in their lifeways in the north country and in their new environment. Prior to contact with outsiders, the Apaches were content with their life in the desert and mountains of the Southwest and Mexico, believing that Ussen's intentions for them were being fulfilled. Their cultural beliefs incorporated a spiritual system that contained some of the ancestral ways as well as new processes of respect that mirrored the conditions of their current homelands. When the Europeans arrived in Apacheria, convinced of the need to religiously and secularly dominate—in other words, to have dominion over—and to attempt to forcibly impose a system of European values, including Christianity, upon them, the Apaches perceived a danger so great that extreme actions were required lest their rich religious heritage be lost for all time. They were correct.

CHAPTER TWO

The Jesuit Period

Northern Mexico

In the late 1530s and early 1540s, Spanish colonial officials in Mexico City listened intently to information about the uncharted geographical region of northern Mexico. Returning explorers Álvar Núñez Cabeza de Vaca, Fray Marcos de Niza, and Francisco Vásquez de Coronado had each lauded the new territory, usually in greatly exaggerated descriptions.[1] Absolutely convinced of the region's spiritual, human, and economic potential, Viceroy Antonio Mendoza and other officials of the Crown approved settlement and economic expansion. Giving life and breath to this plan were soldiers, civilians, and Jesuit missionaries—front-line agents of Spanish political, cultural, and religious imperialism and instruments of the greatest religious campaign since the Crusades. There was no doubt that the Jesuits were equal to their daunting job of evangelizing the Indians, transforming them into Christians by civilizing them, thereby creating new tax-paying citizens of the empire. To a man, the Jesuits were characteristically full of fervor, eager to create and sustain a religious evolution in New Spain at a site they named the Pimeria Alta.[2]

The Spanish Crown favored rapid evangelization and forced indoctrination of the indigenes, if need be, whereas the church favored a slower process resulting in voluntary baptism. Still, by papal authority the kings of Castile had been granted sole

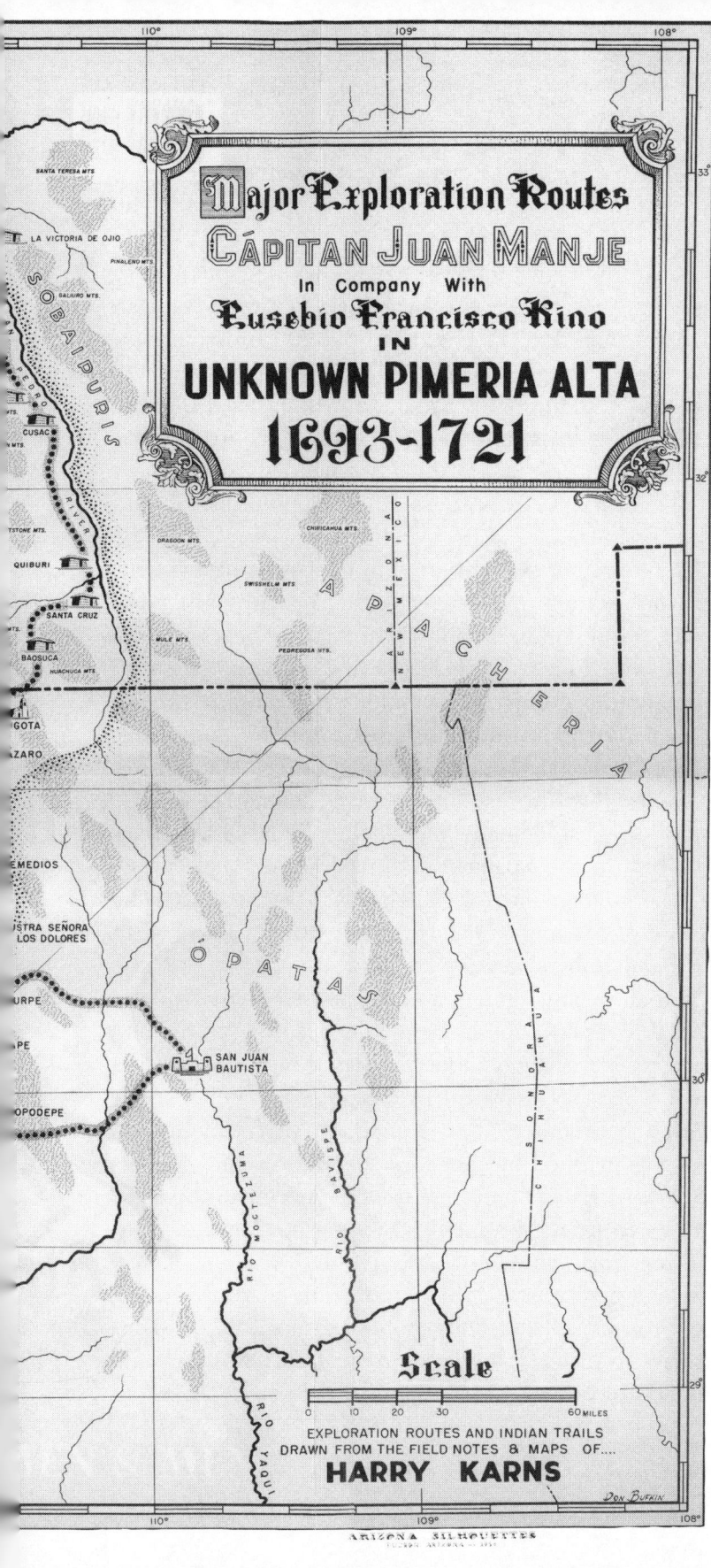

Map 1. Jesuit Father Eusebio Kino's major exploration routes. Accompanied by Captain Juan Manje, he explored the Pimeria Alta during the years 1693–1721.

responsibility for the Indians, and the *patronato real* (royal patronage) policy of 1508 also gave the Crown control over appointments and finances related to the church in America.[3] The Crown became the pope's representative in the New World primarily because of its willingness to support the missionary endeavor with funds from the royal treasury. Wrote Franciscan Kieran McCarty, O.F.M.: "Thus it was that the missionaries' principal task was to bring about the cultural assimilation of the native population."[4] Additionally, patronato real ensured that the Crown would have at least indirect, if not direct, control of the clergy through legislation that continually amended existing laws governing obligations of the priests, their appointments, and reviews of the missions.[5]

Cultural assimilation, as mentioned by McCarty, occurs constantly within social evolution as the wider social setting often dictates the pace of cultural integration. For example, if necessary, the missionaries' advanced forms of society would encourage them to assimilate into another group with a rapidity not characteristic of preliterate peoples. And within the latter category, indigenous tribes (actually, collections of bands[6]) with complex social structures would adapt sooner than the less "progressive" peoples.

An assumption must be made here and applied: the sedentary agricultural tribes on the Spanish colonial frontier, such as the Pimas, were easier to force into assimilation than were the nomadic Apaches because of the more intricate social structure needed to ensure that tribal members' needs were met.

Also essential to any understanding of the events on the Spanish colonial frontier is the indisputable fact that politics and religion joined to coerce indigenous peoples through persuasion first and force when necessary into replacing the faith of their ancestors with Christianity. "The conviction that violence on Indian bodies was justified by the need to preserve Indian souls remained a controversial but enduring facet of the debate about the best means to correct persisting native religious deviance in colonial Spanish America," wrote Nicholas Griffiths.[7]

While Spain's goal was not the annihilation of future Indian subjects, the Crown's self-defeating policy of separating Indians from their tribes in order to "groom" them into Christians and eventual citizens had the effect of limiting their exposure to

European culture by isolating them in mission settings. Another obstacle was the paternalistic Jesuits themselves, who often sought to protect their charges from the dangers of life in the secular world. Nonetheless, David Weber believes that "throughout North America, in ways large and small, Spanish influences changed the cultures of all native Americans. . . . The extent to which change damaged or benefited a people also depended on the nature of their cultures, economies, and polities."[8]

For centuries, various groups of Indians occupying northern Mexico had developed their own religious values, their own cultural customs, and their own methods of acquiring sustenance. Many were agriculturists; farming was usually an adequate means of providing for themselves even though the availability of irrigating water depended on capricious weather conditions. During years of climatic hardships, not uncommon in desert existence, competition for sustenance could be intense, causing raids on Indian villages by other Indians, including the nomadic, hunter-gatherer Chiricahua Apaches.

The Chiricahua Apaches lived in scattered settlements consisting mainly of kinship clusters—immediate and extended families—called "local units" by anthropologists. On special occasions all the Chiricahua bands came together, perhaps to celebrate a puberty ceremony, to gather for warfare, or to console each other on someone's death. Each local unit was independent, autonomous, and only under extreme conditions did one leader assume control by consensus over any Apaches who elected to support him. When the urgency was over, he relinquished his position and the warriors returned to their local units.

In the last half of the 1500s, rain had been absent in the Pimeria Alta for up to four decades.[9] As a land-based tribe with deep spiritual connections to the earth, the Chiricahuas believed that the dryness was an omen—a sign predicting an unknown danger. But until contact with the Jesuit Spaniards and the "extraordinary European conviction of their right to appropriate the world,"[10] wrote Inga Clendinnen, no sign had ever warned of a similar peril.

The Jesuits were members of a religious order founded by Saint Ignatius Loyola and designated by him as "The Company of Jesus." This title was Latinized into *Societas Jesu* in the *Regimini* bull of Pope Paul III, who approved the society's formation on September

27, 1540, and largely freed the Jesuits from control of the Episcopal (bishopric) hierarchy.[11] The society's specific purpose was to propagate and strengthen Catholic faith everywhere, so from the very beginning the worldwide missionary labors of the Jesuits consisted of preaching, teaching catechism, administering the sacraments, and conducting missions. Thus, the Jesuits were, at least theoretically, well suited for northern Mexico, where most of the thousands of inhabitants from many Indian tribes had no idea of Christianity.

The mendicant priests' assignment to the frontier was the result of a shortage of secular priests—those not belonging to an order. Order or "regular" clergy answered to the Crown and were free from the control of bishops. Secular clergy were under the direct authority of bishops, who, in turn, were appointed by the king and his deputies.[12] Had there not been a slump in the number of available clergy, the papacy would have continued its reliance on diocesan priests to carry the Word into northern Mexico. But due to the circumstances, a Papal Bull in 1546 granted the Jesuits permission to indoctrinate the indigenous peoples of the Pimeria Alta into Christianity, to administer the sacraments, to educate the Indians, and to prepare them for citizenship.[13]

Far from Spain and the political jurisdiction of the viceroy in Mexico City, the Jesuit missionaries in northern Mexico took license in designing, adapting, and implementing whatever they viewed as suitable to reach their goals, including educating the Indian children and the sons and daughters of prominent Mexicans of Spanish descent. Although this priestly activity grew dramatically in the mission setting, it supplemented and complemented, but did not supplant, the Jesuits' duty to evangelize Mexico's Indians.

Evangelizing started in earnest in the mid-1600s at a site named Ures[14] and proceeded slowly. Ever present language barriers were frustrating, at least until the Nahuatl language, spoken by Aztec peoples in central Mexico, and Spanish became the lingua francas of the colonial frontier. Unfortunately, shared language skills may not have led to reciprocal understanding. Instead, both tongues probably favored and facilitated the Jesuits' plan by causing them to interpret their initial accomplishments as proof of the unstoppable force of Christianity.[15]

The Jesuits' attitude is important to appreciate, as it underlined the courage needed to endure continued danger from unfriendly tribes. Andrés Peréz de Ribas, the Jesuit provincial—the highest-ranking position within the Jesuit province of New Spain—in Mexico City in the mid-1600s believed that "the Jesuit experience in the New World reflected the unfolding of a divine plan" and that the Jesuits accepted the possibility of martyrdom because they believed "they were living out their lives in fulfillment of a prophecy, continuing the work of Christ and his disciples."[16] And surely another inducement was the missionaries' Eurocentric view of the Indians as needing salvation, a determination that set the stage for deculturation and confirmed their roles as proud and worthy members of the Spanish Empire.[17]

Proof of their cultural superiority was obvious to the Spaniards: they were educated, had better weapons than the Indians, were skilled in working metal to produce tools, had domesticated horses for transportation and raised other livestock for food, and were knowledgeable in the mass production of other subsistence through "modern" farming techniques. In addition, their language was written and many citizens could read and write, an unmistakable sign of supremacy over the indigenous peoples.

Adding to the high opinion of themselves was the fact that these Europeans had laws and governing institutions. They could point to at least one legitimizing legal document, the *Requerimiento*, which granted them license to do anything they wished to the Indians. Written by jurist Palacios Rubios in 1514, the official document stated that the highest pinnacle of humankind was Jesus Christ, who ultimately transferred his power to Saint Peter, who then bequeathed authority to the popes, one of whom bestowed the American continent upon the Spaniards in the form of patronato real.[18]

And so the collision of the Europeans with the indigenes on the frontier was guaranteed. Reff infers that the period from 1591 to 1643, years when the Chiricahua Apaches were permanently established as one of northern Mexico's tribes, witnessed the greatest development of the missions and the influx of Jesuits to staff them.[19] In 1628, 382 Jesuits working in the Pimeria Alta received an annual stipend of 250 pesos each from the Royal Treasury, which also furnished bells, chalices, vestments, and other items necessary for a mission to function. By 1645 there were thirty-five Jesuit missions in the Mexican states of Sinaloa and Sonora, each consisting of from one to four "towns" under the care of a Jesuit and supported by an area presidio.[20]

The venerable Jesuit Eusebio Francisco Kino[21] entered the Pimeria Alta in 1687 and headquartered at a mission complex he founded called Nuestra Señora de los Dolores—Our Lady of Sorrows—dedicating the mission on April 26, 1693. Kino's description has been preserved:

> This mission has its church adequately furnished with ornaments, chalices, cups of gold, bells, and choir chapel; likewise a great many livestock, fields, a garden with various kinds of garden crops, Castilian fruit trees, grapes, peaches, quinces, figs, pomegranates, pears, and clingstones. It has a forge for blacksmiths, a carpenter shop, a pack train, water mill, many kinds of grain, provisions from rich and abundant harvests of wheat and maize, and other things, including horse and mule herds; all of which serve and are greatly needed both for domestic use as well as for expeditions, and for new conquests and conversions, and to purchase a few gifts and attractions with which, together with the Word of God, it is customary to contrive to win the minds and souls of the natives.[22]

Before Kino arrived, the Jesuits had indoctrinated many Pimas and other groups' tribal members into Christianity, a task that was simultaneously easy or difficult, depending on the natives' perceptions of the priests. In some cases, a Jesuit's individual charisma and the church's religious rituals were seen as similar to those of medicine men and were a powerful inducement to comply. The task then facing the missionaries was to keep the Indians interested lest they revert to traditional ways. Gifts such as food and clothing, and other incentives, were continually offered, but Kino had a better idea.

Friendly Indians usually met Kino and his military aide, Juan Mateo Manje, outside their villages and welcomed them by carrying crosses and arches of flowers.[23] To further ingratiate the acolytes, Kino presented staffs to the Indians—usually nothing but tall walking sticks festooned with ribbons. Through interpreters traveling with him, Kino told the natives that the sticks gave them the ability to govern themselves, an impertinent statement because the tribes had been successfully managing themselves for generations. Still,

"PADRE KINO" *as depicted by the El Paso artist, José Cisneros*

Fig. 12. Jesuit Eusebio Kino riding herd on cattle he and his fellow priests introduced to the Pimeria Alta. From Eckhart, "A Guide to the History of the Missions of Sonora, 1614–1826." Sketch by José Cisneros.

the unassuming and unsuspecting natives accepted Kino's gift thereby, to the Spaniards acknowledging and solidifying their perception of their superiority and confirming the Jesuits' ethnocentric impression that the Indians were like children who needed to be guided.[24] This view was consistent with Matthew 18:1–3, in which Christ says, "Unless you change and become like little children, you will never enter the kingdom of heaven."

But there was a political reason as well to infantilize the Indians. The longer these natives remained as "children,"[25] the longer they would remain under the Jesuits' care and not be relinquished to the secular clergy; rivalry among these two groups was heated, for when released to the secular clergy, the Indians would begin paying taxes to support the secular clergy and bishops at the expense of the Jesuits.[26]

Kino, a careful and thoughtful man, stressed mission site selection as being crucial and developed evaluating criteria. After considering an area's importance to the Indians in terms of its ancestral sacredness, its water supply, and the quality of the terrain for farming and livestock grazing, Kino and the other Jesuits applied a significant test: the size of the surrounding Indian population. Were there enough natives in the area to warrant a satellite mission, called a *visita?* Or were there enough Indians to populate a more complex arrangement known as a *cabecera*—the headquarters of worship for one or more visitas?[27]

Regardless of the decision, many of the chosen mission locations had been Indian ceremonial centers and sacred sites that were deliberately selected by the Jesuits to confront the natives' age-old spiritual traditions head-on. Gambling correctly that this unmistakable demonstration of their superiority would overwhelm the Indians, the priests first erected *ramadas*—temporary shelters made of poles and brush—directly atop the natives' sacred grounds, as an initial step in deculturation. Intimidated immediately by this audacity, many of the more timid indigenous tribes soon accepted the Jesuits' presence despite their shamans' wishes and warnings to the contrary. Shamans were the Spaniards' main obstacle to success; the Jesuits looked upon their relations with the Indians as a battle with the devil and his agents, the shamans. Consequently, one of the priests' foremost achievements became convincing a shaman to abandon his traditional ways and endorse Christianity; Reff noted its infrequent occurrence.[28]

After a site was selected, indoctrination of the indigenes into Christianity began through a policy of *reducción/congregación.* Various Indian populations were moved out of their villages (reducción) and resettled into mission communities (congregación), where indoctrination, supervision, and control could be exercised, helped along by the choice of a native, always male, to serve as liaison between the priests and the general Indian mission community. The selected headman's job was to be responsive to the priests' wishes, to follow orders, and to provide information about his tribe and other frontier groups. That the chosen individual might not have any credibility whatsoever among his colleagues was occasionally a positive consideration in the selection, for a leader respected by fellow tribal members would not have been sufficiently submissive to follow the missionaries' directions without question or objection.[29]

In other words, the goal of this aspect of cultural imperialism—deculturation through reducción/congregación—was to significantly disrupt traditional cultures and relocate the natives where the Spaniards could exercise unlimited control, using a so-called leader as their agent.[30] Not incidentally, the policy also left Indian lands open to appropriation by colonizing Spaniards. But not all the tribes cooperated. Importantly, those who resisted remained in their traditional settlements, retained their cultural integrity and autonomy, and defended their ancestral landholdings, at least for the moment.

The mission complexes that materialized from congregación consisted of a plaza—a public square—around which, wrote Herbert Bolton, were located the place of worship, the missionary's residence, the houses of the Indians, "carpenter shops, blacksmith shops, spinning and weaving rooms, corrals for the stock, fields, irrigation ditches and everything going to make a well ordered and self-supporting agricultural unit. . . . Such a mission was a veritable frontier stronghold."[31] It must be kept in mind, however, that this description is of an ideal setting; not all the missions measured up to this standard.

Undoubtedly a climate of tension surfaced periodically in the missions, likely fostered by the Jesuits' objectives clashing with the native residents' wishes. Established mission rules and precepts dictated the type of discipline to be meted out to unruly or uncooperative Indians, ranging from the mildest punishment—withholding food and water—to the humiliation of shaving an Indian's head, to the most severe such as flogging or worse. While reprisal at the hands of the Europeans was a new experience, it was particularly difficult for the natives to understand that, according to what the priests said, being disciplined now would save them from a worse fate of eternal damnation.

This harsh treatment may have occasionally backfired for, wrote Griffiths, "it is highly doubtful whether coercive methods had anything other than a negative impact on the Christianization of native peoples."[32]

Nonetheless, in setting the standards for chastisement, Jesuit Father Provincial Andrés Xavier García wrote on June 25, 1747, "If an Indian is to be punished for an ordinary fault, he will not receive more than 6 lashes. A more serious fault, 12; and the most serious, 25. In case they are women, never more than 8 and always at the hands of the governor or fiscal."[33] The idea of punishment was so intimidating that many timid Indians simply acquiesced to the Jesuits' orders rather than defy them.

One of the most difficult tests of the mission Indians' loyalty was forced labor. For example, to build the foundation of a long, rectangular adobe church, the Indians had to fell timber and haul heavy limbs of trees to a working area at the mission location. Then, under the constant supervision and direction of a priest and armed soldiers, the laborers created square wooden frames for adobe bricks, some twelve-by-twelve inches or larger. Next they dug out the rocky caliche soil, mixed it with water, small stones, and slivers of wood, and poured it into the shells. Days later, when the sun had thoroughly dried and baked the mud, the Indians lifted each heavy brick and carried it to their former sacred site. They piled one brick on top of the other and one or two beside each other, sometimes to a width of thirty-six inches, to raise the mission church's walls. After the sides were standing and secure, roof construction began by peeling bark from heavy tree branches, lifting them, and then setting them across the open width from one side to the other. Next skinny wooden branches of willow, saguaro cactus ribs, or similar materials called latillas were also peeled and placed at right angles atop the beams. Lastly mud, cow manure, grass, and other natural flora sealed the roof.

To prevent deterioration, the Indians hauled, pushed, and pulled tons of limestone boulders to the mission, often from distant quarry sites, burned them with roaring fires in a pit until they exploded, and then pulverized and blended the residue with water. Other natives stood by to smear the mixture by hand onto church walls, frequently standing on shaky scaffolds that could collapse and plunge the men to earth. The Indians worked incredibly hard, and if they hesitated or sat down to rest without permission, soldiers were ordered to discipline them on the spot.

Indian forced labor, not only in building churches but also working in the fields, was justified and organized under two Spanish institutions, the *encomienda* and the *repartimiento*. Donald C. Cutter and Iris Engstrand state that

> the encomienda was utilized to achieve several goals, including Indian control, economic exploitation, and indoctrination. . . . In theory it was a means whereby native people under the guidance of trustworthy Spanish citizens were to be instructed in the way of becoming not only good vassals of the crown but also Christian citizens. In practice . . . it became an opportunity to become wealthy at the expense of the labor of the Indians.[34]

David Weber described repartimiento as a "time honored institution by which Spanish officials distributed native men to work on a rotating basis at tasks deemed to be for the public good."[35] Jesuit Polzer was much more succinct, defining repartimiento as "essentially slavery."[36]

Polzer's definition was closer to the truth, as participation was compulsory, but unlike the common understanding of slavery, the natives were supposed to receive wages, and the length of their servitude was controlled by laws, as was the type of labor they were expected to do. However, according to Weber, "On the frontier, as throughout the Spanish empire, Indians were unpaid, underpaid, paid in overvalued merchandise, unfed, underfed, kept for longer periods of time than regulations permitted."[37] Control through a well-defined hierarchical structure and threats of punishment for disobedience were essential to the Spaniards if managing a large group of Indians was to be even moderately successful. Surely it must have occurred to the Jesuits that their punitive actions compromised the Indians' understanding of Christian charity and love, but the importance of the twin goals of indoctrination and assimilation apparently overrode any other considerations.

The Chiricahua Apaches

The Chiricahua Apaches of northern Mexico, a hunting-gathering tribe, lived with the sacred every moment and, through their cultural appreciation of the universe, recognized the spiritual influence in all things. Unlike the practices of Christianity, which led to salvation or eternal life, the here and now was significant to the Apaches, not the great beyond. To that end, the Chiricahuas saw themselves in a balanced relation with the earth and the cosmos.

In dramatic contrast, Kino's soldier-companion Manje identified the Chiricahuas as "barbarous apostates . . . savages . . . who live by hunting."[38] Despite Manje's perception, it was difficult, if not impossible, on the Spanish colonial frontier to correctly recognize any group as truly "Apache." Mistakes in identity occurred more and more frequently as the Chiricahuas became increasingly visible. Eventually, any group of belligerent or hostile Indians was called "Apaches."

Complicating the situation, true Apache local units frequently consisted of a variety of people from diverse backgrounds, all taking advantage of the ancient Apache custom of cultural fluidity. Under this characteristic, the people always welcomed new affiliates, allowed members of one local unit to become part of another, to start a new group, or even join an unrelated neighboring tribe. Adding to the mix, the long migration from the north centuries earlier brought newcomer Indians into the traveling groups, dropped others off, and births and deaths occurred. As a result, the composition of frontier Apache groups was diverse, and their proportions continued to ebb and flow as cultural fluidity opened doors to new affiliates. Large groups of "Chiricahua Apaches," as we shall call the mixed peoples, brought a measure of security by preventing them from being physically outnumbered by the Spanish military units, and so it was best to welcome everyone to the groups. Still, because of the Spaniards' limited perceptions, most unfriendly or hostile Indians were known simply as "Apaches."

The changing complexion of local units through ethnogenesis—the process by which distinct ethnic cultures re-create themselves as new cultures over time—would have been familiar to the Chiricahuas, whose old stories about Coyote's changing forms and antics were essential to outwit his enemies.[39] Ever open to change, if a particular cultural or religious practice from another society caught their fancy, the Chiricahuas added it to their stories, imitated it, and even temporarily adopted it; if it lost its appeal, they discarded it.

Oral testimony tells of an occurrence in the late 1700s that demonstrates the point. A small group of Indians led by an Apache named Calaxtrain raided a church.[40] One of the warriors stole a glass box, inside of which was a carved, wooden statue of the Virgin Mary wearing a blue cloak. The unbroken box and statue were later found safe in a cave occasionally occupied by some of Calaxtrain's followers. Someone had carefully placed the artifact in a niche in the cave's wall, washed it, replaced it in the niche, and perhaps even adored it. Dancers' pounding feet had trampled the ground beneath the niche, and true believers had stuffed offerings of feathers, birds' bones, colorful stones, animals' teeth, pieces of shell, and other charms into the space around the box. This act appears to be a private religious ceremony, away from the eyes of the priests, combining Catholic veneration of the Virgin Mary with native ceremonial offerings—a syncretic combination of religions and a dual mode of accommodation and resistance.

Raids

Over and over during the Jesuit years Apaches attacked both the cabeceras and visitas, forcing many to become abandoned. The Jesuit letters addressed to other missionaries and high civilian officials—in total numbering tens of thousands[41]—and official documents written about Apache raids were, understandably, deeply partisan accounts. A good example is a letter written in 1764 by Jesuit Juan Nentvig (also spelled Nentuig and Nentwig). He noted that despite the large numbers of livestock that had been sent to the missions from Mexico City, there was often a lack of sufficient cattle, oxen, mules, and horses due to the continuing Apache raids. "The shortage is so acute," Nentvig wrote, "that residents do not have enough beef to slaughter or saddle animals to ride in quest of sustenance for their families." He believed that the deficiency should be blamed only

> on the prowling of the Apaches. . . . One needs only to look at the nearly 300 abandoned ranches . . . that have lost more than 4000 mules, mares, and horses in the last seven years to realize this is true. It is God's merciful design that the Apache scatter

their forces over a large area and do not as a unit attack us, for there could be no place within the entire province that could be held against a united Apache effort. The whole province could be destroyed within a year. . . . Because this enemy goes unpunished, he is able to keep this normally wealthy province impoverished.[42]

Killing mission residents during any of these raids seemed almost accidental during the early years of contact, a fact that has been noted by Maria Soledad Arbelaez, who wrote, "An outstanding feature of [the Jesuit] reports is the constant complaint raised . . . that the main reason for the Indian attacks was to pillage the mission's property. . . . Total destruction was rarely the case since the Indians attacked symbols of domination: church buildings, crosses, and saints' images."[43] In the Apaches' eyes, destroying these religious symbols reaffirmed their power against the authority of the outsiders and their authority over the Catholic religious power.

It is important to understand the reason why raiding, not killing, the newcomers occurred. A pragmatic people, the Chiricahuas recognized that no livestock would reach the area if the Spaniards were murdered and not replaced. It was in their best interests to simply steal the booty, but—and this is quite significant—they believed the priests to be witches. And here is where an intratribal conflict occurred. Through some Apache eyes, witches exhibited unmistakable traits and should be killed. They

1. Are friendly with ghosts—Jesuits recognize and honor the Holy Spirit; they do not consider this "ghost to be an enemy, nor do they take measures to avoid "ghost sickness"—the sure result of interacting with a ghost;

2. Handle the dead without taking precautions—Jesuits conduct funerals without destroying their clothing afterward or rubbing ashes on their bodies to ward off ghost sickness;

3. Use amulets—Jesuits rely on holy oils, incense, etc., during their religious services;

4. Bring sickness—Jesuits carry evil to Apacheria in the form of deadly contagious diseases;

5. Are troublemakers—Jesuits disrupt the traditional life of many tribes by convincing them to leave their villages and live at the missions. The witches then work the Indians like slaves, impose restrictions, insist on them adopting the witches' way, and discipline and punish them severely if they don't obey;

6. Have strange habits—Jesuits pray indoors, eat unfamiliar foods, and dress in long woolen garments in the hot desert environment;

7. Act peculiarly—Jesuits speak a different language, can read and write;

8. Wear beads openly—Jesuits sometimes wrap rosaries around their necks;

9. Are braggarts or misers—Jesuits say their way of life is better but store their excess food instead of sharing it;

10. Are sexually aberrant—Jesuits live without women.[44]

But a nearby, steady, and easily accessible supply of food and transportation took precedence—a major cultural shift—over the traditional ancestral remedy of killing witches, and so the Jesuits were allowed to live.

A transformation in belief and acceptance of the activities that flow from the new concept are noteworthy occurrences in a preliterate society such as the Chiricahua Apaches were on the Spanish colonial frontier. The decision to raid, not kill, flew in the face of ancient cultural prescriptions and would have had to be extensively debated among the leaders before being implemented. Every male above puberty and certain women (wives of important leaders) would possibly be allowed to add their voices as well. The final decision, if protocol prevailed, would have been taken by consensus, with each man's vote carrying the same weight. Despite the "benign" intention to raid, not kill, however, the Europeans used their weapons to defend against the raiders.

When the presidial army retaliated and fired their weapons, the Apaches had to shoot back. The Indians' goals then changed and became twofold: to make off with the livestock and other appealing items, especially Spanish weapons, and to kill everyone who got in the way.

Each attack was carefully planned, a characteristic of a raiding society. Before leaving the campsite the leader consulted with medicine men and medicine women, who were thought to be able to predetermine the outcomes of most situations. If these seers declared that the time was right, the warriors attacked openly and unafraid—screaming in fury atop previously purloined Spanish horses, waving and firing previously pilfered Spanish guns, letting their presence be known in advance but usually not soon enough for an effective Spanish military reaction to occur.[45]

When they weren't charging at the mission, the warriors crawled silently on their bellies across the desert dirt and sand, unseen until too late. There was no pattern to the raids, no way the Europeans could predict the attacks, nor could they prevent them. Their best responses resulted in killing or capturing a number of Apaches and incarcerating them at the missions, where the priests would begin indoctrination.

The Jesuits quickly recognized that, try hard as they did, it was impossible to inculcate these Chiricahua prisoners—men, women, and children—in Christian doctrine; their stubborn personalities and rancorous behavior, especially by the women, permitted no evangelizing. So, the missionaries didn't proselytize them as they did members of other tribes, hoping and literally praying that the Apache captives would observe and be impressed by the Catholic practices close at hand.[46]

Contagion

Abundant information is available about the variety of deadly contagious diseases that, over time, devastated most of the region's peoples. One of the best descriptions of the widespread effect of the successive waves of ailments and deaths was written by Clendinnen:

> We do not even know what age groups were most vulnerable, or in what form death most often came. . . . Certainly the depleted populations . . . must have fractured social life and frighteningly disrupted the reassuring pulse of collective activity. The survivors were reduced to being refugees in their own land, striving to pull together some of the old strands of life. . . . Roles must

have been elided, transformed, even excised, as men strove to sustain the activities and routines they identified as most essential, while organizing to meet as best they could, with what time and energy they could muster, the unpredictable threat from outside. . . . Those little societies had been profoundly transformed. . . . Major adjustments must have been necessary if only because of a massive reduction in population.[47]

Epidemics ordinarily occurred at five- to seven-year intervals. Interestingly, none of the Jesuit documents specifically identify the Apaches as a tribe that had become ill, probably because these nomads had no permanent living structures, no agricultural fields to tend, and no special loyalty to a particular place or settlement; they considered all of Apacheria to be available to them. So, when word of mouth brought the news to a local unit or larger group that sickness had come to a particular mission, the Apaches simply stayed away or literally moved in the opposite direction and were initially unaffected.

The Jesuits sterilized many of their written comments about the mortality and morbidity rates among the diverse tribes of northern Mexico, for it was in their best interests to say as little as possible in their official reports. Detailed and truthful statements about the large numbers of afflicted or dead Indians would have subsequently reduced funding for the missions and caused a concomitant decline in the amount of supplies from the depot in Mexico City, a circumstance that would adversely impact an already medically compromised situation. Still, astute officials reading the Jesuits' reports would have noted the obvious decrease in the number of baptisms and a lower census count during periods of epidemics.[48] Reff notes that "epidemics not only had profound demographic consequences, but . . . undermined the . . . authority of Indian shamans and other elites who could neither explain nor prevent the unprecedented suffering coincident with epidemics."[49]

Had they been asked for an explanation by the natives, the frontier Jesuits would have been able to answer the concerns because they held popular European perceptions of the day about the root causes of illness. One theological theory identified all epidemics as God's punishment of the wicked but in the same breath pronounced that earthly suffering led to grace in heaven.

This concept no doubt influenced the missionaries' mixed attitudes toward ailing Indians, so they didn't become immediately alarmed when more and more natives fell ill, lingered, and then died. Although sad about the deaths, the Jesuits were certain that the dying or dead new Christians or near Christian Indians would find their places in heaven, so, wrote Reff, "disease and culture change had meaning only as manifestation of divine will."[50] Todorov supported that idea, writing, "That the Indians die like flies is proof that God is on the conquerors' side," and he questioned why the Spanish would try to "combat a disease when it was sent by God to punish the unbelievers?"[51]

Reff reported that throughout these stressful times "many natives petitioned for . . . baptism, believing that baptisms and the priests provided protection from and a cure for disease."[52] However, it is difficult to imagine that the Indians continued to be baptized when they realized that it offered no defense. Surely some indigenes saw baptism more critically. Whether or not baptism was seen as a solution or as the vector that spread disease, some mission residents believed that tolling the bells—a daily activity—called the illnesses to the missions, but the Jesuits continued ringing the bells despite the Indians' misgivings.

In an environment in which contagious diseases flourished, statistics showed that if a woman somehow avoided or outlived the contagion and survived attacks from raiding Apache groups, she might bear as many as six or seven children.[53] Still, the average family size was small, only two or three members with only one child or no children. A few of the fecund women in the missions were Chiricahua captives and, in the close quarters, sexual intercourse surely occurred, the result of which occasionally added Apache children to the mission population and statistics to the Jesuits' records. First, though, when possible the priests demanded that marriage and monogamy were imperative and were a prerequisite for living as a couple or a family.

Forced monogamy ran counter to the traditional Chiricahua Apache cultural permission to have several wives, dependent only on how well a husband could provide for his family. But many in the missions who outwardly complied with the Jesuits' instructions, including the Chiricahua Apaches, did so simply to please them, to curry favor, to gain authority, to avoid punishment, or for any other self-interest unrelated to Christian tenets. In these situations, the Apache mission residents' deceitful observance of Catholic doctrines was synonymous with their tacit and silent resistance to Catholicism. However, the church's gaining influence on individual Chiricahuas was not to be denied.

Changes

Between waves of medical catastrophes, the Jesuits needed more and more money and supplies to keep the missions afloat; Apache attacks were also taking an enormous toll. "By the mid-17th century," Reff wrote, "many Spaniards had begun to question the huge sums of money the Crown was spending on missionaries in the New World."[54] Not only the expenditures were of concern, however. After each assault, head counts showed that an increasing number of Christian Indians from several tribes had either been killed or had fled the missions in fear; of these, not many voluntarily returned and the numbers of souls saved diminished.

Aware of the situation, King Carlos III took action by sending the Marquis de Rubi, a trusted member of his staff, to the Pimeria Alta in 1767 to inspect the frontier from Sonora to Texas. Rubi's recommendations included a plan for realignment of the presidios to provide more adequately for offensive and defensive actions against the Chiricahuas and "a systematic extermination of the Apaches and the forwarding of captive families south to be distributed in the interior of Mexico."[55] In other words, kill them or enslave them. King Carlos agreed and, as a result of Rubi's suggestions, issued a new set of regulations for the presidios called the *Reglamento de Presidios*, 1772. Rubi's plan's success was expected to reap one of two rich harvests: either it would destroy the Chiricahua Apaches—genocide now, not deculturation—or it would facilitate assimilation.

Breaking up Chiricahua families in any way, but especially through removing children, seriously violated ancient Apache cultural customs. While many frontier Indian groups recognized the worth of the children, the Chiricahua Apaches held their youngsters in extraordinary esteem. Centuries later it was still apparent, as Opler noted, "The great love of children characterizes the society."[56] As an extension of this cultural trait, historic Apache beliefs proclaimed that relatives of all ages, close and extended, anchored the people to each other, to the tribe, and back in time to their ancient heritage. Any rupture of the kinship system that gave structure and order to this affiliation-oriented culture, therefore, was thought of as being so severe a disturbance that it psychologically and physically weakened the entire band. It is doubtful that Rubi was aware of this characteristic, but he nonetheless had recommended a plan whose implementation would have long-lasting and disastrous consequences.

In that same year, 1767, the king issued a decree ordering the Jesuits expelled from northern Mexico. The order read, in part, "Because of the weighty considerations which His Majesty keeps hidden in his heart, the entire Society of Jesus and all Jesuits must leave the country and their establishments and properties must be turned over to the Royal Treasurer. February 27, 1767."[57] The official notice of removal was received in Mexico City on June 25, and a month later, on July 23, the Sonoran governor instructed the captains of the presidios to have the Father Superior of each group of missions summon the Jesuits from their outlying stations to hear the king's decree. Subsequently, on July 25, 1767, fifty-two Jesuits met in the college chapel of San José de Matapé, Sonora. The church was ringed with barriers, behind which soldiers stood, their guns aimed through the windows at the priests. At the end of the reading, the nervous Jesuits began a march under armed guard to the western Mexico seacoast town of Guaymas, where they were imprisoned in cattle sheds before boarding a boat for a voyage to Matachel, followed by a march across Mexico to Veracruz. Only thirty of the fifty-two lived to reach Spain in July 1769.

The fate of the Jesuits' papers and properties was left to politically appointed, but less than honorable, civil commissioners, who frantically ransacked the missions and stole whatever was worth taking. Deeds reported that the Jesuits' records and possessions "were confiscated by royal authorities placed under the jurisdiction of *temporalidades*, the authority constituted to dispose of them for the crown. Eventually many of them were destroyed, lost, sold, or stored in government repositories."[58]

The Jesuits' experiences on the Spanish colonial frontier had thus come to an unanticipated and ignominious end. During their era they had introduced Christianity to members of a number of

Fig. 13. Mission Cocospera, Mexico, 1934. Courtesy of the Arizona Historical Society, #15957.

Fig. 14. Mission San Ignacio (near Magdalena), Mexico, n.d. Photo by Fr. Charles Polzer, S.J., courtesy of the Arizona Historical Society, #28968.

Fig. 15. Mission San Francisco de Atil, Mexico, n.d. Courtesy of the Arizona Historical Society, #16240.

Fig. 16. Mission Cocospera, Mexico, 1966. Courtesy of the Arizona Historical Society, #28879.

Fig. 17. Mission Tubutama, Mexico, n.d. Courtesy of the Arizona Historical Society, #57696.

northern Mexico's Indian tribes, including the Chiricahua Apaches, indoctrinated many, and demonstrated the benefits—as they perceived them—of observing the ways of the Spanish culture. Although their goal of creating tax-paying citizens was incomplete upon their removal, their religious aims of saving souls had been successful within certain parameters. At the time of the Jesuits' departure, most of the Chiricahua Apaches' local units remained viable, with the exception of a few whose integrity had been compromised by the loss of relatives—men, women, and children—who had been sold into slavery in central Mexico.

A Few Words . . .

Chiricahua Apaches and Spaniards shared several basic religious theories even before contact. However, the Apaches had no need to honor Ussen in a specific structure—a mission church. All of the outdoors sufficed. To the Europeans, however, the missions were the crucibles in which missionary-directed Christianization and Spanish civilization were expected to rise up and engulf the Indians, leaving no overt trace of their traditional cultures. That the goal of indoctrinating the Chiricahua Apaches into Christianity didn't happen exactly according to plan in the Jesuit era is partly explained by the fact that most of the Chiricahuas couldn't be captured during that time and then incarcerated at the missions, where their immersion into Christianity would occur.

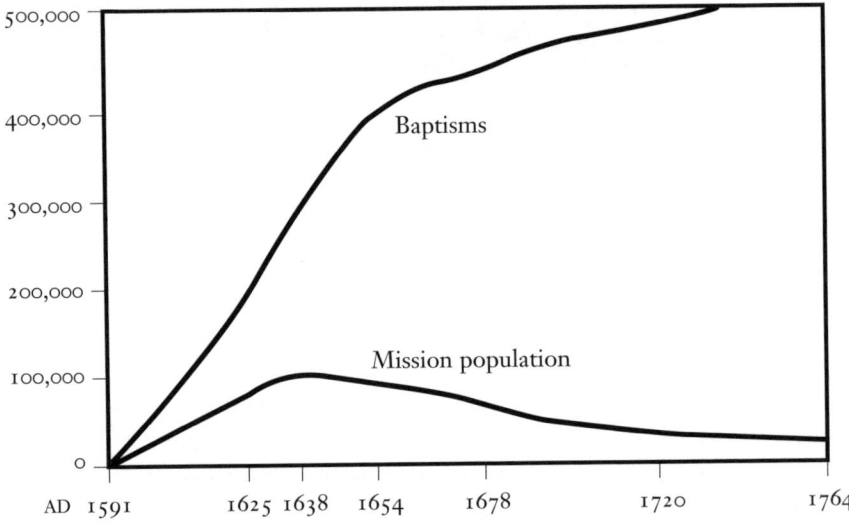

Jesuit baptisms and the mission population 1518 to 1764

Table 1. Jesuit Baptisms and the Mission Population, 1591–1764
Source: Reff, *Disease, Depopulation, and Culture Change in Northwestern New Spain, 1518–1764.*

The Chiricahua Apaches lived in their own spiritual world, an ancient one that protected, satisfied, and inspired them. It brought them into direct conflict with the Jesuits, whose heartfelt duty was to save the Indians' souls, to shape the new citizens of Spain, and to bask in the glory of doing the work of the cross and the Crown during these high and swollen days of empire. As it was, both the Jesuits and the Apaches manipulated each other in a continuing tug-of-war that lasted about a hundred years. When the end of the Jesuit era arrived, there were no clear winners and no clear losers. Although the contest appears to have been a draw, the events on the Spanish colonial frontier under Jesuit administration were so complex that any analysis focusing on indoctrination alone falls short of satisfactorily evaluating the situation.

The predicament was not as simple as a push-pull between the traditional Chiricahua Apache religion and Christianity, because they were not mutually exclusive. Instead, interactions between Jesuits and Apaches—agents of the new and of the old—ebbed and flowed during times of warfare and peace. At all times, individual concessions to Catholicism varied from individual to individual, despite the thin veneer that covered most Apaches' fidelity to their ancestors. Consequently degrees of resistance to Christianity among the Chiricahuas wavered and could not be measured by the European criteria that, absent uniform standards, varied from mission to mission and missionary to missionary. All in all, there was no way to adequately determine the effect of Christianity on the Chiricahua Apaches, individually or collectively, at the end of the Jesuit period.

CHAPTER THREE

The Franciscan Period

Northern Mexico

Fourteen Franciscans replaced the black robes in 1768 and were assigned to eight of the former Jesuit missions that Apache raids had not destroyed. The Franciscans' appointment to evangelize the Indians of northern Mexico was based on precedent: members of the order had already been at work in Mexico's Yucatán peninsula for more than two hundred years.[1] All the newest priests in Pimeria Alta were "men of unusual physical and spiritual toughness and a certain temperament," wrote Clendinnen. The friars would have to "count the people in the morning, preach to them and sing Mass, baptize both children and adults, confess the sick, and bury the dead." In addition, they were responsible for religious lessons that focused on "bowing the head, kneeling, maintaining a hushed silence, and stillness in the manner of Spanish piety. Four main prayers were taught by rote."[2]

Additionally, the routine tasks necessary for the mission to function had to be addressed daily, along with close supervision of any returning Indians, lest they begin to disrupt the order. During the yearlong interval between Jesuit and Franciscan occupations, most of the Indian residents, including incarcerated Chiricahua Apaches captured in battles, went back to their homelands and resumed their traditional lifeways. Only a few chose to stay at the empty missions and continue farming.

With nearly nothing to do during the long and often boring year, the presidial soldiers had become so sloppy and undisciplined that the freely roaming Apaches now mocked them, tormented them, and screamed at them during the military's infrequent excursions into Apacheria. Many soldiers lost heart and courage and deserted their stations, while others simply refused to fight. New recruits seldom stayed long, fleeing in terror after their first encounter with the Chiricahuas, who had begun raiding again as soon as the Franciscans restocked the missions.

On December 14, 1772, a respected Spanish captain named Juan Bautista de Anza sat down to write Viceroy Antonia Mariá Bucareli a long report from his headquarters at the remote and isolated presidio of Tubac, a northern outpost.[3] Along with commanding Tubac and supervising the twenty-one soldiers stationed there, Anza had been charged with evaluating the conditions of all the former Jesuit—now Franciscan—missions in Sonora. His words carried great credibility, for he had an excellent reputation as a military leader, including years of experience fighting the frontier Indians.

Anza had reached the limit of his tolerance—not for the actions of the Apaches particularly, but for the poor and ineffective military responses to the raids in the four years since the Franciscans arrived. He wrote in part, "As for the advancement of these heathens and of those previously reduced, I say that the surest way to attain the worthy goals expressed . . . is to destroy and reform as useless and prejudicial the system up to now observed in the missions."[4] Oddly, despite the esteem in which his superiors held him, nothing dramatic happened as a result of his recommendation, and the relentless Apache raids and killing continued. Perhaps his suggestion to destroy and rebuild the mission system was rejected through silence because of its enormity.

Galvez's Peace Policy or "Peace by Deceit"

Chiricahua Apache raiding and resistance continued, seemingly uncontrollable.[5] Bernardo de Galvez, the acting governor of Louisiana and nephew of José de Galvez, the secretary of the Indies in 1779, was appointed viceroy of New Spain on August 26, 1786.

He issued a document known as the *Instructions of 1786*, which contained three main objectives to subdue the Chiricahuas:

1. Exploit discord among them and form alliances with other Indians against them, with the goal of causing the natives to destroy each other;

2. Continue to wage constant warfare against them up to the point of exterminating them if necessary; and

3. Offer peace terms to those Apaches who asked for them, and, after determining that their intentions were sincere, reward them with amenities designed to foster dependence, such as shelter, food, protection, liquor, and old army guns in varying stages of disrepair.

However, there was a catch. In order to receive the benefits, the Apaches would have to leave their camps, relocate near the presidios or missions in what came to be called "peace establishments," and subject themselves to Spanish supervision. Although these facilities were situated across the frontier, two peace establishments—Bacoachi[6] in Sonora and Janos in Chihuahua—were expected to receive the largest number of Apaches.[7] The missions' original purposes, that is, indoctrination and assimilation, were, for the most part, eclipsed now by the emphasis on the military provisions of the policy, but the friars were nonetheless expected to continue proselytizing the native groups and to play a major role in Christianizing the Apaches if and when the policy became successful.

BACOACHI

"The Franciscans were in charge [at Bacoachi]," stated Father McCarty, adding that the

> Spanish policy [operated] under the assumption that the Franciscans were enlightened and had a higher morality than just about anybody else. If I were a Franciscan on the frontier trying to convert the Apaches, I would try to first learn what they

thought, their own beliefs. . . . They came to Bacoachi of their own free will to get the fringe benefits—usually bushels of corn. The problem, though, was concepts. The Indian often couldn't understand what we were saying. They didn't have the words to understand Father, Son, and Holy Spirit. Still, Christian lessons on the frontier included that doctrine and the idea of morality. It's part of the Franciscan ethos. Love and peace.[8]

The consequences of the escalating Spanish military actions, along with the promise and expectation of regular meals cooked from the "bushels of corn" McCarty referred to, were also the reasons many Chiricahuas voluntarily opted to live at Bacoachi. In late September of 1786 the first group of Apaches appeared at the peace establishment. Whether they were aware of the "peace policy" this soon—it had been in effect less than a month—is arguable. But they undoubtedly reasoned that moving to Bacoachi removed them from the immediate danger posed by the newly inspired Spanish soldiers. And they certainly were aware of the intensified warfare. However, the temporary asylum at Bacoachi left them vulnerable during Apache raids conducted by their own relatives and friends and additionally exposed them to death from periodic epidemics of communicable diseases. The trade-off was a staggering predicament.

At Bacoachi the friars established a daily routine to control and manage the growing number of Indian residents coming from all tribes. Each day began with religious services, followed by a small breakfast, after which the laborers walked to the fields to work all day at planting, tending, and raising crops such as wheat, corn, and melons. Their reward had to wait months, until harvesttime, when each resident Indian family was allotted a certain amount of the surplus left after a large part of the crop was sold at a profit to the military, civilian neighbors, nearby mining communities, and other population centers. The excess grains were then stored in a general warehouse, to be consumed in time by the community at large.[9]

At sunset each day the tired workers returned to the villages and, by a standing order, stopped at the mission to say "the Doctrina and prayers . . . in the plaza in front of the church," reported Bernard Fontana. "The problems of administering confession and communion were unusually difficult. But at regular missions most

Fig. 18. Franciscan missionary on Mexico's northern frontier after 1767. From McCarty, *Desert Documentary*, 64. Sketch by José Cisneros.

Franciscan Missionary

of the Indians were at least able to confess in Spanish. On special feast days, notably those of Mary, processions were organized and the rosary was recited or chanted."[10] Religious processions and chanting were familiar to the Indians through their own traditional rituals, some of which included aspects of one or both actions. On the other hand, confession and communion and their connection to sins were troubling to the potential Christians.

Kidwell states the reason that confession and communion posed obstacles to the priests' successful indoctrination of Indian peoples was "the lack of specific terms for such concepts as sin, guilt, and salvation made it difficult to convey some of the basic tenets of Christianity,"[11] especially since many indigenes had absolutely no frame of reference for the idea of, say, sin. If the missionaries were successful in conveying the theory, David Murray states, "the recognition of sin might well be a key moment, the point at which an alien element becomes fundamental, and a spiritual dependency is created."[12]

In contrast, baptisms were easily understood by many indigenes because of their similarity to various rituals performed on newborns in many tribes. As frequent baptisms of large numbers of indigenes added more numbers to the statistics that were routinely sent by the friars to their Franciscan superiors, the priests eagerly pursued every opportunity related to the rite. They encouraged conception, favored fecund young women with small gifts, and regularly counseled married couples regarding fertility. One inducement in particular often appealed to parents who were initially ambivalent about baptizing their baby: the priest was willing to give his own name to the Indian child. "Thus we found [a child named] Francisco Hermenegildo Herran, who was almost certainly baptized by Father Francisco Hermenegildo Garces," wrote Alfred Whiting, adding, "Judging from birth dates, such names came into use only after the coming of the Franciscans. . . . The Jesuits . . . rarely recorded a family name for any Indian."[13]

During their time at Bacoachi, harmonious relations among the Chiricahua Apaches and Spanish citizens remained mostly elusive. Wary by nature and past experiences, some Chiricahuas also mistrusted the other resident Indian groups, to say nothing of their suspicion of the Europeans, and the feeling was mutual. Still, the Chiricahuas continued to add to the Bacoachi census. Reported Max Moorhead:

> Additional groups of this tribe [Apaches] came in voluntarily, and although one band became suspicious and fled to the mountains again, there were still two hundred and fifty-one Chiricahuas of both sexes congregated . . . at the end of March 1787. . . . The infants had been baptized.[14]

Three months later, in mid-June of 1787, a total of 283 Chiricahuas were at Bacoachi and "all indications there pointed to a permanent and peaceful Apache community," according to

Moorhead. During the same month 119 men, women, and children changed their minds and left Bacoachi quickly, followed by another sixty-four Chiricahuas eight days later.[15] By leaving at will, the Apaches were practicing their timeless custom of cultural fluidity—the right to come and go without recriminations. Adhering to this traditional belief demonstrates ongoing resistance to the Europeans. But as more and more Apaches voluntarily arrived at Bacoachi, the army carefully looked them over and selected certain men to persuade to become allied against their own people. Bribery, using food, gifts, and special favors, seduced certain Apaches, but exactly why their cultural allegiances ruptured so easily remains to be explored and understood in detail.

Said Father McCarty about the betrayal, "The peaceful Bacoachi Apaches were the strongest military element in the white man's favor because they knew their own people. It is amazing to most, I suppose, that they would fight against their own people, but they did. The Apache ethos is not generally peaceful, but [most of] these Bacoachi Apaches were content with the arrangement of getting rations, at least to the extent of staying at the presidio and not finding any cause to behave differently."[16] Characteristic pragmatism could have motivated these Apaches, especially since McCarty mentioned a regular supply of rations. Since military actions were increased, it was quite difficult for free Apache men to leave camp to hunt without risk; relieving hunger would have been a strong contributing factor in the practical decision by families to voluntarily enter Bacoachi.

Occasionally, contact between the Chiricahuas at Bacoachi and area settlers led to intermarriages and an attempt by the indigenes at compulsory monogamy. For years, polygamous alliances had been an accepted practice among the Apaches, but to now comply with the Christian tenet of monogamy was an innovative cultural shift toward the Europeans' ways. Even so, several Bacoachi Apache women had already given birth to children fathered by the soldiers, without benefit of marriage. After the priests baptized these babies, some were turned over to childless Hispanic couples who lived nearby.[17]

Monogamy and other aspects of mission life were unfamiliar to the increasing numbers of Chiricahuas reporting to Bacoachi, and the new experiences were often disturbing. For example, Apaches had historically eaten only when food was available, such as after a successful hunt, when high-protein meat, heavily loaded with animal fat, was abundant. If hunters came back empty-handed, the people went hungry or relied on small rodents for nourishment. While this erratic food supply created periods of gluttony that alternated with times of starvation, the Chiricahuas' physiology had adjusted. At Bacoachi this familiar routine was replaced with two regular daily meals, and the Apaches' bodies rebelled. Constipation or diarrhea afflicted most of the people, and they soon learned that the priests had no effective remedies and their traditional remedies were inaccessible.[18] Another adjustment—being forced to work—was especially distressing because it was contrary to the volunteerism and cooperation that had always characterized their society and given meaning to the surrounding world.[19]

Despite problems like these, the peaceful mission Apaches cooperated for the most part with the friars, at least superficially. In time, as many became increasingly unhappy with Bacoachi's daily routines and duties, concerns on both sides mounted. Periodically an unknown number of Apaches walked away and returned to their former campsites in the deserts and *barrancas*. Back home, when they told of the free food, liquor, and the promise of material goods offered by the Spaniards, many other tribal members showed interest. Access to alcoholic beverages was certainly an inducement, even though the Chiricahuas were no strangers to intoxicating drinks. For years the medicine people had made a fermented brew called *tiswin*, but the Chiricahuas had not tasted distilled liquor until contact with the Europeans. The lure was so enticing to some that despite the negative descriptions about aspects of life at Bacoachi, more and more Chiricahuas took the dramatic and unprecedented step of turning away from the lifestyle of their ancestors to become dependent on the Spaniards,[20] including complying with the religious requirements.

Attempting to explain the behavior of many Indians in accepting Christianity, Kidwell, Noley, and Tinker state that "in the face of the overwhelming power of the advancing white world, conversion was an attempt to stave off continuing disaster and to access for themselves the perceived power of whites."[21] While that idea may hold generally true for most Indian tribes who encountered Europeans, whether it totally applied to the Chiricahuas is arguable.

Apache egocentrism, manifested by confidence in its own prowess and bolstered by victorious warfare actions and the mistaken belief that they had driven the Jesuits away, would not have perceived the Spaniards as having "overwhelming power." But drawing upon the power of the Christians' God, lesser deities, and saints surely would have been appealing to many astute warriors incarcerated at Bacoachi, as it would have been thought to enhance their own abilities for future use when they returned to their campsite.

In March 1787 a new viceroy, Manuel Antonio Flores, took office and soon made no secret of the fact that he mistrusted all Apaches. He urged his generals to treat the Apaches "so badly that they will obey the Spaniards,"[22] inferring that Apaches captured in battles could be abused and held up as models of what might happen to everyone who resisted. These pronouncements didn't faze the Chiricahuas still riding freely in Apacheria; they went on with their fierce attacks, which were now matched and even occasionally surpassed in intensity and brutality by the presidial soldiers.

One glaring example occurred during a 1784 military expedition to rout Apaches. Led by Captain Pedro Allande y Saabedra, the soldiers spied a lone Apache mother and son hurrying on foot across a valley to escape. Instead of detaining them as prisoners of war after the two were captured, an officer named Captain don Manuel de Echeagary baptized the boy and then ordered both their heads to be cut off.[23] Similar violence became more and more common among Spanish troops once they recognized that their actions had the support of their superiors, which is not to overlook the fact that the Apaches responded in kind. When Commandante General Jacobo Ugarte y Loyola offered his troops a bonus for each pair of Apache ears cut off during battles or while on patrol,[24] horrified Chiricahuas reacted by cutting off the ears of soldiers they had captured alive.[25] Women messengers carried these trophies back to the presidios, hefting high tin or wooden crosses as a sign of nonaggression as they approached, ensuring that the delivery wouldn't be met with gunfire.

These types of exchanges continued to rage and escalate in savagery on both sides. In time the growing number of Apache captives confined to Bacoachi—especially those who were wounded—became an urgent military problem. Many of the injured died slowly, agonizingly, and each of their deaths had an emotional impact on the other Chiricahua men, women, and children—volunteers and captives—at the peace establishment. Worried about possible uprisings, the officials watched some Apaches grow sad, some become more submissive, some more resistant, and some furious. Soon, due to the intensified military actions, Bacoachi was overwhelmed by numbers of dying, dead, and alive Apaches of all ages. A solution had to be found before an emotional explosion occurred.

The answer was provided in an earlier order, the Reglamento of 1772, which had directed Apache captives to be marched to Mexico City, where the men would be distributed as laborers and the women and children were to be placed in homes as domestics.[26] When the order was reenforced, large numbers of Chiricahua prisoners walked under guard to the capital city, there to be disbursed as slaves but relieving, for the moment, the overcrowding at Bacoachi. Not all Chiricahuas were consigned to slavery, however. Some had teamed up with unsavory Hispanics living near Bacoachi and were practicing a lifestyle that was either criminal or felonious in other ways. Also, so many Apaches had begun to imitate the bad habits of the Spaniards and Mexicans with whom they were constantly interacting that in May of 1795 Franciscan Pedro de Arriquibar, the *doctrinero* (preserver of the existing faith) for the Christianized Indians and non-Indians and chaplain for the presidial troops at Bacoachi, complained in a letter to the president of the missions, the Very Reverend Father Francisco Antonio Barbastro. Arriquibar wrote that some Apaches had admitted to him that they had learned all their vices, including promiscuity, from the Christians at Bacoachi.[27]

Arriquibar also reported that along with adopting offensive social habits, other circumstances also worried him: the Apaches' abominable—to him—eating habits. His complaint was that when they received rations, they ate everything in sight all at once and asked for more, leaving nothing for the next meals. (Had Arriquibar been interested enough to learn about the Apaches' cultural heritage, he would have understood that historically they had never had a reason to conserve food for the next meal, for fresh meat or plant foods were abundant in their homelands under normal climatic conditions.)[28]

The next source of distress that Arriquibar noted was the

Apaches' work habits. They tackled a job in a frenzied way, he wrote, not stopping for a second until they were exhausted. Then they would collapse and refuse to do anything else the rest of the day and even the next day. Or so it appeared. The element of Apache trickery was probably at work here, for most of the Chiricahuas who were not sick and able to work were strong and vital, in excellent physical condition with stamina to spare. Fooling the missionaries into believing their energy was spent would have been a hilarious joke, saved and savored in private after dark. But if their actions were not deliberate, this example addressed the differences in thinking between members of two disparate cultures. The Spaniards thought linearly, getting as soon as possible from point A to point B, as it were. The Apaches, on the other hand, thought in a more circular fashion, and since they had plenty of time, there was no need to rush to the end of a task.[29]

One more of Arriquibar's written grievances was the way the Bacoachi Chiricahuas appeared at catechism: bare. "It is not proper for them to come to the catechetical instruction naked, especially the women and children. We therefore have this great difficulty to overcome," his letter concluded.[30] As modesty was a Chiricahua cultural trait, Arriquibar's statement may have been an exaggeration and an attempt at gaining attention from his superiors. If true, however, nakedness was an expression of the Apaches' resistance to the wishes of the Spaniards, a tacit opposition they talked and laughed about in private.

Father Barbastro forwarded Arriquibar's letter to Commandante General Don Pedro de Nava on June 29, 1795, with the recommendation that for "the Apaches to be properly instructed, they ought to be completely separated from all the Christians in Bacoachi. . . . Pueblos should be founded for them with their own church and missionaries who would have no other occupation. . . . Because they have seen and heard so many things which are contrary to the law they are to profess, they must be taught repeatedly that these Christians whom they have seen living with such license will be severely punished by God."[31] He also recommended that each peaceful Apache be given a parcel of land and be taught how to farm it and that they immediately learn how to sow cotton, harvest it, and use it for clothing. Barbastro's final recommendation to Nava was to provide Catholic schooling for the

Chiricahua youngsters in the hope that education would affect the children's parents as well.[32]

Nothing of the sort occurred, of course, either in Bacoachi or at a counterpart facility called Janos, a peace establishment in the state of Chihuahua.

JANOS

In 1680 Apache raiders destroyed the original Jesuit mission at Janos[33]. Six years later a military outpost was garrisoned there, but the mission itself waited until 1717 to be repopulated by the Jesuits with frontier Indians other than Apaches. The terrible Apache raids continued until the years between 1790 and 1795, when a relative degree of peace with the Chiricahuas occurred. Ten to sixteen Apache settlements at Janos, all headed up by different chiefs, then dotted the countryside. The clusters of wickiups and cooking arbors resembled the traditional local units, making the arrangement familiar and comfortable for the Apaches at first. However, when dozens more tribal members arrived and were assigned to the existing settlements, the congenial atmosphere could quickly change.

In earlier times, disputes among the Chiricahuas were often resolved in the time-honored way by one of the unhappy parties moving to another band or starting a new local unit with those who supported his point of view. The physical and cultural restrictions at Janos, along with the inherent emotional stresses associated with confinement, prohibited this customary way of conflict resolution, so resentments simmered and often exploded violently. Frustrated Apaches bolted from the peace establishment and went back to their homelands, taking with them their newly acquired skills, such as farming, range and livestock management, cooking, craftwork, ability to sing and play musical instruments, and a limited ability to speak Spanish. Bilingual Chiricahuas were a great asset to the still roaming local units, especially during their main "business" venture—trading stolen livestock, farming tools, and other useful plunder with friendly Spanish ranchers.[34]

Initially, purloined horses and mules obtained in raids had simply enhanced the tribe's mobility and increased its food supply.

Horsemeat, for example, became such a big favorite, and they ate so much of it, that Jesuit writer Och noted:

> The still untamed Apaches outdo all others in feasting. Their greatest delicacy is horse and mule meat which they roast and prefer to beef. The most particular delicacy for them is the following: when they have speared a horse or donkey and cut open its belly, they remove the intestines, roll them up in the animal's fat, including even a fetus in the caul, throw it on the fire where this sausage is roasted amid an unbearable stench, and then eat it with the same relish as they would the best kraut sausage. Because of their constant eating of horseflesh, these Apaches smell quite uniquely and their weapons give off a most repulsive odor. Horses can smell Apaches, their enemies, for a distance of as much as a quarter of an hour, and reveal through snorting and mane tossing the presence of Apaches concealed in the bush.[35]

Apaches had long recognized that animals, equipment, and merchandise were valuable frontier commodities, and they quickly devised a plan to capitalize on the situation. Surprised ranchers and farmers living in the vast region around Janos asked no questions when a small number of peaceful Chiricahua men appeared on the property and one or two of them shouted in broken Spanish that they were traders, not enemies. Willing Spaniards were always eager to enhance their own herds and happy to swap items such as blankets, hats and clothing, coffee, tobacco, kettles and pots and pans, and salt. If the exchange frequently appeared lopsided in favor of the Spaniards, it was because fair market values were never part of the transaction; only the appeal of the other's possessions mattered. For example, trading several horses for a pound of sugar or salt was common. Ultimately, Apache raids of presidios, missions, and peace establishments and subsequent trading of stolen animals and goods expanded commerce all across the frontier. Before long, the reciprocal exchange network stretched northward into southern New Mexico's ranching country and eastward toward Comanche lands in Texas and added another dimension—that of friendly merchant—to the Chiricahuas' reputation.[36]

This economic venture also had another advantage: goodwill and trust developed between buyer and seller, especially when one or the other made good on previous damages. For example, Chiricahuas brought along an extra cow or two to make up for shortages that occurred during their last trip. And ranchers presented more than enough valued goods to apologize for a shortcoming they had inadvertently caused in the past. While a mutual admiration society never developed, the Spanish military probably was exasperated by the limited circumstances of the new friendships.

These trades sometimes included a human element. Spanish women and children previously abducted by the Chiricahuas were bartered, often miles away from their homes, for items such as a bottle of shaving lotion or a bolt of colorful cloth. The opposite also occurred: enslaved Apaches were sometimes repatriated by Spanish ranchers or farmers in exchange for livestock such as stallions, mares, mules, cows, or bulls.

Ironically, the booty helped promote and expand the imperialistic and economic roots of the Spanish Empire through its distribution. The trading network also benefited the Apaches by providing them instant gratification with desirable goods and supporting their new noteworthiness as trusted promoters of frontier commerce.

All along the trade routes the Spanish-speaking Apaches became invaluable as negotiators and suppliers, taking orders from ranchers and farmers without too many misunderstandings due to language incomprehension and impressing their buyers with their honesty, reliability, accommodations, and pleasant demeanor. In time, the intercultural trading networks grew more complex and had unintended and unanticipated results, particularly in the area of new commercial alliances, some of which probably were social and romantic as well.[37]

When the army's campaigns disrupted the recently established commercial patterns by killing, capturing, or deporting Apaches, those Spanish ranchers, farmers, merchants, and dealers in black market goods who had profited from their association with the Chiricahua local units became upset and angry. Their animosity created a situation so controversial that few officials dared to tackle it publicly. And so the new role of Apaches as entrepreneurs grew steadily even though their good reputations as traders were in direct contrast to the army's experiences.[38]

In 1795, during the swirl of trading and raiding Apache activities around Janos, the military's central command was directed to cut costs and to decrease the number of Apaches receiving rations. In an innovative action, military officials responded by urging Janos's peaceful Apaches to return to their local units. It was an odd request, at first confusing, but most Chiricahuas complied and headed for their old campsites.

When the practice of releasing peaceful Apaches had been in effect for about a year, nearly 70 percent of the former mission residents were back home. A year before, 850 Apaches had been counted at Janos. In the late months of 1796, only 200 Apaches remained, and a year after that the number fell to 130 persons. Of course, the costs of administering the peace establishment dramatically decreased due to the downturn in population, but the policy certainly didn't benefit the Franciscans. Fewer Apaches meant limited opportunities for the Janos friars to attempt to indoctrinate and that, in turn, meant not as many Indians were on the path toward Christianity and assimilation into Spanish society as tax-paying citizens. The outlook for the Franciscans was not completely bleak, however. As long as Apache prisoners remained confined at Janos, they were exposed daily, directly and indirectly, to Roman Catholicism and grew familiar with Catholic doctrine.

One other Spanish policy—deportation—also had the effect of reducing the population at the peace establishments. "By 1789, deportation of the Chiricahuas to Havana, Cuba, was a generally accepted activity," according to Christon Archer.[39] Upon arrival, all possible efforts were to have been made to place the prisoners with Cuban families as "servants"; those who could not be placed were put to work building fortifications, for example, the landing docks and forts. Families receiving prisoners had to agree to educate the Apache children as Roman Catholics, but not surprisingly, the actual result was a situation akin to slavery.

On the frequent marches under armed guard from Janos to the seacoast at Veracruz or the capital of Mexico City, diseases such as smallpox often struck. For example, in a group of forty-nine Chiricahuas on their way to Mexico City, only twenty-nine survived.[40] These prisoners were held under maximum security lest they find some way to return northward, as unknown numbers did. Archer reports that "even the very young Indians of ten to twelve years of age could escape and eventually find their way back to the north, posing a serious threat to the Spanish because of knowledge they had picked up along the way."[41]

Violence and physical resistance along the route was also common; soldiers didn't hesitate to use their weapons, and so many Chiricahuas died before being loaded onto boats sailing for Cuba. The jails that held the Apaches until the next crowded and cramped boat left Veracruz were filthy and rodent infested. When they overflowed, the prisoners were herded into outdoor pens with barbed-wire walls and no shelter from the blazing sun. If food was available, it was often ears of raw corn thrown haphazardly into the corral.

In the late 1790s, the captain general of Cuba, the Marques de Someruelos, tried to stop the policy, claiming that the arrived Apaches caused numerous inconveniences and disruptions in Cuba. Apparently the long land and sea journeys had reinforced the prisoners' opposition to their enemies rather than breaking their will, as had been hoped. Someruelos's opposition failed to change the policy, and the Chiricahua prisoners kept on arriving and going on rampages in Cuba, being arrested, and attempting to escape custody. During one of the escapes, several Apache men murdered a black slave. All but two Apaches—Raphael Bitaqui and Oste—were killed. In the ensuing trial, the two men received sentences of ten years' imprisonment each.[42]

With an ulterior motive to demonstrate goodwill, the Crown periodically exercised compassion regarding certain Apache prisoners, as in the case of two others who were jailed in Mexico City. One of these men was totally blind, and the other could barely distinguish figures and objects. While incarcerated, the first man had requested and received baptism into the Catholic Church; the other man quickly decided to do the same. Archer reports that "during their long stay in prison, the two Indians became well instructed in the Faith by clergymen who visited them regularly and removed some of their terrible solitude." The archbishop took a personal interest in the case, believing that their medical disabilities would make the chances of surviving the trip to Cuba very slight. Additionally, their conditions would prohibit their escape and eventual return to the homelands to cause trouble. So the men remained in jail and were told that, as a favor, they were expected to help quiet the other Chiricahua prisoners who would be deposited in the same jail before deportation.[43]

Word about the deportation and concomitant breakup of families spread back into Apacheria, and many Chiricahuas, leery now of these consequences of warfare, decided to again take up residence at Janos for protection; in effect they surrendered. Janos filled up quickly once more and was hampered again by the continuing lack of adequate rations. In time, so many Chiricahuas arrived at Janos that the frontier authorities feared trouble. Henrique de Grimarest, a high military official, stepped forward with a solution. He proposed that the government offer four pesos for each dead Apache or dead Apache's head that the peaceful Chiricahua volunteers could deliver. The response from resident Apache men was immediate. Many temporarily left Janos, determined to kill their relatives and friends before they arrived at Janos so the amount of rations allotted to each person would not be further reduced.[44] For the first time in the long cultural history of the Chiricahua Apaches, loyalty to one another had been seriously compromised as the Janos Apaches took up arms against their kin, an unprecedented action and a major cultural shift from hundreds of years of tribal and family allegiances toward an uncertain future with strangers.

The existing documents are silent about what happened to the Janos Apaches who killed their relatives for four pesos and then returned with their trophies. However, if these collaborators imagined that they were safe from harm because they were under the protection of the Spaniards, they were wrong. Believing they were witches or had been bewitched, loyal Janos Apaches would have set upon them when the time was right. Kinfolk still out in their homelands would have learned through word of mouth who had done this horrible deed. So when the Chiricahua warriors next raided Janos, the traitors could have been specifically targeted.

Janos Apaches who had refused to participate in this murderous campaign—mainly women, children, and ailing or elderly men—believed that no one would deliberately murder friends and relatives, even for food, unless the killers were witches or had been bewitched. The loyal Apaches didn't hesitate to use witchcraft to cause harm to their friends or relatives who had taken part in the killings or to bewitch their exploiters. Deeds states, "In some cases, the [Indians] performed acts intended to exact revenge against priests who had punished transgressors. Several missionaries claimed they nearly died from strange illnesses passed to them by witches."[45]

Apaches surely also considered some of the Pimas to be witches. For years, they and some men from other allied local indigenous groups had been recruited by the Spaniards to rid the countryside of the Chiricahua Apaches.[46] In the late 1700s, for example, the Pimas were the Spaniards' main mercenaries, fighting beside the soldiers to kill or capture Apaches. Since Janos was then overflowing with Indians, Spanish administrators gave the Pimas permission to sell the captives at low prices to Tucson individuals and families. Most of the sales were of men and children because the contentious Apache women were the least desirable as servants. If the Pimas couldn't sell their female prisoners, they simply killed them, believing correctly that there would be no retribution from any of the authorities.

Completely aware of this political change from a policy of indoctrination into Christianity and assimilation to a policy of enslavement or murder, the Franciscans were nonetheless reluctant to stop it. At least one friar noted his feelings in writing. "There is absolutely no other way to save these captives from inevitable death if there's no profit to their captors," recorded Diego Miguel Bringas de Manzaneda y Encinas, known simply as Father Bringas. He approved of the sales, informing his superiors in writing, "Orders should be given to the military commander of Sonora that the frontier captain should not prevent the Papagos and Gila Pimas, our friends and allies, from selling or trading so many head of hostile Apaches who are taken captive and brought to our presidios and towns. If there are among the barbarians any adult males or women, they should arrange to acquire them at the lowest price possible."[47]

By endorsing sales of Apaches to Spanish Catholic families, Father Bringas could have sincerely trusted that the receiving families would bring them to the altar of Catholicism. Not surprisingly, some of these enslaved Apaches never had any exposure whatsoever to Christianity, but other families acted in good faith, as shown by the 1798 Arizpe, Mexico, census. Fifty-two former Apache captives between the ages of three and twenty had been distributed to twenty-five Spanish households and, according to James Officer, "sacramental registers from communities in northern Sonora reveal that most, if not all, the Indians who wound up in Hispanic homes during the last dozen years of the eighteenth century became Catholic converts."[48]

Although ridding Janos of captives helped reduce the drain on funds from the royal treasury, the endless outflow of monies was still a significant problem and of growing concern to viceregal authorities. In the late 1790s, relief arrived from an unexpected quarter: smallpox. Most of the resident Apaches fled back to the local units, abandoning Janos, at least for the moment.[49] By the early 1800s, Spanish children on the frontier were inoculated against smallpox, but there is no evidence that Apache children received similar protection.

Simultaneously, U.S. officials were talking about territorial expansion, an action that would seriously affect all of Mexico and its ethnic populations in the future. In 1803, the United States purchased a huge parcel of land known as the Louisiana Territory from France for $15 million—a major step in opening America's westward movement.

Mexican Independence

Rumblings of revolution began around 1810. Issues such as excessive taxation, a great and growing disparity between the haves and the have-nots, painful class distinction, overt political favoritism, and a boisterous disrespect for authority among citizens stirred the Mexican people's emotions to a high pitch. Many Franciscans lost faith in the presidios' ability to guard the frontier facilities, so they moved on, vacating several peace establishments. All active efforts at evangelization had long since ceased, but the remaining stalwart Franciscans' continuing presence around Janos served to remind Christian Indians of their religious obligations and responsibilities.

Uncertain of the future, Indians from various northern Mexico tribes had also walked away from Janos. Those who elected to continue with the routines of life at the peace establishment became acutely aware of the increasing effects of the pending war with Spain. "Spanish administrators," wrote Park, diverting troops and money to meet the [war] crisis, weakened the northern defenses. Morale at the presidios deteriorated and soldiers turned to graft and illegal trade with the Indians to compensate for the reductions in pay. Riots flared among the Apaches settled nearby when commanders attempted to cut the rations or assign fieldwork. When renegade factions left the reservations, presidio commanders launched half-hearted campaigns and made patched-up treaties, allowing the Apaches to keep the plunder they had taken in adjacent provinces. Emboldened by such signs of weakness in the presidial line, the Apaches openly deserted the military settlements. The twenty-year respite of peace ended in a flame of revolt that burned brightly for many years thereafter.[50]

The frontier colonial institutions were theoretically and practically also on the verge of collapse. But for those Indians of northern Mexico's tribes who could survive on an unpredictable supply of minimum rations, life at Janos just went on.

Victorious in its battle with Spain, the newly independent Mexican government initially showed a lack of commitment to the many policies of the Spanish period. That understandable disregard, however, affected the circumstances at the peace establishments, as did the remoteness of the northern provinces from the seat of the unpracticed officials in Mexico City. The inexperienced political administration dealt first with the problems it could see and hear, and those were numerous. Paramount among the issues was paying the incurred costs of the newfound independence, and so continuing to bear the expenses of the peace establishments became an unwelcome drain on the Mexican treasury. Yet the Mexican government realized it had to keep the frontier mollified, and it did so for ten years after 1821 by continuing to provide, albeit erratically, the minimal rations and supplies the Indians had been receiving under the Spaniards' jurisdiction. However, dramatic changes once again hovered over the frontier during this time, motivated by money and politics.

For nearly ten years Mexico's native-born citizens had been becoming increasingly envious of peninsula-born Spaniards living in their country, which was now ostensibly free of Spanish control. However, many of the resident Spaniards still thought of themselves as superior, had business advantages, and were still receiving favors from the Crown. The citizens' concerns were taken to the federal congress.

Explaining, Father McCarty wrote, "Five days before Christmas 1827, the [Mexican] federal congress passed the long-expected Decree of Spanish Expulsion. Except for special circumstances, the decree included all but one of the Franciscan missionaries residing in the *Pimeria Alta*. The state congress . . . followed suit on January 30, 1828. It outdid the federal decree by allowing only thirty days for peninsular Spaniards not exempted by the federal decree to leave the state."[51]

For the second time in less than a hundred years, Spanish missionaries to the Indians of northern Mexico were purged. However, the German and Basque Franciscan priests who had also come to the frontier since 1768 were permitted to stay, as were a few of the very eldest Spaniards for whom the trip back to Europe would be life threatening. By 1830, only four older Spanish friars remained in all of the north to keep up their work.

Appointed civil commissioners once again, as they had in 1767, took charge of the missions around which a small number of Christian Indians chose to live; the properties immediately fell to ruin. Manuel Escalante, the concerned head of the political jurisdiction known as the Arizpe Department, wrote a note to Governor Francisco Iriarte on January 13, 1830, in which he urged the governor to return the administration of the mission properties to the four Franciscans "before the totality of mission wealth is either squandered by the civil commissioners or destroyed by the Apaches." Not incidentally, he also asked the governor to order more priests into the area.[52] The governor was convinced of at least one aspect of Escalante's request and on January 22, 1830, he gave back the spiritual and material administration of the missions to the four aging friars. Not unexpectedly, the responsibilities related to duties covering all of northern Mexico soon overwhelmed them.

In 1831, the Mexican government totally ceased its support of the frontier institutions, rationalizing that suspending rations and other benefits would force idle Indian residents to go to work. Actually, there simply was no money in the treasury to continue to support the peace establishments. Secular diocesan priests replaced the four Franciscans and tried to build up the missions as churches that would be supported by their parishioners. Three years later the Mexican legislature passed a law secularizing all the remaining missions in the country, counting on the fact that the action would release the Indian populations to work as a labor force in the growing mining and ranching economies and live as tax-paying citizens.

After persistent reports of Apache attacks and thievery, on July 3, 1834, the Sonoran legislature, sitting at Arizpe, authorized a massive military offensive. The Chiricahuas' bold raids had dramatically increased over the previous three years, and they were rapidly becoming the commercial lords of northern Mexico—a situation the new government realized it had to stop. "By 1835," Robert Stevens notes, "numerous haciendas and ranches in northern Sonora had been abandoned. It was reported by one Sonoran official that some 5,000 persons had lost their lives in the early 1830s because of the raids. If this figure is accurate, it means that from five to ten per cent of the Sonoran populations were casualties during those years."[53]

It wasn't until the early 1840s that officials in the state of Chihuahua came to terms with the situation and called for a general peace and return to the former Spanish policy of supplying sufficient rations and rewarding benefits at the old peace establishments. Census data from 1843 reveals that over four hundred Apaches were then administered in Janos. As had been so in the past, many were just taking advantage of the opportunity to eat regularly and receive other benefits.

In February of 1844 a smallpox epidemic caused most of the Janos Apaches to flee in terror, followed within the year by all the others.[54] By 1845, Janos was empty of Chiricahua Apaches.

A Few Words . . .

The Franciscans' frontier years were different from the Jesuit era in that a number of Apaches—volunteers and captives—lived at the missions. The friars believed their duty was to execute the will of God by saving the Indians' souls and simultaneously "civilizing" them. Apache, missionary, Spaniard, or Mexican each underestimated the other's dedication and perseverance and so the warfare and bloodshed went on, halted neither by the god of the Apaches nor the god of the Christians. Both of these deities, it seemed, wanted no part of solving the terrible conflicts in northern Mexico.

The early years of the nineteenth century reflected a complex and dynamic interplay of Indian and Hispanic strategies—political, social, military, and religious. Some members of certain tribes, the Chiricahua Apaches included, had accepted the Spanish spiritual and material imports quite willingly. Through an admixture of accommodation/resistance, others exploited many aspects of the Spanish culture but preserved aspects of their own heritage, remaining faithful to their ancestral ways through a complicated mix of erratic religious and secular syncretism.

Several cultural shifts characterized the Apaches' experience— adjustments that would not have been tolerated in a less culturally fluid and more rigidly structured society. New foods, apparel, language, livestock, and weaponry entered the ancestral culture and produced lasting changes. These were pragmatic choices, indicative of the power of one culture to permanently influence another and certainly demonstrating the Chiricahua Apaches' psychological willingness to alter and change their own customs when desired.

Transforming ancient ways was not a new internal practice. Julia Cruikshank notes that in the far distant past, trade between the Tlingit and the Apaches' Athapaskan ancestors long existed around the Yukon and that "Athapaskan peoples incorporated Tlingit themes into their storytelling traditions."[55] Obviously, the intellectual foundation needed to endorse and support differentiation had been long-standing inside the culture and was also responsible much later for the influence employed by many tribes the Chiricahuas met during their generations-long migration from the Arctic Circle to northern Mexico.

So, another significant addition and enhancement, however limited, to the Chiricahua Apache traditional religious culture was Roman Catholicism and Christian dogma. For the most part, however, despite a few individuals subscribing to Catholicism, it appears that the people's identity as Chiricahua Apaches who practiced the religion of their ancestors remained strong at the end of the Jesuit and Franciscan missionary period in northern Mexico. Resistance remained.

CHAPTER FOUR

The Apache Diaspora

Florida and Alabama

In the late eighteenth century, the frontier Franciscans had come under increasing pressure to secularize the missions, meaning that the friars would be replaced by priests who were not of a particular order. The missions would then become parishes and the resident Indians would be required to assume responsibility for paying the priests since their status too would change—to Christian. When that goal was reached, three more major changes would occur: (1) the government would be relieved of its financial burden, (2) the Indians would also become tax-paying citizens, and (3) the surplus of the former Indian properties would be opened for purchase.[1]

While the theory sounded plausible, actual practice was quite different. Personal resistance of varying degrees among the indigenes was a factor, as was the situation of a minority—the Franciscans—attempting to persuade through several means—not always pleasant—a majority to totally change their lifestyle and comply with the demands of a European culture that most could not yet understand. Still, the zealous Franciscans were determined to fulfill their obligation.

Despite their best intentions, however, a complete collapse of the Mexican mission system occurred at the end of the country's successful decade-long struggle for autonomy from Spain. Predating the victory, however, in approximately 1810, officials in

Mexico City had to divert funds from the northern missions in order to pay for wartime supplies and personnel. By the end of the war, some four years later, virtual chaos characterized the missions. Government aid no longer reached the frontier, so troops stationed in the presidios had not been paid and looted the missions for food and other supplies. Apache raids continued, almost unchallenged. Many Indians, Christian and non-Christian, left the mission complexes to return to their homesites and ancestral ways. The missions themselves were bare and practically nonfunctional in the mid-1820s. Still, approximately 1,127 loyal neophytes remained in the eight Pimeria Alta missions.[2]

Adding to the friars' ongoing difficulties was the lack of new recruits, a consequence not only related to the war but to an egocentrism among the Franciscans, who depended on Spain as the source of the next generation of frontier missionaries; Mexicans had not been trained. Weber wrote,

> Between 1821 and 1846, economic, political, ecclesiastical, military, and demographic changes combined to alter frontier society and culture more profoundly than in any previous twenty-five year span. . . . Change took place at different rates, depending on particular local circumstances. . . . In isolated Southern Arizona successful Apache offenses caused the frontier to retreat in the 1830s before new influences made a notable impact.[3]

One example of the "new influences" Weber mentioned is the expulsion of Spaniards from Mexico, a direct consequence of newfound independence. Spanish-born Franciscans were ordered out of the Pimeria Alta in 1828 and replaced by lay overseers whose "corruption, combined with intensified raids by Apaches, left the mission properties irreparably damaged."[4] Although the missions were returned to the Franciscans two years later, the clock could not be turned back successfully. The cattle and horse herds had either been stolen or wandered away, the fields were overgrown from lack of attention, destruction of the properties was virtually complete, and the native residents, regardless of their position along the road to Christianity, had drifted on. Noting that not much was left in the years after the end of the war with Spain, Hall wrote,

"The rebellion drained the country's resources, leaving little to spend on a northern frontier. This led to the disintegration of peace with nomadic groups."[5]

Fewer than twenty years later, America's complex difficulties with Mexico led to another war. While it is not within the scope of this book to discuss the topic in detail, several factors can be listed: claims by American merchants of mistreatment, war as a natural outgrowth of American expansionism, and a boundary controversy that included a border clash have all been cited. The war began on May 13, 1846, and ended a little more than one year later, on September 16, 1847, when American troops under General Winfield Scott raised the flag over Mexico City.

On February 2, 1848, the U.S. representative, Nicholas Trist, and members of a special commission from Mexico's collapsed government met at a town just outside of Mexico City. Called Guadalupe Hidalgo, the town lent its name to a treaty ending the war and an agreement that added 1.2 million square miles to the United States. The Senate approved the treaty in May of 1848.[6] Importantly, under the terms of Article XI of the treaty, the United States assumed responsibility for preventing "border Indians from making incursions into Mexico," wrote Shelly Hatfield.[7]

In the years that immediately followed, successive political administrations in Mexico City fell into dire financial straits. Between June 1848 and January 1850, sixteen different finance managers controlled the recovering country's funds. In August of 1853 President Franklin Pierce sent James Gadsden, a railroad executive, to Mexico City to negotiate for the purchase of lands that would give the United States a southern railroad route from the Mississippi River to the Pacific Ocean. Needing capital quickly, the Mexican government agreed to a $10-million sale of 29,142,400 acres of land within the present states of New Mexico and Arizona. The deal, known as the Gadsden Purchase, received the consent of the Senate, and the president signed it on June 29, 1854. With this, the retreat of the Mexican frontier was complete.

Winning the war brought three particular directions in American federal policy toward Indians, including the Chiricahua Apaches, who now were under the exclusive jurisdiction of the United States: (1) military protection had to be provided to citizens threatened by Indians in the Southwest, (2) Indian title to lands had to be formally extinguished, and (3) some type of human situation had to be created to address the needs of the Indians.[8]

If the Chiricahuas now knew they were legally under the supervision and jurisdiction of the United States, they certainly didn't care. Hatfield declared, "Apaches could not understand the U.S. government's assumption that it now owned Apache land because it had conquered the Mexicans."[9] To the Apaches, the territory was still Apacheria. Their actions communicated contempt and complete disregard for the newest bunch of outsiders as they continued to freely ride all across their homelands—to them the U.S. border was nothing more than an artificial barrier, if that.[10] American ranchers, however, were now a new market for stolen livestock and other trade goods that the Apaches could swap, so time and again the Indians stampeded a Mexican herd of horses or cattle and drove the animals into the corrals of southeastern Arizona ranches. In time the reverse would occur and the Apaches raided American ranches and drove their stock southward into Mexico. According to Hatfield, "Mexico blamed American Indians for the continued raids and the United States was convinced that Mexican Indians were responsible for the plunder of the frontier."[11]

The U.S. government's fiscal reports dated 1866 showed that America had by then spent half a billion dollars on all the Indian wars across the American West. The expense of killing just one Indian was calculated at $1 million, not including the enormous costs in terms of lives and livestock lost, manpower hours, and supplies and equipment. To bring an end to the conflicts and allow its citizens to safely settle the vast territory west of the Mississippi, the government resolved to place all Indians on reservations.[12]

The first bureaucratic steps to legitimize this action were nationwide "hearings" to be held to determine exactly how crucial the situation was and, by eyewitness testimonies, establish without question the necessity of controlling the Indians by creating reservations for them. But there was more to it. The reservations—monuments to the concept of Manifest Destiny—would be on Indian lands with clear boundaries but would encompass only part of a tribe's total traditional landholdings. The remainder would be open to Americans for settlement and especially to the railroads for purchase, settlement, and development. Thus, the outcomes of the proposed hearings, that is, the need to settle the Indians, were predetermined, transparent, and deliberately designed to foster America's westward expansion and economic goals, a striking similarity to the earlier Spanish policies on the colonial frontier. The public sessions went forward unashamedly and substantiated the government's case brick by brick. Absent at the hearings, of course, were declarations by Indians as to why they should not be forced to live on reservations and surrender their traditional lands. But even if tribal members had testified, the juggernaut of American imperialism could not be stopped.[13]

President U.S. Grant's Peace Policy

Established by President Ulysses S. Grant in 1869, this official policy was ostensibly designed to bring an end to the widespread and well-known corruption among political administrators in the Indian Bureau and stop Indian hostilities. Written in response to demands for reform, several main points characterized this plan:

1. Indians would be placed on reservations, keeping them from contact with white settlers, teaching them how to be farmers, and exposing them to the aid of Christian organizations;

2. When necessary, Indians would be punished for misdeeds, which should demonstrate the efficacy of following the government's advice rather than continuing their traditional ways;

3. High-quality supplies would be furnished to reservations;

4. Through religious organizations high-quality agents would be recruited, who would fairly distribute goods and aid in uplifting the Indians; and

5. Through Christian organizations, churches and schools would be provided, which would lead the Indians to appreciate Christianity and civilization and educate them to assume the duties and responsibilities of citizenship.[14]

If this sounds familiar, it was. Although similar Spanish and Mexican policies at pacification, missionization, and Christianization had not succeeded, the Grant administration was willing to try its hand at "civilizing" the Indians by implementing aspects of the failed efforts south of the border. One wonders why history wasn't studied, why one country's sad ineffectiveness was ignored, and how the American ego became so inflated that it thought itself invulnerable to the mistakes of the recent past.

Grant's proposal gave churches—mainly Protestant—important control over reservations through his appointment of agents selected from their congregations.[15] Most Protestant-Americans supported the innovative policy because the citizenry believed, at the time, that civilization and Christianity were conjoined; that is, the United States was a Christian nation and the government should aid religion in improving American society.[16] A majority of politicians—and most Americans—agreed that appointing churchmen as reservation agents would help correct the embarrassing corruption in Washington and raise politics and politicians to a respectable position once again.[17]

The need for change was apparent. "Politicians were at the top of the pyramid of corruption," wrote John D. McDermott. "Members of Congress and officials in the executive branch of the federal government used their powers to secure selection of their friends as Indian agents, traders, and contractors." These political leaders were partners, according to McDermott, with the Indian agents, who "had many ways of acquiring wealth at the expense of his charges." For example, agents withheld food and other goods and sold them elsewhere for personal profit. Like their counterparts on the Spanish colonial frontier years earlier, they also inflated the number of Indians under their supervision so that sufficient supplies would be sent to accommodate the exaggerated totals; agents could then sell the surplus and pocket the proceeds. Another member of this so-called Indian Ring was the trader, who worked in collusion with the other two partners and often received the diverted goods from the agent. The trader then, true to his calling, swapped the supplies to the Indians for fur pelts from which he in turn could realize a profit. One more member was the contractor, who supplied the agent with the actual foods and goods, for example, providing useless items such as mosquito netting and umbrellas at prices exceeding market value. And the last member of the "Ring" was the merchant interested in keeping troops in the field, such as provisioners and transportation contractors. For example,

McDermott cites Wells, Fargo & Company and accuses them of "staking out . . . broken down horses where Indians might easily steal them, the government having agreed to pay for such losses."[18]

Along with eliminating corruption, a basic, underlying assumption of the peace policy was its trust that Christians would not succumb to fraudulence and that the churches could stop the unscrupulousness that for twenty years previous had given the Indian Bureau a terrible reputation. And, the theory went on, the righteousness of the handpicked Protestant agents could produce peace among the Indians. On the other hand, the minimal risk was that failure would cast doubt upon the moral power of Christianity and bring disgrace upon the sects.

Like Galvez's peace policy nearly a century earlier, Grant's program was also designed to contain Indians for the benefit of non-Indians. Although the details of Grant's plan were somewhat different than Galvez's, the expected successful end result was similar: remove obstacles to white settlements on former Indian lands.

Combining church and state in mutual purposes was comfortable in the American mind of the 1870s. Many citizens looked upon their government as being divinely created—the idea of the separation of church and state was unthinkable—and as an institution that would assist men (women were not considered) in moral and religious redemption. Consequently, school prayers were routine, Bibles were read at home almost on a daily basis and, if not, certainly more than once a week, and sermons from the pulpit stressed the unselfish need of helping the less fortunate; most Americans believed that Christianity deserved the government's support. Grant himself was convinced that the religious and educational work by missionaries who had been previously stationed among the Indians had started them on the road to Christianity and that assigning churchmen to reservations would enhance and expedite the process.

He was correct in at least one regard. For years Protestant and Catholic missionaries had served as agents of a sort in the government's involvement with peaceful Indians. During a typical day, along with prayers and devotions, the clergymen living among the tribes performed a variety of tasks: they settled disputes among Indians and non-Indians; saw that rations were distributed fairly, that individuals were treated equally, that white men didn't take advantage of the Indians and vice versa; and generally acted as stabilizing forces, particularly in remote areas. The ground had been broken.

Grant informed the nation about the new politico-religious proposal in his first annual message to Congress in December 1869, reporting that "[Quakers] are known for their opposition to all strife, violence, and war, and are generally known for their strict integrity and fair dealings. These considerations induced me to give the management of a few reservations to them and to throw the burden of the selection of agents upon the society itself. The result has proven most satisfactory."[19]

Church officials from Protestant sects other than Quakers spoke out and made known their wishes to also participate, so the process of selecting the religious agents became more expansive. Most appointed agents were extremely dedicated to causing change for the better among their Indian charges. For example, a twenty-two-year-old Dutch Reformed congregant by the name of John Philip Clum was recruited to be the Indian agent at the San Carlos Apache Reservation.[20] Clum was openly ambitious and took his job seriously, even demanding that the government leave him alone to accomplish his purposes on the reservation—and they did, at first. Within a short time he established an Indian police force and a court administered by native judges. Under Clum's tutelage, many of the San Carlos Apaches became farmers, growing impressive amounts of corn on fertile stream bottoms. But in the long run, circumstances conspired against him and, very unhappy with the job, he resigned in 1877. Initial good intentions notwithstanding, Grant's peace policy failed that same year. Many of the reasons for its collapse appear to be similar to those on the colonial frontier years earlier, especially the lack of adequate funding.

Congress was not willing to appropriate the monies necessary to sustain the reservations during emergencies such as the widespread disappearance of game. Political infighting resulted in supplies arriving late or not at all on reservations, school funds were depleted, "agencies were in debt, and employees unpaid," stated Dr. Henry E. Fritz.[21]

Problems with Indian tribes also added to the policy's demise. For example, many Chiricahuas refused to relocate permanently at San Carlos after their reservation near Fort Bowie (agreed to by

Fig. 19. The children of Geronimo's band, photographed by C. S. Fly in March 1886.

Cochise in 1872) was withdrawn from federal supervision in 1876 and remained "out" in their now American and northern Mexico homelands, away from regulation by any U.S. authorities. Led by an upcoming warrior and medicine man named Geronimo and other headmen, several young Chiricahua men continued to raid back and forth across the border, stealing livestock, causing mischief, raising havoc, fighting, and frustrating the armies of both countries.[22]

Apache religious beliefs regarding warfare were an essential component of all the raids. Wrapping aspects of combat in a cloak of sacred traditions had always been a part of the Apaches' religious observances. For example, as soon as the agreement to go to war was made, all related actions assumed a religious significance. In particular, the warriors spoke a "warpath language" when talking together as they rode to and from the scene and during the actual engagement. Part of this specialized vocabulary was holy names: a horse was referred to as a "warhorse" or "charger"; an arrow was called a "missile of death." At this special time the men were addressed by temporary names to which the words *brave* or *chief* were appended.[23] And upon returning from a successful fight or raid, the customs of the victory feast, the distribution of the plunder, and the enhanced social status of the raiders were all rooted in a traditional religious complex and were considered to be signs from Ussen that they must keep Apacheria free from intruders.

With Geronimo's final surrender in 1886, twenty-seven years of captivity lay ahead for *all* the Chiricahuas—those who helped the U.S. government fight their own people and those who didn't. For those Chiricahuas innocent of hostilities against America, there was, as Captain Bourke wrote, "no more disgraceful page in the history of our relations with the American Indians than that which conceals the treachery visited upon the Chiricahuas who remained faithful in their allegiance to our people."[24] For the descendants of those who, with their parents and grandparents, had held out against the Spanish, the Mexicans, and now the Americans, imprisonment brought a bitter end to what they believed was their sacred duty to protect their homelands and the way of life Ussen had specifically designed for them. It had been a noble and outstanding effort.

Incarceration in Florida: Fort Marion—St. Augustine

This former Spanish fort was never intended to be a prison, as it had room for no more than 150 persons, and that was crowding.[25] It was here, however, that 130 *families*, totaling about 502 Chiricahua Apaches,[26] were confined, squeezed cheek by jowl on the fort's parapet into Sibley tents.

Apache women cooked outdoors over open fires in spare corners of the ramparts. When it rained, as it frequently did on the seacoast, the fires couldn't be lit and the people didn't eat. The meals varied little: the daily dish was a soupy beef stew made with flour and fat, not unlike the food Apache ancestors had eaten at the Spanish colonial missions. The exception was fish, in abundance in

Fig. 20. Chiricahua Apache prisoners of war being transported to Florida, September 1886. Geronimo and Naiche in front row, third and fourth from right. Courtesy of the Smithsonian Institution.

Fig. 21. Chiricahua Apache prisoners of war preparing to board the train at Bowie Station, Arizona, for St. Augustine, Florida, in 1886. Courtesy of the National Park Service, Castillo de San Marcos. Sketch by James Calvert Smith.

Fig. 22. Some members of Geronimo's band photographed by C. S. Fly in March 1886. Postcard photo, n.d.

Fig. 23. Castillo de San Marcos, now known as Fort Marion, Florida. Postcard photo, n.d.

Fig. 24. Interior of Geronimo's living quarters at Fort Pickens, Florida. Courtesy of Wesley Billingslea.

the eastern waters and on the army's menu for the Apaches. But to the Chiricahuas, fish was taboo, forbidden, and so no one would eat it. According to Geronimo, "Ussen did not intend snakes, frogs, or fish to be eaten."[27]

In a report to the U.S. Senate, Lieutenant Colonel Loomis Langdon, the fort's commanding officer, wrote, "[They] will not eat fish, as they seem to have a religious objection to fish as an article of food."[28] A fish meal was frequently distributed to the prisoners but then ignored and sent back by them. Coupled with unfamiliar climatic conditions, especially the rain and humidity and the exposure to contagious diseases carried by white people with whom they came into contact, the erratic and scant rations caused many to weaken and fall ill with tuberculosis, pneumonia, and other diseases. Approximately eighteen to twenty-four men, women, and children died during nearly eight months at Fort Marion. None of the medicine men's religious rituals could keep death away, but there is one report of a traditional Chiricahua Apache healing ceremony that tried to do just that.

Understanding that his religious paraphernalia was absolutely vital to the survival of his people, back in Arizona the medicine man called Ramon had carefully packed his sacred attire and artifacts and brought them with him to Florida, taking care to protect them during the long train journey. This very special clothing, body paint, and equipment was indispensable to the Chiricahua Apache religion, and had he forgotten it, he could not have performed any similar healing ceremonies. The traditional ritual, to be conducted for an ailing child, did not include any overt Christian practices that might have been adopted by ancestors and handed down.

First, the Mountain Spirit dancers prepared their bodies with sacred colors, a basic green-brown with yellow on each arm and an insignia in yellow on their backs and chests. Then they dressed in the traditional hide skirts with jingles and put on their knee-high boots with the turned-up toes. Each dancer held two wands ornamented with representations of blue lightning. The ailing child was strapped to a cradleboard and resting inside a tent in the northwestern sector of the terreplein, and so the dancers shuffled to that area first. They stomped on the damp brick floor, stabbed at the air with their wands, and cooed the timeless sound, all in an effort to drive the evil spirits away.

Fig. 25. Courtyard at Fort Marion, St. Augustine, Florida, 1991. Photo by author.

Fig. 26. Chiricahua Apache prisoners of war on the terreplein at Fort Marion, Florida. Tourists/sightseers mingle with the Apaches (left of center). Courtesy of the National Park Service, Castillo de San Marcos.

At a specific moment, a woman appeared out of a tent, knelt before the dancers, and held her sick baby up toward them. They swooshed their holy batons around, over, under, and upon the cradleboard that held the baby as the mother turned her child toward the four directions. Each of the dancers in turn took the cradleboard in his hands, pressed the baby to his breast, lifted the carrier with the child in it to the sky, lowered it to the earth, and turned to the four directions, all the time making the cooing sound that echoed from long ago. The child's mother and her friends simultaneously pierced the night with their shrieks, trills, and ululations.

Unfortunately, there is no record of whether that child recovered, nor is there a description available of the soldiers' reactions to the Apache ceremony. That is unfortunate, for it would be most informative to learn what these soldiers thought about their first experience with the Chiricahua traditional religion.[29] Importantly, this particular Mountain Spirit dance—possibly the first ritual of its kind performed in captivity—is testimony not only to the continuing power of religious belief but is also a potent political symbol of resistance, cultural survival, and tribal identity. Undeniably, among a people forcibly removed from their land base that Ussen gave to them and having no concept of what lay ahead for them as prisoners of an alien society that hated them, this Mountain Spirit dance anchored them to their ancestral beliefs and provided a measure of surcease from the stress and fear caused by their immediate surroundings.

EDUCATING THE YOUNGEST CHILDREN

More than 164 children of all ages were American prisoners of war at Fort Marion. To its credit, the U.S. government realized that it had an obligation to do something with the youngest, but what? Educating them seemed correct, but how and by whom they would be taught was undecided at first.

The first phase of the endeavor began when public notices and solicitations for educational services were posted. In negotiations that would determine the government's fiscal responsibility for the Chiricahua children, the foxy Mother Superior of St. Augustine's

Congregation of the Sisters of St. Joseph, possibly hoping for a windfall, requested a contract guaranteeing $20 to $40 per month per child, depending on the grade, to teach the youngest twenty-six girls and forty-two boys. The Commissioner of Indian Affairs rejected the amount as being outrageously high and countered with an offer of $7.50 per pupil instead. After evaluating the situation and (not incidentally) privately acknowledging that they needed the money, the sisters reluctantly accepted the government's offer. To complete the negotiations, the bureaucrats further demanded that the nuns agree to an annual limit of no more than $900 for all the students, which they reluctantly did.

Here again, combining church and state through federal funding was not considered to be unusual or prohibited. For that matter, through oral testimony and oral history, the Apaches themselves were familiar with both entities being one, as reflected in their ancestors' historical experience with the Jesuits and Franciscans on the colonial frontier.

Since no school building was immediately available for use in St. Augustine, the nuns appropriated one of the cavernous rooms at the fort, called casemates, as a classroom. Initially the children began their instructions under the direction of a young French woman, Mother Alypius, and her colleague, Sister Jane Francis. Lessons in English, Spanish, reading, writing, drawing, singing, and Catholicism were conducted daily from nine o'clock in the morning until noon. The children wore hats, shoes, dresses, shirts, and trousers that had been generously donated by the town's citizenry; books, tablets, and pencils were also part of the contribution.

Always protective, Apache men stood in the fort's plaza outside the casemates, watching over their children. They became so interested in the lessons that they too were soon drawing with crayons and singing religious and patriotic songs. "The Apache men and women grew quite fond of Mother Alypius," said Sister Mary Albert, in 1991 the community archivist at the Congregation of the Sisters of St. Joseph, adding,

> When another nun temporarily took her place, the adults were very reserved toward the new educator. . . . Although the government expected the children to learn only numbers and letters from the nuns and paid them only to teach the children,

there was much more. [Being able to speak and understand some Spanish, many] adult Apaches also became part of the [religious and academic] lessons taught at the fort, were very eager to learn, and were quite impressed with Mother Alypius. Because of the tribal concept of respect for authority figures, the Chiricahua Apaches accepted the teachers. . . . They knew the nuns were instructing their children at the request of the United States government. Contacts between the nuns and the Apaches were wholesome. There was good humor and a good climate of relations.[30]

Occasionally the children were removed from the fort and allowed to walk to the convent under the supervision of the younger nuns. The children then skipped and fussed and behaved like any other group of boys and girls. At the convent they used a bathhouse on the premises to change their clothes and then played in the ocean, carefully watched over by the nuns. Later, when the youngsters were taken into the church for their lessons, said Sister Mary Albert, "like electricity they jumped from bench to bench, so educating these children was not just a matter of teaching the ABCs. Their mental health was also important." The nuns also instructed the children in how to behave in the larger society. They believed they were making progress. "The mingling of these children with people from another culture broke down resistance. Because they were cooped up at the fort, walking to the convent also gave them some sense of freedom, as did the interaction between the younger nuns and the Apache children."[31]

In talking with Eve Ball many years later, Warm Springs Apache James Kaywaykla remembered his youthful experiences with the sisters. "I will never forget the kindness of those good women, nor the respect in which we held them. For the first time in my life I saw the interior of a church," he said, "and dimly sensed that the White Eyes, too, worshiped Ussen. I realized more fully that not all White Eyes were cruel and ruthless, but that there were some among them who were gentle and kind."[32]

It is certainly possible that at this juncture—late 1886—some of the children's parents, and especially their grandparents, knew more about Catholicism than was immediately obvious to the nuns. Their previous familiarity from the experience on the colonial frontier, handed down through oral testimony where appropriate, would probably explain why these former skillful warriors suddenly became passive parents whose youngest children were being forced to learn the enemy's ways. Then again, the pragmatic Apaches could have simply accepted their fate without any reluctance whatsoever, believing that to resist would mean their death under conditions of captivity.

Incarceration in Florida: Fort Pickens

The train carrying Geronimo and his followers eastward from Arizona toward imprisonment in Florida was detained at Fort Sam Houston, Texas, to await a decision from government officials regarding exactly what would happen to the small group.[33] A number of influential citizens of Pensacola, Florida, had petitioned their congressman, P. N. M. Davidson, requesting that he use his influence to designate Fort Pickens, a deserted structure on Santa Rosa Island in Pensacola Bay, as the warriors' place of confinement.[34] Incarceration there would segregate them from their friends and relatives—a good idea to the military since a rumor told that many peaceful prisoner Apaches at Fort Marion blamed Geronimo's efforts to stay free for their current status as prisoners of war; they were angry with him and seeking revenge.

Geronimo's group remained in San Antonio, not knowing their fate, until October 20, 1886, when Lieutenant General Philip Sheridan ordered the warriors and their interpreter, George Wratten, to be sent to Fort Pickens. The eleven women, six children (including a baby several weeks old, Geronimo's grandchild), and two enlisted scouts were to be separated from the warriors and sent to Fort Marion in St. Augustine.

On Friday, October 22, 1886, at four o'clock in the afternoon, a special train left San Antonio and was expected to arrive at Pensacola early Sunday morning. The railroad cars separated there, with the one containing the women and children scheduled to continue on to St. Augustine. Upon reaching Pensacola, the coach containing the Apache men and thirty soldiers from the Sixteenth Infantry was switched off to a side track. The warriors left the train and were marched single file between double rows of soldiers

Fig. 27. Geronimo, ca. 1905. Postcard photo.

Fig. 28. Geronimo, ca. 1906. Photo from author's collection.

Fig. 29. Geronimo, ca. 1900. Courtesy of Western History Collections, University of Oklahoma Library.

toward a steamer that was to ferry them across Pensacola Bay to Fort Pickens.

More than two thousand citizens had gathered at the Pensacola, Florida, depot, hoping for a glimpse of Geronimo. So large and restless was the crowd that soldiers formed double-file lines to enable the men to walk unmolested to a small boat that would ferry them across the bay to Santa Rosa Island. Geronimo became frightened of the large body of water and insisted he be allowed to face forward, to sit in the bow, and be chained to his guards' wrists.[35]

A reporter from a local newspaper, *The Pensacolian*, recorded the arrival.

> The special train from San Antonio, consisting of four coaches, chuffed into Pensacola at 2 A.M. on October 25. Aboard were 15 Apache warriors, their women and children, and a 30-man detachment from the 16th U.S. Infantry commanded by 1st Lt. E. F. Woodbury. At 8:30 o'clock the steamer Twin pulled into the railroad wharf, where the two cars with the 15 male Indians and their guards had been parked. The Apaches were soon aboard the ship. . . . The Indians and their guards landed on the rickity [*sic*] Fort Pickens wharf, and Captain Woodbury turned his prisoners over to Captain Wilson. As one of the warriors was leaving the Twin, he reportedly exclaimed, "Won't see Mexico no more."

An editorial published on October 23, 1886, in the same newspaper had declared, "We welcome the nation's distinguished guests and promise to keep them so safely under lock and key that they will forget their hair raising proclivities and become good Indians."[36]

While confined to Fort Pickens, Geronimo sent at least one letter to two of his wives and a son and daughter at Fort Marion. Writing through the white interpreter, George Wratten, Geronimo talked about being satisfied and working hard, saying it was healthy to work, and expressed his loneliness. "It seems to me that the Great Father and God are very closely united. I do hope he will let us see one another soon. As sure as the trees bud and bloom in the spring, so sure is my hope of seeing you again. . . . We are at peace now, and by God's help will remain so."[37]

His reference to God by name was unusual, given the fact that his exposure to Christianity had been minimal if at all at this time. Even if Wratten changed Geronimo's reference from "Ussen" to "God," Geronimo's connection of the Great Father with God reveals his understanding of American political power and, by extension, provides a clue to his comprehension of the immediate situation.

Intelligent, highly skilled, and naturally pragmatic, Geronimo and the Apache men were so obedient to authority at Fort Pickens that the army eventually allowed twenty wives and eleven children to leave St. Augustine on April 27, 1887, by train and join their husbands. Reconciling families was successful and pleased Langdon, the commanding officer of both Florida forts, so much that he allowed the Chiricahuas to hold a Mountain Spirit dance on June 10, 1887. There was only one condition: the dance had to be in front of spectators. No private religious ceremonies were permitted. At Langdon's invitation three hundred Pensacolans—at a charge by the army of fifty cents per adult and twenty-five cents per child—left the Palafox Street wharf aboard three steamers and landed at a dock recently repaired and shored up by the Apache prisoners. A newspaper item the next day reported the ancient ceremony, writing, "A large fire had been built in the center of the parade [grounds]. Near the east front, a buffalo hide had been placed on the ground, its hairless side up. Squatting around it, holding long switches, were Natchez [sic], Geronimo, and about eight other men. A crude drum was positioned before one of the Indians forming the circles." The reporter then described the Mountain Spirit dancers' attire and the dance steps, concluding with, "This kept up until time for the Pensacolans to return to their vessels at 10 o'clock. The dance, however, continued till dawn."[38] As the medicine man Ramon had at Fort Marion, these Apache men had brought their sacred dance attire with them from Arizona, indicating the value the men placed on the artifacts and their hope that the apparel wouldn't be taken from them.

Local journalists had taken an interest in the Apache warriors and periodically published items about any occurrences at Fort Pickens. Reporter Wheatley was a frequent visitor to the fort and wrote a story for *Cosmopolitan Magazine* about the Apache prisoners. Much of the information was written from his observations, and some of it was made up, for the Apaches refused to answer many of his questions. One of his boldest inquiries was about the Chiricahua religion. When no one responded, Wheatley drew his own conclusions and wrote:

> Strange as it may seem, these feline creatures are religious, believe in communion with the Supreme Being, pray to Him, and also to the sun, the light, the darkness, and the listening Earth-Mother. Some remnants of Roman Catholic teaching and more of primitive tradition, linger in their minds. Superstitious, too, they are, and reverence the eagle, owl, all perfectly white birds, and also the bear, whose flesh they refuse to eat. But they don't like to talk on these subjects. Even Geronimo keeps his eye peeled when he lets himself loose on these subjects, least some lurking brother should overhear what he says.[39]

One wishes Wheatley had understood that the Apaches did not pray to the sun or that he had explained the "remnants of Roman Catholic teaching." With regard to the latter, the reporter could have observed the results of the wives' and children's contact with the nuns at Fort Marion. On the other hand, Wheatley could have seen Christian religious activities that were the consequence of colonial influence.

The Chiricahuas' relationship to the owl and bear, construed as "reverence" by Wheatley, revealed the age-old cultural taboo about owls and bears. From childhood Apaches are warned that owls and ghosts are related and that they make people sick. Bears cause evil influence and exert their power through smell, bringing pain and sickness to the victim.[40]

While they continued to respect the ancestors' beliefs, a form of silent resistance, the normal workday routine for the men addressed the vegetation that had overrun Fort Pickens in prior years. The former warriors cleaned the grounds of weeds and dirt, scraped, painted, and piled shot and shell, killed snakes—also a major taboo because of the serious illness that results from an encounter—rooted out from the chinks of the walls the plants and young trees that constantly sprouted there, and planted Bermuda grass in the parade ground. One chore was digging wells among the sand dunes to obtain water for cooking and washing.

Killing snakes was an example of an activity that was forced upon the prisoners, as no Apache would dare to risk "snake sickness" through contact. Opler reported that the snake "should be held accountable for serious skin ailments of all kinds . . . swelling appears as a symptom in a specific case," and even "mention of the snake is usually avoided except in invective."[41] I have been unable to discover any medical records from Fort Pickens that specifically addressed the prisoners' ailments and so am unable to determine whether snake sickness actually occurred.

Living together in the vast open area of Fort Pickens and relaxing at the end of their workday, the men and women surely reminisced about their lives of freedom in Arizona and Mexico. In more private moments Geronimo and other medicine men must have held the sacred dance clothing, examined and talked about it, and then put it back for another time. Homesick for the desert and mountains, they could have repeated the tales told to them by their ancestors about Catholic processions that honored the saints' feast days on the colonial frontier. The older prisoners might have remembered or been told by their parents about the cruciform design of colonial ecclesiastical architecture and the wooden, silver-plated, or tin crosses on the walls of the mission churches. Other recollections may have recounted the dozens of crude, hand-hewn crosses that had been planted in the earth all across northern Mexico by loved ones at the site of sudden deaths by Apache attacks.[42] At this time in their cultural history, the cross still represented the four directions to many Chiricahuas, but other tribal members were aware of the joint meanings—traditional and Christian.

Mount Vernon, Alabama

Popular Indian advocacy agencies, such as Philadelphia's Indian Rights Association, monitored the deteriorating health situation at Fort Marion and were alarmed, but all they could do was lobby Congress and contact their local newspapers to report the circumstances. Eventually damning publicity embarrassed the government so badly that President Grover Cleveland and his cabinet agreed to move all the people to another site, hoping the relocation would quiet the nation's concern.

Fig. 30. Chiricahua Apache prisoners of war at Mount Vernon, Alabama. Interpreter George Wratten stands in background on right with hand at left trouser pocket, ca. 1890. Courtesy of the State of Alabama archives.

Fig. 31. Female student prisoners of war, presumably a school class at Mount Vernon, Alabama, n.d. Courtesy of U.S. Military History Institute.

At one o'clock in the morning of April 27, 1887, the remaining Fort Marion Chiricahua families—those who did not join their men at Fort Pickens—were put on trains bound for Mount Vernon, Alabama, the newest prison camp.[43] Thirteen months later, on May 13, 1888, the warriors and their wives and children were moved again, this time from Fort Pickens to Mount Vernon.

In conversation with Eve Ball, Eugene Chihuahua, a survivor of the imprisonment years, recalled:

> We had thought that anything would be better than Fort Marion with its rain, mosquitoes, and malaria, but we were to find out that it was good in comparison with Mt. Vernon Barracks. We didn't know what misery was until they dumped us in those swamps. . . . It rained nearly all the time. . . . The mosquitoes almost ate us alive. . . . Babies died from their bites. . . . Our people got the shaking sickness. . . . We burned one minute and froze the next. . . . No pile of blankets would keep us warm. . . . We chilled and shook."[44]

During the next eight years of confinement in Alabama more than three hundred men, women, and children died from contagious diseases and were allegedly buried in unmarked graves in a field adjacent to the main compound.[45] "They [the Chiricahua Apaches] sneaked the deceased out of the tent or wherever the death occurred," the late Arthur Capell, a former information specialist at Mount Vernon, stated in 1991. "Under the cover of darkness they carried them to a secret burial place to which no one ever returned."[46]

Capell's statement implied that some of the Apaches practiced traditional burials, which is not surprising because Christianity was still not a major influence in many lives. However, an example of later Apache exposure to the Christian religion at Mount Vernon was provided by Belinda Jones, another information specialist.

> The government thought that it would be better for the children if they got some education. This again was to try to instill in the younger generation the ways of—they used the term "White Man"—and to educate them and teach them things. Well, they got two teachers to come down. Sophie and Margaret Shepard

came from somewhere in the east. I believe there were teachers here before that, however, because I have a record that shows they had classes outside. They strung up a blackboard between the pines and tied it off. At first they encouraged only the Apache men to come to class; women didn't mean anything back then. I think they also had the responsibility of some Christian teaching as well.[47]

The government built a schoolhouse in 1889 and encouraged the children to attend, which seemed to be acceptable. In fact, oral history passed on by Ms. Jones reported that Geronimo would round up the children and make them attend. Actually, however, Sophie Shepard "installed Geronimo as school disciplinarian," believing that "his influence as an 'element of torture' was too valuable to risk losing."[48]

One of only a few documents I could locate about this period in Chiricahua history shows that on January 5, 1888, a Miss Isabel B. Eustis wrote a letter to a Mrs. Hemenway regarding a visit she (Eustis) had paid to Mount Vernon. Along with descriptions of the surroundings, the letter stressed the need for missionaries. "We held a service for the Indians under the pines each Sunday afternoon while we were at the Barracks," Eustis wrote.

> It was impressive to watch the eagerness with which they tried to catch the words of life from the lips of our little interpreter. Their intent hungry faces preached to us more effectively than we talked to them. Your own plan is most wise and pressing of sending some missionary teacher to live among these people and supplement the work of the officers. The War Department will provide for their physical comfort and probably for their industrial training. But they need food for their minds and their spiritual natures. Some one should teach them that life has hope in it still for themselves and their children. No one could talk to these keen thoughtful men without desiring to help them. . . . The present need is for mission work at Mt. Vernon.[49]

Did the Shepard sisters travel to Mount Vernon as a later result of this letter? Neither Capell nor Jones could fill in the missing pieces of the puzzle. The director of Information and Community

Services, a Dr. Patric Howley, added his voice in August of 1999, saying, "I have not much to give you on religious activity among the Apache prisoners of war at Mount Vernon. I do know, however, that the Catholic Church people were very active in our area at that time because of the many French and Spanish settlers here."[50]

Mount Vernon's Roman Catholic St. Thomas Church, with Father Henry O'Grady as pastor, was built in early 1890, and a dedication was planned for the first Sunday in May. Blessing the new church was a big event that had captured the attention of the press in Mobile, about thirty miles south of Mount Vernon, and stirred great public interest. Excursion train coaches left the city in mid-morning and arrived in time for the eleven o'clock ceremonies. Following the mass and lunch, a number of visitors walked up a hill to the site of Apache incarceration, hoping to steal a glimpse of Geronimo and buy Apache-made trinkets, which were a popular item among visitors.

At two o'clock that same afternoon, the crowd returned to the church in town to witness the first baptism of an Apache child, the two-month-old son of Chief Chihuahua. Named William St. Clair in honor of the former commandant of the prison camp, the baby's sponsors were two local citizens, a Mr. Thomas Rogers and his daughter, Miss Maggie. Records show that the child fell ill soon afterward and died.[51]

Documents describing the ritual in detail are not available, so the events leading up to Chief Chihuahua's decision to have his child blessed, and the ceremony itself, can only be imagined. However, one may fairly assume that his previous exposure to Catholicism had taken place at Fort Marion and probably continued in the Apache village at Mount Vernon, as had interaction with the local Catholic residents who became the baby's godparents.

Oral testimony must be considered in understanding Chihuahua's acceptance of Catholicism. Undoubtedly the adult generation to which he belonged had heard their parents and grandparents talk about the conditions on the Spanish colonial frontier. Some of the stories necessarily included portrayals of the efforts of the Jesuit and Franciscan missionaries to bring Christianity to their ancestors and coupled with the more recent good experiences at Fort Marion with the sisters of St. Joseph might have combined to create an acceptance of Christian doctrine among some of the incarcerated Apaches. Chihuahua appears to be one who was affected by his family's history.

Try hard as he did, the Protestant army chaplain at Mount Vernon, a Methodist minister named William H. Pearce, could not convince a single Apache to follow Protestantism. Pleasing their military captors and surviving on a daily basis was probably enough of a drain on their energies, particularly since contagious diseases such as tuberculosis were rampant in the camp, so they had very little, if any, vigor to dedicate to a new endeavor, such as learning the tenets of Protestantism. However, at one point the Methodist minister wrote that there was a "desire on the part of the men to marry in accordance with the customs of the Whites. There have been four such marriages. This involved giving up their custom of polygamy and what is of equal importance, their custom of divorce."[52] If he was not exaggerating and the four marriages he cited were the beginning of a trend, these several Apaches had either accepted Protestantism or were reflecting the ways of their ancestors, who had given up polygamy at the urgings of the Jesuits and Franciscans on the colonial frontier.

Two months after Chief Chihuahua's late infant son received the sacrament of baptism, in July of 1890 Geronimo appeared at St. Thomas Church with his wife and young daughter and asked the priest to baptize the family members. As Father O'Grady proceeded with the ceremony, Geronimo allegedly knelt and watched attentively. His wife took the Christian name of Maria and the girl was called Frances. Although Geronimo himself asked to be baptized, the priest refused. He apparently was not convinced of Geronimo's sincerity and needed more time to think about it before proceeding to educate him in the doctrines of Catholicism.[53]

Father O'Grady drove the Geronimo family back to the Apache village and visited with the Chiricahuas, some of whom guided him to a woman lying under an oak tree, dying from tuberculosis. O'Grady tried to talk with her while showing her the crucifix. She smiled and reached for it, causing the priest—unaware of the traditional representation of the four directions—to conclude she was a Catholic. He left her bedside and hurriedly drove back to the church, returning with the items necessary to administer extreme unction. As he anointed her, watched closely by more than a hundred Chiricahuas who had gathered by then around the tree, she grasped the crucifix once again and wouldn't let go. Father O'Grady wrested it from her grip and remained with her until she died that night.[54]

Profoundly influenced by the priest's devotion in staying beside the dying woman, a few days later the Apaches brought many of their children to the church to be baptized. As they stood in line, O'Grady realized he had to make a decision. Routine baptism would not be given automatically, he stated, and further announced that the parents and youngsters must receive religious instructions. Most of the Apaches in attendance agreed, and formal lessons were scheduled.

One somewhat amusing anecdote is told about a prisoner called Go-kliz. A San Carlos Apache by birth, he had married a Chiricahua woman and, reluctant to leave her and their children, he remained at her side as a prisoner of war. After all their children perished from contagious diseases, he petitioned the government to be able to return to San Carlos with his wife, but his petition was rejected. As pragmatic as the Chiricahuas, he made the best of the situation, including trying to understand the white man's religion. One day Go-kliz approached a teacher and asked for a picture of her God. Miss Marion Stephens carefully explained that there was no such thing and offered instead a picture of Jesus. Go-kliz pondered the gift for a long moment and then, obviously disappointed, shrugged and said, "Yes, I guess Jesus will have to do."[55]

Go-Kliz's hesitation was understandable. That Jesus died on the cross for the sins of humankind was incomprehensible to many Apaches, who were nonetheless able to relate Jesus to the culture hero called Child-of-the-Water, but Child-of-the-Water had never died *for* the Apaches. On the contrary, he *gave* life to the people by being one of their mythical ancestors. It was so perplexing to many Apaches that they ignored the captors' religion and simply went about their lives. Others just said they trusted and paid lip service to the complicated Christian concepts. Still others were true believers.

Watchdog organizations of the day continued to keep their eyes on the conditions at Mount Vernon. The Indian Rights Association, concerned about the prevalence of communicable diseases in the camp, sent inspectors to evaluate the circumstances. After a site visit, the concerned examiners publicly protested the smallness of the area, the unhealthy conditions that were due mostly to the climate, the overwhelming presence of tuberculosis, and the idleness among the prisoners. As a result of their intervention, government officials held a conference at Mount Vernon about a move eastward to a reservation near Wilmington, North Carolina, on June 24, 1889. Among nongovernmental notables in attendance were Professor Charles C. Painter of the Indian Rights Association, Captain John G. Bourke, Assistant Surgeon Walter Reed, M.D., and most of the Chiricahua chiefs and headmen. George Wratten, an old friend of the Apaches, translated. In the course of the discussion, Chato, a formerly ferocious warrior and later army scout, replied to a point Painter made by saying, "I am glad to listen to your talk. It seems as if my brother had come to me. God is your Father sure. I pray to God that we could once more have a farm, that some one would come to us to talk about it where we could raise cattle and crops. I pray for such a home every day."[56]

Chato's words reveal the influence of Christianity in his life, but it is difficult for me to believe that he was sincere in his flattery and references to God. Like most other Chiricahuas at Mount Vernon, Chato had assessed the situation carefully and adopted a position vis-à-vis his captors. The Apaches were so miserable at Mount Vernon that they would have done anything to be relocated anywhere that showed more mercy than the humidity and swamplike environment in Alabama. Consequently, if Chato had lied about God and prayer, his actions would have been seen as necessary from the Apache perspective; anything that brought about beneficial changes to their situation was fair game. Ultimately, though, the proposed transfer to North Carolina was canceled and the Apaches remained at Mount Vernon. The children continued receiving academic and religious instructions in a one-room schoolhouse from teachers Vincentine T. Booth and Marion E. Stephens,[57] both of whom had been at the post since February 1889.

By the time school closed for the summer, on May 31, 1889, attendance figures were up to as high as thirty men and thirty children. No women were noted in the records. Teacher Stephens came back in October, but Booth didn't return, so Sophie Shepard,[58] a native of Mobile County, took her place. The enrollment by pupils of all ages was impressive and climbing. "This number includes nearly all men and children of suitable age, and all come with more cheerfulness and display much more interest than at first," wrote Lieutenant W. H. Kellogg, the military commander at Mount Vernon. "It appears that many of them hesitated to send their children, fearing that if they attended the school they would be sent to . . . some other place away from here; but now, as they seem to understand that that will not be done, they are willing and many of them now anxious, not only to attend themselves but to have the children attend also."[59]

As Christian missionaries, the teachers also started a Sunday school, with twenty-five children, but no adults, enrolled. Finally one Apache woman, known as Annie, took the big step of attending the Sunday afternoon services the teachers held for the adults. Annie was George Wratten's wife, and news of her "acceptance" spread throughout the camp. Still, she was the only Apache woman to attend both church and school during the first year the teachers were at Mount Vernon.

The religious instructors were thrilled by a gift of an organ from a congregation in far away Litchfield, Connecticut. It caused quite a commotion, particularly since the only convenient spot to set it up (so the minister said) was in the breezeway of Geronimo's cabin. Everyone gathered around as the music blared through the damp forest. Children and adult males sang hymns together, but the ever-suspicious women stood by and just watched.

A hundred years later, in December 1989, the prisoner of war location at Mount Vernon had long since served Alabama as Searcy Hospital, a state-run mental institution. As the facility's holiday greeting, it published a nostalgic look backward at "Operation Santa Claus," the first Christmas celebrated by the Chiricahuas in Alabama. The card reads as follows:

> During the weeks prior to Christmas the teachers worked hard to enlighten the Apaches regarding the history of Christmas. The story of the birth of "the Babe in the Manger, watched over by angels under the Eastern Star," held the children's attention as nothing else could. The children were told over and over that "Christmas was the birthday of this Holy Child."
>
> The story that there was to be a tree bearing gifts was purposefully spread around; expectations were high in the Apache village.

On Christmas Eve, 1899, after breakfast the ladies [military wives] gathered and went to the school where they found very clean children standing at the door. The children were so radiant with expectation that "it was hard to resist the temptation to deal out fruit and candy on the spot." After the women entered the school, they locked the door and tacked newspapers over the windows to add to the mystery which nearly boggled little Apache minds. The children refused to leave, staying nearby all day. Every now and then an amazed little face would pop up above the newspapers for just a brief moment.

By dark everything was ready. Major [William H.] Kellogg appeared and ordered the lighting of the many candles that were on the tree. Then only one door of the double doors was opened and a steady stream of wide-eyed youngsters entered the room.

A few Apache men entered the room also because of their importance. Included among them were Naiche, chief of the Chiricahuas, and the "school's friend," Geronimo.

"I can never forget the look of delight on those faces," wrote a happy and pleased Sophie Shepard, the children's teacher.

The tree was beautiful, an exquisite holly tree covered with red berries. Its top rose majestically into the arched roof where a white and silver pink-cheeked angel presided over the 400 cornucopias, burning candles, dolls, assorted ornaments, wreaths of pop-corn balls, and other items. The body of the holly tree rose out of a pyramid of golden oranges and red apples. Tables were covered with packaged, labeled gifts.

Then Santa Claus appeared. He was dressed differently from any Saint Nicholas that appeared in other places. Although it was unseasonably warm even for South Alabama, Santa Claus was dressed in Mrs. Kellogg's fur coat; he wore a black fur cap, a white cotton beard, and a real moustache. When Santa Claus greeted the children in their own language, they knew it was the interpreter, George Wratten. He distributed his bags of candy with Apache witticisms which elicited peals of laughter. These ecstatic yells and confusion "was the happiest kind" which all, even Geronimo, could forgive.

After Wratten passed out the gifts, the youngsters were seated. Major Kellogg ordered that the adults be allowed to see their children, "as it would have been cruel to shut out the sight

Fig. 32. Walter Reed, M.D., physician to the Chiricahua Apache prisoners of war at Mount Vernon, Alabama. Courtesy of Armed Forces Institute of Pathology, Washington, D.C., n.d.

of them." The newspapers were removed, the windows were raised and the doors were opened wide. Apachedom gazed on a sight unique in their history. Each child had received gifts of a top, a bag of marbles, a pencil, a slate, a horn, a picture book, "all cheap," but precious in their eyes.[60]

It was a wonderful time for everyone at Mount Vernon, especially the children, but very sad for those Apache sons and daughters who had been sent away to school in Carlisle, Pennsylvania. For them, homesickness was their gift every month of the year.

A Few Words . . .

While at Mount Vernon, some of the Chiricahua Apache prisoners of war came under the influence of Catholicism as certain of their ancestors had on the Spanish and Mexican colonial frontiers. The immediate similarities were striking: confinement, regimentation, a strange diet, sickness, and death. The political situation, while somewhat comparable in that the Apaches were constrained by governments they couldn't understand, was quite different as well. Under Spanish and Mexican jurisdiction, the potential to return to their camps was possible for those who volunteered to live at the missions; cultural fluidity prevailed. American control prohibited freedom. Still, speculation among today's Chiricahua Apaches is that some women fled into the woods around Mount Vernon under cover of darkness and eventually melded into one or more of the Alabama tribes in the region. Laughter and disbelief by Apache men is always part of this discussion, for they insist that no sane Apache woman would forsake an Apache man and become a member of another Indian tribe. Chiricahua women, hearing this exaggerated response, howl and deride the men.

Those Apaches who decided to adopt Catholicism at Mount Vernon, as Chief Chihuahua did, had no problem participating in Christian ceremonies. In their eyes, fidelity to the ancestors' religion had not been compromised; it simply had been enhanced, and in so doing, they maintained the relationship through time from the past to the present without any loss of cultural identity.

CHAPTER FIVE

With Jesus in Boarding School

Pennsylvania

Following cultural customs, most Chiricahua Apache parents provided a protected atmosphere for their children so they could be emotionally enriched by the myths, stories, lessons, and their loving relations with others. Cultural identity was thus maintained, and that it didn't happen as planned, or wished, was more a consequence of external circumstances rather than any societal shortcomings.

Cultural integrity, through ceremonies culturally prescribed at certain stages of an infant's life, was instilled from the moment of birth, when the newborn's mother or her midwife blessed the child with water; if none was available, sputum was the source. The baby was then dried and sacred pollen sprinkled on its body.[1]

Disposal of the placenta was also a religious ritual. Placed in a piece of cloth or blanket, it was deposited in the branches of a nearby fruit-bearing bush or tree. The bundle was blessed by the midwife, who recited a small prayer at the site, such as, "May the child live and grow up to see you bear fruit many times." The family forever considered that place to be sacred, and the parents and child might return there many times in the child's life. Legend has it that Geronimo went back on several occasions to the place of his birth to lie on the ground and roll over and over toward the four directions in acknowledgment and respect. (Burial of the placenta was out of the question because animals could dig it up and thus, the culture teaches, cause harm to come to the child.)[2]

A baby was usually named during a religious ceremony that was held immediately after delivery or, depending on the circumstances, could be postponed. The name given to an infant at birth was often not permanent and may change several times during an individual's lifetime.[3]

A special ceremony was held when the child was about one month old, before he or she was placed into a cradleboard. The infant was first marked with hoddentin and then the carrier was lifted by a medicine man or medicine woman to the four directions with the baby inside if it was a boy; if a girl, an empty cradle was lifted on high. Amid prayers, the cradle was faced toward the east and after three ritual thrusts, the baby girl was finally placed inside. As an infant matured, charms were sewn onto the slats to protect the child.[4]

The cradleboard was made four days or more after the birth of the baby. It was not unusual for medicine men or medicine women, at the request of a family, to construct a carrier. They often prepared the materials in advance, sometimes working on the outer frame for a day and then setting it aside, awaiting the moment when they finished crafting the crosspieces and the canopy. Once actual construction began, however, it usually was completed within one day. The cultural assumption was that the medicine man or medicine woman would say the appropriate prayers for the coming child's welfare and long life during each step of creating the cradleboard.[5]

First haircuts were given to youngsters in the spring of any year with a medicine man or medicine woman in attendance. Locks of the child's hair were buried under a fruit tree, ensuring a full head of hair.[6]

The ceremony known as "Putting on Moccasins" derived its power from Child-of-the-Water.[7] This rite was performed by a medicine person when the child took his first steps in an imitation of Child-of-the-Water, who underwent a similar ritual when he began to walk. Cultural memory guaranteed that performing the continuing legacy would ensure that the child would be as strong as this supernatural benefactor.

Even though both parents took primary responsibility for their offspring, as the infant matured, certain adults in the extended family took an interest, including informing him about his cultural and religious heritage and its expectations of him. A child's behavior was greatly influenced by the creation myths and sacred stories, most of which set standards and impressed the youngster with the need for control of himself in public and private settings. Often the stories described spirits and the powers of animals that can cause humor or hurt. Each of these tales had a moral, or an example to heed, and if it wasn't apparent to the child, the storyteller explained it again and again until the listener understood.

In early life boys and girls were physically trained together, with no distinction as to gender-based duties until they became a bit older.[8] "The training process was such," said Leland Michael Darrow, the Fort Sill Chiricahua/Warm Springs Apache Tribe's historian, "that essentially everybody had the same training but with different emphasis. Everybody was supposed to know how to do everything, whether they do it or not. [Boys] would need to know how to cook and sew because there might be an occasion when they would need to do that. [Girls] would need to know how to ride horses and follow tracks."[9] There was one distinct difference, though, and the culture imprinted it: a female was obligated to lifelong obedience to her parents. A male, on the other hand, was released from this duty when he married and moved in with his wife and her family, but he then became beholden to his in-laws.

By the time the children reached the age of cognizance at about seven years, both boys and girls could hunt small game, use a bow and arrow and a slingshot, whittle a dart, throw a stick, handle a knife offensively and defensively, cook a meal, help tan and sew hides, help butcher an animal, prepare medicinal herbs and treat small wounds, manage the livestock, and care for younger siblings. Rarely did a child refuse to participate in the training sessions or become unruly and hard to handle, but when that happened, mild disciplinary measures such as sending him away on a wild-goose chase taught him a lesson. Once in a while a small cup of cold water had to be poured over his head or he was put in a gunnysack to calm down, but these types of punishments were not routine.[10]

Along with learning good behavior from his parents and the sacred stories, the actions of a youth were also shaped by peers, especially among the boys, who followed their older friends around as they shot at birds with darts or their slingshots. Physical strength was emphasized, and a boy was tested as to how far and how fast he could run, his ability to lift heavy rocks, and his skill in hand-to-hand fighting. Exceptional youths were watched carefully by their extended family members and others, for they tended to rise to prominence and bring honor and respect to their parents, as did youths who showed an interest in the supernatural; these youngsters were apprenticed to medicine people.

A girl's future duties as a wife and mother were made very clear to her while she was still a child being taught to help with the work of the home. For example, she was shown how to bring wood and water to the camps and often carried bundles of twigs on her small back as practice. But her principal duties were to assist the adult women and to receive continuous training from them, including how to weave baskets, which were needed to collect seeds and carry water. A girl's thin fingers were especially capable of tightly entwining reeds together so that a woven water jug would not leak. As she matured, the girl was informed about sexual etiquette, how to make herself attractive, and how to be a good wife and mother. When menses arrived and the puberty ceremony was held, she was ready for marriage and her own children.

These revered rituals meant absolutely nothing to the U.S. government and one of its agents for Indian education, the Carlisle School's superintendent, Captain Richard Henry Pratt.

The Carlisle Indian Industrial School

"Kill the Indian, save the man." This harsh slogan, created by Pratt, clearly and concisely reflected his public and private attitude.[11] Arrogant, self-confident, and stubborn, he was completely convinced that he knew exactly what had to be done to civilize the children of America's Indian groups and didn't hesitate to broadcast his opinion. Because of his excellent reputation in dealing with American Indians, allies and advocates alike listened.

Pratt's interest in Indian education started in April 1875, while he was a U.S. Army captain. Seventy-two warriors from the Cheyenne, Comanche, Kiowa, and Caddo tribes were imprisoned under his military supervision at Fort Marion, in St. Augustine,

Florida.[12] He viewed these captives as military adjuncts, issued them old army uniforms, and forced them to cut their hair, polish their buttons, press their trousers, and clean their shoes. Eventually he taught the men how to read and write, and by the end of their incarceration three years later, seventeen of the prisoners expressed a desire to go on with their schooling. At Pratt's request, the all-black Hampton Institute in Virginia enrolled them.[13]

After studying Hampton's philosophy of training students to return to their communities as leaders and professionals, Pratt formulated a similar model for Indians only. His goal was to take children from the reservations, remove them to a school far away from home, family, and tribal influences, and transform them into Christians and honorable, productive American citizens. If Pratt's idea was successful, Indian students would closely resemble their Euro-American counterparts. In other words, his plan was not unlike the effort made during Spanish colonial times to "Christianize" the Indians and groom them to be tax-paying citizens.

Pratt made no secret of his intentions, believing that the more he publicly stated his belief, the more support it would engender. He trusted that America was still ripe for the idea, having recently experienced the effects of Grant's peace policy and the dual roles churchmen could take with regard to Indian issues. In an address to a convention of Baptist ministers, Presbyterian Pratt proclaimed, "In Indian civilization I am a Baptist, because I believe in immersing the Indians in our civilization and when we get them under, holding them there until they are thoroughly soaked."[14]

Pratt's analogy to baptism is understandable because of the religious affiliation of his audience, but under other conditions his choice of words would be poor and give the listener the impression that he advocated any means to an end. Still, his zeal for educating American Indian children was looked upon by public officials as one answer to the perplexing problem in the late 1870s of what to do with the Indian peoples; Pratt appeared to have a partial solution.

After extensive lobbying in Washington for public funds and subsequent appeals to humanitarian and civic reform groups for private monies, Pratt opened the Carlisle Indian Industrial School on November 1, 1879. In time, the annual amount of congressional allocation per student at any of the nation's Indian schools would eventually reach $167.00, a far cry from the $7.50 per student the nuns were paid at Fort Marion.[15] But time and circumstances had shifted interest from Spanish Catholic Florida to Protestant Pennsylvania, and that change made a difference, as did the religious affiliations of high government officials. Pratt's rich friends and most of the political, administrative, and congressional policy makers of the time were Protestants in a now expanding Protestant America. By authorizing monies for Pratt's idea, Congress trusted that the school would emphasize the popular Protestant ethics of work and morality and promote "the superiority of the American Protestant culture."[16] Here again is an example of a similarity with the Spanish colonial officials and missionaries: the presence of imperious egocentrism that elevates one culture over all others.

The Carlisle School publicly endorsed the four accepted truths of Indian education at the time:

1. Teaching Indian students the rudiments of "American" education, that is, the ABCs and the English language, was the first step toward civilizing the children.

Commensurate with their exaggerated opinion of themselves, many Protestant Americans believed they were obligated as Christians to "raise up" the natives a little higher, but not so high that the Indians would become competitive. Through education the Indians were expected to recognize the worth and inevitability of the American/Christian way, discard ancient tribal customs, and begin thinking as Americans did—all giant steps toward becoming civilized as they defined it. A logical extension was the widely accepted belief that once educated, Indian fidelity to reservation life would fall by the wayside as more and more civilized Indians opted to leave home for urban areas. Then abandoned Indian lands could be opened for settlement by emigrant Americans, who eagerly subscribed to the theory of Manifest Destiny.[17]

2. Individualization—the certain result of education—was expected to change the Indian's traditional role as a consumer to the more significant role of producer.

In the late nineteenth century, Protestant America measured prosperity by individual accumulation, which was completely opposite of Indian societies, in which wealth was determined by how much an individual or family could give away. Through education, it was believed, the Indian would unhesitatingly adopt the belief in the Christian ethic of work and profit, recognize and appreciate the significance of ownership, become a producer, and thus benefit all of society. Not incidentally, tribal values would then disappear and be replaced by individual interests, which would predominate in the newly educated Indian's mind as he came to value personal property over community sharing, one of the hallmarks of civilization. If tribal values vanished, so would the tribes—a publicly unstated goal to be sure, but one that would guarantee no resistance to the government's aims.

3. Christianization of all American Indians was absolutely necessary in a society anchored in Christian ideals and morality.

Many Indians had already embraced Christianity—both Catholicism and Protestantism—by the time Indian education became a reality, but there were still resisters within the tribes. These holdouts, whoever and wherever they were, had to be brought to the altar if Indians were to assume responsibility for their own behavior and act as citizens. Permitting natives to reject Christianity and remain traditionalists would drain the country of some of the energy it needed to move forward as a Christian nation as well as thwart the government's economic and other intentions.

4. Citizenship training included learning the basic principles of American democracy, the rights of Americans, and the rule of law in a democratic society.

When Indian students recognized and fulfilled their obligations as good citizens, it was assumed that they would endorse the advantages of civilization over their tribal customs. Education would instill loyalty and devotion to the United States in the Indian youngsters and would cause them to agree with the dominant society's efforts to dispossess the tribes of their land bases. With this concurrence, educated Indians would support everyone who coveted Indian lands.

Taken together, these educational aims ensured that Indian children would be totally transformed into "Americans" who would respect and support the nation's policies, including those that went against their own people. When that happened—when assimilation, acculturation, Christianity, and civilization saturated native children as completely as Pratt wished—the goals of Indian education would be reached. Hidden behind all this, of course, were the political and economic ends—many personal—of American leaders from all areas of society that couldn't be accomplished if the Indians stood in the way.[18]

To begin to reshape the Indian children, Pratt believed in regimentation and established several processes that would alter former tribal behavior.

ROUTINES

Carlisle students woke up each morning at six o'clock, ate breakfast at six-thirty, cleaned their rooms at eight, started school at nine, and ate lunch at twelve and supper at six. Homework was scheduled from eight to ten at night, and then the lights went out. The pattern never varied, nor did the students' clothing. The boys wore military-style uniforms, and the girls dressed in proper Victorian attire. They marched together in groups to and from their classes and to the dining room for meals. Regular drill practice was a feature of the boys' daily life, as was ranking them and assigning military grades according to their abilities.[19]

With such a strict schedule, students had very little time to concentrate on the homesickness that must have filled the air. After ten each night I believe crying and sobbing could be heard throughout the dormitories, at least until time began to heal the incredible loneliness for their families that the children must have felt. Some Apache students remained away at school without seeing their parents for up to ten years, during which time their initial reaction to being away from home became a thing of the past and adaptation was a continuing way of life.

RELIGION

According to one observer, at the Carlisle School there was a pervasive

> religious influence. . . . Religious service is held in the institution each Sabbath afternoon, usually conducted by a minister of one of the congregations in the city of Carlisle. The students all attend this service; also a prayer meeting in the evening and they

can attend the church services in town in the morning. A large percentage of the students have been converted. . . . Nearly two hundred are members of the Young Men's Christian Association, and a larger number of the young ladies are members of "The King's Daughters' Circles." Some of the students belong to the Christian Endeavor Societies in town. It seems very evident that Carlisle School is largely blessed of the Lord, to whom be the praise.[20]

In describing the religious backgrounds of the Indian students, David W. Adams noted that

many came from communities characterized by religious factionalism. . . . Many . . . came from cultures that either had managed to integrate various aspects of Christianity into their own religious system without destroying the latter's essence or had simply accepted and compartmentalized it. . . . Finally, and this point cannot be overstated . . . nearly all students entered . . . with only a partial understanding of their tribal belief system and ceremonial cycle.[21]

All of the students were indoctrinated into Protestant Christianity as part of their lessons. No exception. Adams believes many of the students were confused by the constant proselytizing that accompanied their academic pursuits, particularly when they were forced to repeat biblical verses and sing hymns using words that initially had no meaning to them. He cites one Hopi student who "probably went through the motions, kept [her] counsel, and endured the hours of preaching and praying as best [she] could."[22]

Christian tenets were taught daily in the classroom as well as sermonized from the Sunday pulpit. During the week the teachers discussed the chapters of the Bible, the Ten Commandments, the Beatitudes, and the Psalms. They talked about Adam and Eve, the Garden of Eden, Moses, David and Goliath, angels, and, importantly, the resurrection of Christ. Since death was not new to the Indian children, stories about Christ's ascension were especially tantalizing, but at the same time the notion of rising from the dead was as perplexing to many of these youngsters as it had been to their ancestors.

Fig. 33. Chiricahua Apache children prisoners of war arriving at the Carlisle Indian School from Fort Marion, Florida, November 4, 1886. Courtesy of the Smithsonian Institution.

Adams recorded a statement from a boarding school teacher that soothed the children's concerns. The teacher related, "When I found the place in the Bible, and read about the holy city which we all hope to enter, their merry eyes opened wide and their little faces grew thoughtful, and they wondered if the little boy who died last autumn went there and asked, 'Did the angels come to take him?'"[23]

Moral training for all children shared equal footing at Carlisle with academic and religious instructions in classrooms. Teachers were obligated to instill in the children's minds the Christian ideals of chastity, pure thought, respect for the Sabbath, honesty, and temperance. (Alcohol had already begun to take a dreadful toll among Indians, and many of the children were familiar with its devastating effects.) The idea of sin and all its manifestations was carefully explained over and over until it was clear. When the instructors were

Fig. 34. Chiricahua Apache children prisoners of war after four months at the Carlisle Indian School, March 1887. Courtesy of the Smithsonian Institution.

certain that the youngsters comprehended the concept, they discussed at great length the notion of guilt because of having sinned. And as a natural progression, ideas of heaven and hell were then raised in the classroom.

Adams documented the pain felt by Harry Raven, a Carlisle student who believed he had sinned in some way and, acknowledging his guilt, wrote a letter to Captain Pratt. "I only believe that God has the power to take way our sins," the child lamented. "So please Captain help me and pray for me to come out of this wrong where I am in. I will promise you that I will never write nor say such words to any body here after this. . . . From today I will commence my way to follow the Christians. If I do fall into sin I will get up again. . . . Pray for me that I may become Christian and I will give my self to Christ. I have long sin and gives me but a sorrow life."[24]

CHIRICAHUA APACHE STUDENTS

October 23, 1886, was a special day for Pratt. After receiving permission from the government, he, his officers, and their wives spread out among the Chiricahua Apaches imprisoned at Fort Marion and selected more than ninety-five children, who were to be sent immediately to the Carlisle School. All five of the boys from Fort Pickens were also tapped, bringing the total to exactly one hundred new recruits. Helplessly watching their children pulled away from them by strangers was a terrifying experience for the parents, to say nothing of the children's horror, a repetition of the situation their ancestors endured as captives on the Spanish colonial frontier. Some adults at Fort Marion responded quickly and cleverly by hiding their youngsters from the authorities. For example, Ruey Darrow, daughter of prisoners of war, said, "My father [Sam Haozous] told us his mother put him in a rain barrel so he wouldn't have to leave."[25] Other parents weren't quite so fast, so in the confusion and crying, some of the older children invented their own ways to avoid being selected. Mildred Imach Cleghorn said her father was one of a group of boys who were marched out of the fort and onto the beach, where they were lined up by height—tallest down to the smallest. "My father said he caught on fast that the soldiers were going to take the tallest boys to Carlisle, so he dug his bare feet into the sand, slouched over, and made himself as small as could be. It didn't work. He was chosen and had to go."[26]

Young James Kaywaykla, the boy who so loved being with the nuns, apparently was at the age—eight or nine years old—where he could have been either overlooked or selected. Despite already being enrolled in the fort's classes for the youngest children, he was separated from his mother and placed with the group of older children who had already been segregated. "I was the youngest child to go," he told author Eve Ball.

> Part of us went by train, part by sea. I was with the latter. We were under the care of an officer and his wife; and except for the terror of another separation from our people, and the uncertainty of what was to be done with us, we were well treated. Being out of sight of land frightened us, but not more than the bewildering experience of crossing New York City.

Fig. 35. Chapo Geronimo, son of the warrior, on the right with unidentified friend, n.d. Courtesy of Frisco Native American Museum, Frisco, North Carolina.

At Carlisle we were subjected to the indignity of having our hair cut and being forced into trousers. Our clothes were sent to our families in Florida so that they might know that we still lived. How that could have convinced them I do not know but that is what we were told.

Both Kanseah [Geronimo's nephew, age thirteen] and Chapo [Geronimo's son, age unknown] were among the students [chosen]. Jason [Betzinez, Geronimo's second cousin, age twenty-six], too, went and he was a mature man. Again we encountered climatic conditions new to us and fatal to many. Chapo became tubercular and was returned to his people to die. Kanseah was unhappy and not interested in school. . . . Daklugie [son of Apache chief Juh of the Nednhis, a small group of

Chiricahuas, and nephew of Geronimo] made rapid progress in school; and I think I must say without boasting that I did. The Apache children learned to communicate with Indians of many other tribes who were in school; and eventually some of us learned the sign language which our people had never used. We learned English, too, both in school and in the homes in which we were placed to work during the summer.[27]

In this exchange, Kaywaykla didn't say how each of the children received their Christian names, possibly because the subject was incredibly painful to him. However, according to oral testimony, the children were placed in rows of twenty-six, by height. The tallest then received a name that started with *A*, the shortest with *Z*. From that time onward the children were known by their new Anglicized names and most traditional names were lost. Simultaneously each child was assigned an arbitrary birth date based on physical appearances, which were evaluated by Euro-American standards.

Even though the U.S. government preferred that Indian students keep their original tribal names and issued an instruction in that regard, most of the tribal names were quite difficult to pronounce and record in a ledger. Many administration officials in the Indian schools disregarded the directive and simply assigned names that could easily be spelled.[28] At least one such experience was documented that involved an Apache child. "An Indian policeman rode up to the government school and delivered a little boy to the superintendent. 'What's his name?' inquired the official. 'Des-to-dah,' replied the Indian employee as he rode away." The superintendent, assuming that Des-to-dah was the boy's family name, assigned the Christian name Max to him. "It turned out, however, that *des-to-dah* was the Indian word for 'don't know.' The policeman had simply said he didn't know what the boy's name was," but from then on the child was known as Max Don't Know. Further, "Max was one of four brothers in the same school, no two of whom had the same surname,"[29] a common situation that has made tracing Indian genealogy difficult.

The first batch of Apache children did so well at Carlisle that in April 1887, Pratt and the military officers selected sixty-two or sixty-four (accounts differ) more children for the school. Jason

Betzinez was among this group. Much older than the other Apache students, Betzinez was determined to be a good pupil in every way, and he succeeded. He studied in the mornings and worked in the school's blacksmith shop in the afternoons, learning that trade from the ground up. Not too long after he arrived at Carlisle, though, he was sent to a farm owned by Edward Cooper in Bucks County, Pennsylvania, as a participant in the outing system.

Designed for both boys and girls, the outing system enabled the students to spend at least one year in a country home, supervised by its owners, many of whom were Pennsylvania Dutch families. During this time the pupils also remained under the jurisdiction of the school and were paid periodic visits by the outing agent, who wrote a report concerning the students' health, condition, and progress. The farm homes became a vocational training ground for the children. Female students worked as domestics in the homes, while the boys labored as farmhands in the fields. Each participant was paid one dollar to fifteen dollars per month in proportion to the kind of work they did and the ability and skill shown in doing it. Earnings were deposited in individual bank accounts, which were accessible to the students for necessities. As an added benefit, many families became quite fond of the students and kept in touch with them long after they returned to their natural parents. To show their respect and gratitude, a few Apache children took the first or last names of the local families as their own.[30]

The outing system at Carlisle was Pratt's own plan "to promote the assimilationist goals of the federal government by placing Indian children in intimate contact with 'civilized' American society."[31] But, claimed Robert A. Trennert, "academic learning clearly played a subordinate role," especially with regard to the girls, who "spent no more than half a day in the classroom and devoted the rest of their time to domestic work." At Carlisle, wrote Trennert about the girls, "the first arrivals were instructed in the manufacture and mending of garments, the use of the sewing machine, laundry work, cooking, and the routine of household duties pertaining to their sex." Consequently, when their education was completed, the young women "could find work, but only in the artificial environment of Indian agencies and schools . . . protected by a paternalistic government. Here they continued to perform tasks of domestic nature without promise of advancement. Nor were they assimilated into the dominant society as had been the original intent of their education. . . . Women were trained for an imaginary situation that administrators of Indian education believed must exist under the American system. . . . Few rewarding jobs were available in white society, and status was an impossibility."[32]

Betzinez's experience with farming lasted only about three months, after which he had to return to the school as a result of an accident. After a serious injury to two of his fingers had healed, Betzinez went back to the farm. He studied at Carlisle for nearly nine years, but when he was about thirty-five years old and in the eighth grade, he gave up his formal education and entered the workaday world. The next year, while working in a Pennsylvania steel mill, tuberculosis struck, but the ailment was not fatal. Betzinez became a Christian during this time and was selected from his congregation at a Dutch Reformed Church to become a delegate to the national convention of the Christian Endeavor Society in Washington, D.C. He was a devout member of that church and later married one of its missionaries, Anna Heersma. Jason Betzinez lived to be one hundred years old and died from injuries received in an automobile accident. He is buried in the Chiricahua Apache prisoner of war cemetery at Fort Sill, Oklahoma, close to Geronimo's grave.[33]

Even though Betzinez, Kaywaykla, Daklugie, Kanseah, and other Apache students survived the educational experience, many Chiricahua and other Indian children died at the boarding school from contagious diseases, primarily tuberculosis. When the death rate of Apache children at Carlisle rose so dramatically that the newspapers publicized it, Pratt became alarmed. Writing to the commissioner of Indian Affairs in Washington, D.C., on May 24, 1889, he stated:

> The cause of death, so far, has been, without exception, inherited consumption from venereal taint. While climate may to some extent have an influence in aggravating and bringing a speedier termination, I think the deplorable and almost hopeless conditions surrounding them have a greater influence. They have no home, no country, no future, and life has become hardly worth living. I hope that at the earliest practicable date something may be arranged covering the disposition of the whole

party. If thoroughly sifted and the unhealthy disposed of, there is no possible objection to the others.[34]

Pratt coldly told the truth as he saw it and devised a clever method for reducing the school's death rate. When sick Apache students reached the terminal stages of their illnesses, he loaded them on trains and shipped them to their parents in the prisoner of war camp in Alabama. Along the way, some died in their seats. When the trains arrived at Mount Vernon, the children who were still able to function carried their friends' corpses out of the cars and placed them lovingly in parental arms.

Dead children and those who died after being returned to Mount Vernon were interred by their relatives in unmarked graves in fields on the outside perimeter of the Alabama prison camp.[35] Their heartaches did not go unnoticed by the military supervisors and troops, many of whom sympathized with the Apaches' loss but were helpless to change the terrible situation. In the meantime, Pratt's mortality and morbidity statistics improved and he continued to be funded.

GERONIMO'S VISIT

Apache youngsters and other Carlisle students had a big treat in March 1905. Geronimo, still a famous warrior although incarcerated, visited the school en route to Washington, D.C., where he was to ride in the inaugural parade of President Theodore Roosevelt. "My friends," Geronimo said to the assembled pupils, "I am going to talk to you a few minutes. Listen well to what I say.

> You are all just the same as my children to me, just the same as if my children are going to school when I look at you all here. You are here to study, to learn the ways of white men. Do it well. You have a father here and a mother also. Your father is here, do as he tells you. Obey him as you would your own father. Although he is not your father, he is a father to you now.
>
> The Lord made my heart good. I feel good wherever I go. I feel very good now as I stand before you. Obey all orders, do as you are told all the time and you won't get hungry. He who

owns you holds you in His hands like that and He carries you around like a baby. That is all I have to say to you.[36]

Geronimo's inference, oddly, was that disobedient students would become hungry, which he might have deliberately stated to impress the Indian pupils; there is no evidence that food was ever withheld from the students as punishment. However, there can be no doubt about Geronimo's explicit reference to the Lord—an indicator of his 1903 acceptance of Christianity. On the other hand, he could have used the word *Ussen*, but the translator—nephew Asa Daklugie?—substituted the word *Lord*. In any case, it is fair to assume that Geronimo made his point.

LETTERS FROM HOME

Interpreter George Wratten and letter-writer Isabel Eustis served as writers for many prisoner of war families at Mount Vernon who wanted to contact their children. Some of these letters have been preserved, and I will quote verbatim from some of them, misspellings included.

To Betzinez from his mother Natklekla.

My dear child:

I am thinking about you. I have no friends. I sent my one child to Carlisle. I loved you long ago. It is long since I have seen you. You are my son. You must write to me often. I want you to learn. I have no father or no mother. There are just we two. Perhaps you work. I don't know. I work too. You do not write to me. You must write to me. You must work for I am working too. We are living well here. None of your friends are sick. Do write to me. Good-bye.

Your mother.

From chief Becathlay.

My dear child.

I am going to talk to you. You must learn. Your friends are all well. We all try hard to do right and you must do so too. When you went away I talked to you. You must try to do everything right as the teachers tell you. You must be good. We are trying too. We work every day. We have nice clothes. We work and get nice things, coats and dresses and every thing we want. Your friends are all well. Nobody is sick. You must write to us again.

Your friend,
Bakathlay.

To Chiskio from his mother [a medicine woman]

My dear children.

Are you happy? You must be happy my two boys.
I see well yet and I talk kind. When you went away from me I cried every day. I feel better now. We live very well here. I think we shall see each other again. You must not think about me. I don't think about myself.

Your mother
Chenlozite.[37]

The heartsickness these parents felt is obvious, but the children's reactions were not recorded, nor could I find letters from the youngsters to their parents. One can only imagine the emotional pain both experienced.

THE STUDENT NEWSPAPER—THE INDIAN HELPER

Along with publications such as the "Carlisle Arrow" and "The Red Man" (especially published for the general public and the public and private agencies responsible for funding), the school's printing shop, staffed by Carlisle boys, issued a student newspaper each Friday. The publication supported Carlisle's motto of "Into Civilization and Citizenship" by printing poems with Christian lessons and guides and reporting school events, human interest stories and their lessons, and religious activities. *The Indian Helper* was read by the student body and also mailed to alumni and other interested persons who paid ten cents a year to subscribe. In Pratt's words, "[*The Indian Helper* was] printed weekly for the special edification of the pupils both past and present and for circulation among their parents and people in their remote homes."[38]

Each issue's general circulation was estimated at about ten thousand copies, but editor Pratt was unhappy with what he considered to be a low number of readers. The October 14, 1898, edition urged students, faculty, and supporters to solicit new subscriptions so that circulation would double. "You want to do missionary work," he stated in an item addressed to alumni and members of religious organizations. "What better missionary work is there than to let the people of our country know that the Indians are the same as other people if they have the same chance for development? And how can they better find that out than through the HELPER?"

Supplementing the preserved records, Barbara Landis, the historian at the Cumberland County (Pennsylvania) Historical Society provided additional information about religious influences at Carlisle. "Protestantism was emphasized," she wrote. "There were Catholics missioning to the Indian children, but these influences were barely tolerated by the school staff as Catholics were considered foreign, likely to be under the spell of liquor, and some priests didn't speak good English, so they were suspect."[39]

Part of Pratt's animosity toward Catholics and Catholicism was based on the fact that several Catholic missionaries among western Indian tribes refused to send students to Carlisle.[40] Pratt was so angry at them that at one gathering of educators, he publicly castigated the Catholic Church. Reaction to his stance was widespread, and he was severely criticized for it by public and private agencies alike. Intimidated by a real or perceived threat of having his funding suspended, Pratt retreated somewhat and in 1901 issued a statement:

The Catholic sisters meet the Catholic students in the schoolrooms from six to seven Tuesdays and Thursdays of each week. They also have a meeting at the church between nine and ten on Sundays, the same hour we have for Sunday school for the remainder of the children here. In all these services the Catholics have all the boys and girls belonging to their denomination. . . . We have a Sunday afternoon preaching service and a Sunday evening meeting at which all students without reference to creed are required to be present unless there should be some special service in town at which the minister requests the presence of his members, but such occurrences are very rare. There has been no objection on the part of the Catholic church to the presence of the Catholic students at morning prayers of the school in the dining room, nor at the Sunday afternoon and evening services.[41]

In his own self-interest he swallowed his emotions and eventually developed a tolerable working relationship with the Reverend Henry George Ganss, the pastor of St. Patrick's Church in the town of Carlisle. Yet Pratt's unending anxiety about the Catholic Church and its influence on his students was never assuaged and even extended into the school's outing system. Pratt worried that without his constant supervision, some students would be placed with Catholic families and all of the Protestant teachings they had received at the Carlisle School would dissolve into thin air. Even though that never happened, Pratt carried his terrible obsession with him for the rest of his life, masking it sometimes in an overt attitude of cooperation with funding authorities. At other times he couldn't keep it hidden and it burst out in embarrassing statements or diatribes for which he later apologized.

Pratt's insistence on the religious instruction of Carlisle's pupils is evident from the plentiful references to it in the *Helper*, particularly through poems that were published on page one of an edition. Examples of themes from selected issues published during the last months of 1898 follow.

A poem titled "The Helper," written by James H. West, reinforced the Christian teachings the students received at Carlisle.

He who the light to one dark soul shall bring
Among the sons of men is more than king.
No word thou utterest, or good or ill,
But sounds forever—wild or soft or shrill,
Fast held within the vibrant air's embrace,
If words of thine shall brighten one sad face,
Thine accents ease a brother's heavy load
The daily task reveal where truth is stowed.
Then rest content! For there shall come a year
—And soon shall come—when back into thine ear
With ten-fold power the words or ill or good
Shall speed with force that may not be withstood.
Then happy thou if in thine ear shall ring
Words that shall crown thee, servant, helper, king.[42]

A poem titled "Souls are Houses" equates the soul with fastidiousness, conveying the thought to readers that religion is hygiene and that God is watching.

SPIRIT, how is it with those rooms of thine?
What front the world look very clean and fair.
The curtains are so white, thy windows shine;
Are dirt and cobwebs hanging anywhere?
Ah! Souls are houses: and to keep them well
Not spring and autumn mourn their wretched plight,
To daily toil must vigilance compel,
Right under God's scrutinizing light.[43]

Another poem, titled "The Best We Have," was meant to inspire the students.

Christ wants the best. He in the far-off ages
Once claimed the firstling of the flock, the finest of the wheat,
And still He asks His own with gentlest pleading
To lay their highest hopes and brightest talents at His feet. He'll
not forget the feeblest service, humblest love;
He asks only that of our store we give to him
The best we have.

Christ gives the best. He takes the hearts we offer,
And fills them with His glorious beauty, joy, and peace.
And in his service, as we're growing stronger,
The calls to grand achievements still increase.
The richest gifts for us on earth, or in the heaven above,
Are hid in Christ. In Jesus we receive
The best we have.

And is our best too much: O, friends, let us remember,
How once our Lord poured out His soul for us.
And in the prime of His mysterious manhood
Gave up His precious life upon the cross.
The Lord of lords, by whom the worlds were made,
Through bitter grief and tears gave us
The best He had.[44]

Obituaries about fellow students were rarely published, but one is of particular note. An Apache boy named Bruce Patterson was sent to Carlisle from Florida but subsequently transferred to the Albuquerque Indian School in New Mexico, where he died from a lung hemorrhage, probably the result of tuberculosis. The superintendent of the Albuquerque School notified Pratt, who published the notice.[45]

The item is notable, not only for the detailed description of the way the boy died, but because Pratt had repeatedly insisted publicly and privately that the Apache children had inherited venereal disease and it was this ailment that killed them, rather than tuberculosis acquired at Carlisle. Pratt's own words, though, belie his pronouncements. When he stated in the obituary that Bruce Patterson went to New Mexico, where the climate was higher and drier, he clearly was describing a popular remedy of the time for tuberculosis. Venereal disease, inherited or acquired, could not be cured by the Southwest's climate.

The obituary of another Apache boy, Naneco Antonio, noted that he had died due to tubercular meningitis. Pratt took pains to report that the boy was buried in a "Catholic rite" conducted by the priest from the town's St. Patrick's Church.[46]

Table manners were addressed in one issue through publishing a list of "don'ts" rather than a list of "dos."

Never smack the lips when eating.

Never pick your teeth at the table.

Never put your finger into your mouth.

Never drum with your fingers on the table.

Never put your knife in your mouth.

Never put your elbow on the table.

Never scrape your plate or tilt it to eat the last drop of anything it contains, or wipe it off with a piece of bread.

Never play with your knife and fork or salt-cellar, or balance a spoon on your glass.[47]

The admonition about never putting "your knife in your mouth" struck a chord with Apache children, who always used a knife when eating. Food was placed on the dull edge of the knife and then into their mouths.

Pratt often used *The Indian Helper* to make announcements of upcoming changes in procedures. For example, one issue contained a notice that "on Thursday and Friday of each week a few minutes of the opening exercises of school will be devoted to the practice of new hymns."[48]

Another announcement reported that old Geronimo abstained from liquor and was meant to influence the students. Wrote Pratt,

We have had Geronimo's children and grandchildren as pupils. If what the following clipping from the Indian Journal says is true, some of us may gain a lesson in the life of the famous chief, now on exhibition at Omaha. The Journal says "Old Geronimo, the famous Apache chief is stationed at Fort Sill, and he spends most of his time playing monte. He is 90 years old, but straight and active with an eye like a Rocky mountain eagle. Notwithstanding his years, he occasionally gets permission to go hunting and seems to enjoy the sport as much as ever. He has been fighting the whites during most of the time since the war of 1812, but is now reconciled to them and lives peacefully on their bounty, toothless, propitiatory, and composed. He has been a total abstinence Indian all his life and his age and state of preservation show that it has been a good thing for him."[49]

This story is absolute propaganda, designed, of course, to favorably impress the Carlisle students and financial contributors by holding Geronimo up as a role model and by reporting his change of ways that purportedly occurred under the influence of the surrounding culture. The errors in this news item are several: (1) Geronimo was not "stationed" at Fort Sill but imprisoned there; (2) in 1898 Geronimo was not ninety years old but approximately sixty-nine; (3) he had not been "fighting the whites since the war of 1812," because his birth date was sometime in 1829; and (4) he had certainly not been "a total abstinence Indian all his life," because he had been frequently drunk while still a free man and drank to intoxication every chance he could while a prisoner of war. Carlisle's Chiricahua Apache students probably got a good laugh out of this piece.

Christian activities outside the school were encouraged and popular, as this item reveals:

> The school's Young Men's Christian Association sent four delegates to the YMCA District Convention held the previous week. Although the weather was disagreeable, attendance was good and the meetings were interesting and helpful, according to later reports. When asked about the purpose of the trip, a delegate replied, "It has been said by some of the students that we go to such conventions to have fun or a good time. We go to meet with the good Christian people and to learn the different ways to be a good Christian."[50]

At least three Chiricahua Apache children—Viola Zieh, Hugh Chee, and Vincent Natalish—were still at Carlisle as the decade ended and the century turned. Most of the other Apache students had either graduated or dropped out and gone "home" to Fort Sill, Oklahoma—the newest prison site, which received the transferred Indians in 1894.

Educating the Apache children continued in a school constructed on the military reserve with teachers who were, for the most part, missionaries from the Dutch Reformed Church—the latest religious group to attempt to evangelize these Indians.

A Few Words . . .

From 1879 to 1918, the Carlisle Indian Industrial School was the model for a "nationwide system of government-run Indian boarding schools intended to 'civilize' American Indian children by teaching them [the ABCs], farming, and trades while squelching their language and traditions."[51] Approximately 164 Chiricahua Apache children attended the school for various periods beginning in 1886 and ending a few years after the turn of the twentieth century.

Many of these children were old enough to have experienced some of the entire rich store of ancestral ceremonies but, while not totally tabula rasa, they were nonetheless vulnerable to religious pressures from Pratt and his staff. The degree of fidelity to traditional ways varied from Apache child to child while at Carlisle as did a shifting back and forth between a wish to remain faithful to the ancestors' teachings and heartfelt acceptance of Christianity. Cynthia Radding has named this vacillation "resistant adaptation"[52] and concluded that it was a dual theme, the other part being cultural perseverance.

A good example of this dual theme was expressed by Asa Daklugie, who had attended the Carlisle School for eight years. He looked back and told Eve Ball, "I began to realize that some of the things . . . required of us were beneficial."[53] Yet other comments he made to Ball led her to conclude, "Daklugie so disliked the white race and its laws that he would not admit having gained anything from conditions forced upon the Apaches,"[54] including education, no doubt. Given the natural pragmatism of the Chiricahuas, it is simple to conclude that many of these youngsters, like their ancestors on the Spanish colonial frontier, told the authorities what they wanted to hear but kept their forebears' ways close to their heart.

Most assimilation and acculturation models preferred by anthropologists and historians fail to provide a platform for interpreting this inconstant behavior,[55] which is inexcusable because this "middle ground," so to speak, was probably more characteristic of most Carlisle students than was the either-or model that positions rigid adherence to ancient ways against total commitment to Christianity. In this instance, "middle ground" may be defined as a dynamic site that Carlisle students moved onto and away from—a theoretical place that accommodated their changing loyalties.

Regardless of their allegiance to either religion, however, the Chiricahua Apache children, like other students, were expected to participate in classroom lessons involving Bible stories, Christian dogma, and examples of moral behavior—all designed to civilize them. Extracurricular, involuntary church activities added another dimension of learning to the experience, one that could not be denied. When an Apache student's education at Carlisle culminated—either by choice or graduation—and he returned to his prisoner of war parents, the results of his education contrasted dramatically with his family's lifeways and, even though he still favored and honored some of the traditional ceremonies—as some did—he often found himself as alienated from his kinfolk as he had initially felt years earlier when arriving at the school. This time, however, he was totally on his own to make a decision regarding his future course.

CHAPTER SIX

The Protestant Period

Oklahoma

During eight years of confinement at Mount Vernon nearly three hundred Chiricahua Apaches had died from contagious diseases. Statistically, the original group had been reduced by almost half and had not been supplanted by as many births. Sympathetic newspapers of the day dramatically reported the situation nationwide and, as during their confinement in Florida, the news once again aroused widespread public support for the Apaches. Government and military officials felt pressure to transfer the prisoners to a healthier climate. But where? When word leaked out that officials conducting high-level political talks were considering returning the Apaches to the Southwest, furious territorial Arizonans—still smarting from their deadly experiences—raised such a ruckus through their elected representatives in Congress that another location had to be found. After reviewing eight possible sites and rejecting seven, Fort Sill, Oklahoma, in the southern part of the state not far north of the Texas border, was chosen.[1]

On October 4, 1894, 259 healthy and sick Chiricahua Apache prisoners of war were loaded onto ten train cars and moved out of Alabama; two more baggage cars followed containing their baggage. Along with supervising the prisoners, Fort Sill's job was to somehow stem the tide of death, to rejuvenate the ailing Indians, and to do it visibly so that the public's adverse reaction to their

Fig. 36. Two Presbyterian missionaries visiting an aged Apache woman in Anadarko, Oklahoma, November 3, 1898. Courtesy of the Western History Collections, University of Oklahoma Library.

treatment by the American government would be quieted; indoctrinating the Apaches into Christianity was not initially part of the challenge.[2]

Most of the wooden structures that had been the prisoners' homes in Alabama were dismantled and piled into two or more of the train cars in the convoy. Although plans were designed to reconstitute new villages at Fort Sill using this same lumber, fate intervened. While standing on a sidetrack in New Orleans, the cars caught fire. When the blaze was extinguished, the Apaches' disassembled homes and much of their household items had literally gone up in smoke in the freight yard of the Louisville and Nashville Railroad.[3]

"When they got to Fort Sill, they were back in tents," said Capell.[4] He estimated that two hundred cabins had burned, but eighty homes is probably closer to the actual total. Consequently, the prisoners spent the first winter at Fort Sill, an exceptionally harsh one, living out-of-doors in hastily constructed traditional wickiups made of branches, boards, and tarps provided by the military. Given the fact that many were ailing with tuberculosis, the cold and damp Oklahoma winter exacerbated the disease, and many of the weakest died soon afterward.[5]

So-called healthy prisoners built seventy-one homes that next spring of 1895, when timber, available some twenty-five miles away, could be felled by the men and transported by horse and buggy to the military post. Twelve small villages scattered across twenty-five thousand acres of the western end of Fort Sill were soon on the map, each settlement led by a designated headman chosen by his followers and responsible for all the activities in the immediate vicinity. This arrangement was both similar to and different from the Spanish colonial policy of congregación: similar in that it gathered the Indians in a village, and different in that each headman's leadership role was designated and accepted by his followers—not imposed as the Spanish had done. And held over from ancestral customs was an individual's right to move among the groups as he pleased—cultural fluidity—but by this time most Apaches remained satisfied with their choice of affiliation. In essence, these prisoner of war villages were the latest incarnation of the traditional local units, consisting of nuclear and extended families, albeit some children were missing because they were still attending the Carlisle School. It was not quite like a total return to the ancient lifestyle, but it was one that was closer to the ancestral ways than ever before.

One year after their arrival at Fort Sill, able Apache men were working the land, growing hay, and running cattle, purchased through a congressional appropriation that had been introduced in the House of Representatives, debated halfheartedly, and approved. When the federal dollars arrived and cows and bulls were purchased, the Apaches branded the symbol "U.S." on the animals' flanks. Although running cows became a favorite occupation, farms and gardens were also tended and productive.[6]

First, though, they had cut fence poles, dug postholes, stretched wire, and fenced their lands—all on foot as horses were

Fig. 37. Chiricahua Apache children prisoners of war at Fort Sill, Oklahoma. Courtesy of Frisco Native American Museum, Frisco, North Carolina.

not yet supplied by the government. With the pasture adequately enclosed, they then dug stock tanks where the cattle could drink and built earthen dams with shovels and their hands. After the herd was of sufficient size and maturity, the industrious men sold their beef to the military at a profit and looked forward to the day when they could purchase farm machinery, to be used communally, with the proceeds from sales of cattle and crops.[7] While relaxing in quiet times, they dared to believe they could create a future for themselves and their families. The outlook seemed promising, even though tuberculosis and other contagious diseases still plagued the people. The annual death rate, however, was on its way down, and, in general, the conditions of their lives seemed to be improving. Apache men had even formed three baseball teams

Fig. 38. Chiricahua Apache prisoners of war at Fort Sill, ca. 1895. Left to right: Arthur Guydelkon, John Loco, Eustace Fatty, Richard Olsanny, unidentified boy. Courtesy of Frisco Native American Museum, Frisco, North Carolina.

and a football team but had not had much success in defeating their soldier opponents.[8]

Those children not away at school in Pennsylvania were taught in secular facilities built on the military grounds and at a Catholic school in Anadarko, St. Patrick's Mission, about thirty miles north of Fort Sill.[9] Any separation from their youngsters worried the Chiricahuas, who clearly remembered the pain and anxiety at Fort Marion when their children were sent to Carlisle. To allay their fears, many parents often frequently walked the distance between Fort Sill and Anadarko to visit their youngsters and bring them small gifts. It was a labor of love and, naturally, the walk back to the fort always seemed longer.

Coming to Jesus

In August 1898 the first Protestant missionary, Reverend Dr. Frank Hall Wright (son of Chief Allen Wright of the Choctaw Tribe) of the Dutch Reformed Church in America (now the Reformed Church in America, or RCA) sought access to the Chiricahua Apache prisoners of war at Fort Sill. Especially did he want to meet with the children, for as far back in time as 1628, the philosophy of the Dutch Reformed Church in the New World had been to concentrate on winning over the children. To reach that goal, it seems, it was often necessary to separate the children from their parents and then place them "under the instruction of some experienced and godly schoolmaster . . . especially in the fundamentals of . . . Christianity," wrote Gerald F. DeJong.[10]

Wright had been successfully evangelizing for four years among the nearby Comanche children and adults, during which time he learned that the Chiricahua Apache prisoners of war lacked exposure to, or any guidance from, local religious authorities. It was not an oversight. The U.S. War Department, tired of a bad press, had consistently denied all churchmen's requests to visit and speak with the prisoners. Wright's efforts, however, bore fruit in a conversation with Lieutenant Francis H. Beach, a young officer who was assigned to the prisoners. Turcheneske wrote that "Beach told Wright he wanted him to preach to the Chiricahuas. . . . Beach then consulted the Chiricahua headmen."[11] Shortly after that meeting the Chiricahuas expressed a strong desire—it could even be considered a demand—to have a mission established and to begin receiving religious instruction. The spark that set everything in motion created a response apparently so sincere and impressive that the War Department officials atypically reversed themselves and agreed to allow the minister and members of his faith access to the Chiricahuas, adults and children.

Indeed, something untoward had happened to the Apaches that made them amenable to becoming Protestant catechists. One possible explanation for their behavior spotlights a crucial, decisive event: the children returning from the Carlisle School as devout Protestants. These children, many old enough now to be adults, arrived over time in small groups of two or three, even singly. They were educated and acculturated, well groomed, tailored, spoke

English well, and overtly worshiped a Christian god. Some, like Asa Daklugie, compartmentalized aspects of traditional ancestral ways and Christianity. Others, like Benedict Johze, Jr., told Ruey Darrow, the chairperson of the Fort Sill Chiricahua/Warm Springs Apache Tribe, that "we all came back from Carlisle as little missionaries."[12] Of course he didn't speak for all of the former students in this generalization, but if there was resistance to Christianity among Carlisle's Chiricahuas, it is fair to ask what forms resistance took or what constituted resistance.

Cynthia Radding stated that "individual acts of rebellion or non-conformity"[13] constitute resistance, but there is little evidence of this behavior among the Apache students. For example, there was no collective action taken, such as a boycott of classes, nor did any of the youngsters flee in protest after they were given permission to withdraw. Daklugie, as a leader of the Apache students, was convinced that adaptation to the white ways was best but that acculturation didn't mean surrendering his ancestors' religious customs. His leadership took the form of overt cooperation that ultimately had the effect of using Pratt's educational system to introduce the children to the ways of the surrounding culture—another example of Chiricahua Apache pragmatism. Radding has also stated that there was a "dual theme of resistant adaptation and cultural persistence through the changing quality of relations between dominant and subordinate actors over an extended historical period,"[14] and many of the Carlisle students may certainly be included in this statement. However, not all the Chiricahuas fit Radding's description. Jason Betzinez, for one, wrote about the missionaries' efforts to teach the children at Fort Sill, declaring, "The day school children and the parents make endless trouble and undo much of the helpful work done for the children by workers of the orphanage." Still, the RCA personnel held firm and continued their work unaffected by the Apaches' resistance, all, that is, but worker Anna Heersma, who had "a nervous breakdown."[15]

At their return home from Carlisle, the ex-students' families were excited and happy to see them, but many of the young adults had mixed feelings about their traditional relatives. Some of them had been away for as long as ten years, with no visits "back home" in the interim, and their kinfolk were outsiders to their assimilated way of life. Many of the students had grown away from their heritage, from their culture, from their relatives and, at Carlisle, had increasingly identified with their teachers, the clergy, the farm families they lived with in the summers, and Christian Indian friends. Seeing their parents still wedded to an old-fashioned lifestyle—as much as they could manage during incarceration—was a shock to some of these now baptized and "civilized" believers. As could have been predicted, more than a few turned toward the missionaries' way of life rather than emotionally, spiritually, and physically rejoining their families. These matured Chiricahuas volunteered to help the Dutch Reformed ministers and workers evangelize the prisoners, an act that conveyed the clear impression to their kinfolk that they knew what the future held, that observing tradition was backward, that adopting Christianity and worshiping in the Protestant way were the right things to do, and that those who refused to do so would have to be left behind. (For purposes of clarity, it must be stated here that this is my original conclusion and one that has not been previously expressed. It is based on my decades-long relationship with the grandsons and granddaughters of the prisoners of war and of the returning Carlisle students. It has been substantiated by several Chiricahuas who wish to remain anonymous, but Apache Ruth Spearman, in an interview published in a later chapter of this book, supported my conclusion openly.)

Because of the great love Apaches had for their children and recollections of heartbreaking past experiences, most parents acknowledged to each other that they risked losing their sons and daughters once again if they didn't keep up with them. This awful realization served as a major turning point in the history of the Chiricahua Apaches, expedited by the adult children. And it is at this moment in time that the traditional religion's emphasis on the value of children ironically facilitated the transfer to another religion with an ease that would not have been possible without their children's background in Christianity. Unfortunately, one can never know what was truly in the parents' hearts or what form, if any, their resistance took.

So many adults told army officials that they wanted to learn "the Jesus road" and asked Wright to "teach [us] and we will be glad"[16] that the minister didn't need a second request. In September 1898 he sent a message to the church's headquarters and a controlling body, the Women's Executive Committee, about his apparent good

Fig. 39. Group photo of the Christian Endeavor Society (CES) at Apache Mission, Fort Sill, 1903. Asa Daklugie is at the center of the back row, Jason Betzinez to his right. Note the presence of women matrons and a minister, top row, left. Courtesy of Fort Sill National Historic Landmark collections, photo #P1006.

luck. That organization raised over $1,000 to get him started, and later contributions brought the final figure to just about $1,500.

Even though his spirit and enthusiasm were strong, Wright was not in the best physical health. A long siege with tuberculosis had caused him to be frail and weak and had depleted his energy, so, understandably, he felt an urgency about his new obligation to indoctrinate the Apaches. Endorsed by Fort Sill's military administration, in the summer of 1899 Wright and another RCA missionary, Dr. Walter C. Roe, erected a tipi for themselves and held the first camp meeting just north of Geronimo's village. The aim was to determine whether the people were truly willing to learn and accept the Protestant way of worship and would allow the evangelizing missionaries to live among them. As the day proceeded, there was no doubt: the Chiricahuas responded enthusiastically and the stage was set for another Apache experience with organized religion.[17]

Betzinez was one of the first returning Carlisle students to wholeheartedly affiliate with the church people. Years later, in 1942, he wrote a long article that described the early days of the missionaries' presence among the Apaches at Fort Sill, beginning with the summer of 1899, when the missionaries first began their work among the Chiricahua Apache prisoners of war. Betzinez credits one of the missionary workers, Miss Maud Adkisson, with the first organizing efforts that eventually interested the Chiricahuas. However, there was a lapse of attention during the winter of 1900, when a brief revitalization of traditional ways occurred, a fact that disturbed Betzinez greatly.

Coppersmith attributes this resurgence to "illness and mortality from tuberculosis, and the excitement resulting from the opening of the Comanche Reservation to Euroamerican settlement,"[18] but it also represented an obvious attempt at resisting Christianity. According to Betzinez, a Mountain Spirit dance occurred, attended by friends and relatives from his entire village, who sat huddled on the ground under blankets because of the biting cold. Many, including the dancers, fell ill afterward with pneumonia. It is difficult to determine if Betzinez objected strongly to the dance because of its traditional origin or if he was worried about the tribal members' health. I prefer to believe that Betzinez, in his unceasing efforts to curry favor with the authorities, had selfish motives when he reported the dance. In any case, the dances continued and were even embellished by having a youth dance group participate, the first ever.

The following spring, 1900, saw the creation of a Sunday school and the Christian Endeavor Society. Still, Betzinez believed it was "up and down" with the Indians, meaning that Christianity vied with traditional beliefs and that vacillation between the two was usually present in the twin forms of resistance or accommodation.

Substantial private donations and congressional appropriations continually flowed to Fort Sill and were expended to build a church compound. The complex of centrally located buildings was situated between the Apache villages and the fort's administrative building at a site close to a location called Medicine Bluff. Included in the complex were a grade school with a laundry, a combined orphanage and kindergarten with a dormitory and mess hall, a mission church, and a large camp meeting tent. Still needed were an American flag, maps and pictures for the school's walls, seats and desks for the stu-

Fig. 40. Group photo of the Apache Missionary Society of the Apache Orphanage at Fort Sill. Courtesy of Fort Sill National Historic Landmark collections, photo #P975.

dents and teacher, books, slates, and pencils, and lamps for the church service, which was also initially held in the schoolroom. Routine appeals for funds to purchase these items went out across the land to every Dutch Reformed Church, and the response was most generous.[19]

Sundays among the prisoners of war were devoted to church activities. In time a small Christian Endeavor Society came alive, and Sunday school lessons were started. Most of the former Carlisle students gladly took an active part in religious exercises, serving as assistants to the ministers and leaders of the congregation. The missionaries depended on these young men and women for help in spreading the Word in the villages and at the school. Parents and other adults looked with unmistakable respect at their children, and soon more than one mother or father came to trust the missionaries and believe what they said, as their adult children had recommended they do.[20]

Each Sunday, Roe preached his weekly sermon while his wife, Mabel, played the organ and Dr. Wright sang the hymns. Initially, most Apaches attended church only sporadically, but on later occasions the growing number of congregants sat beside several young white women—laypersons loosely known to the Chiricahuas as "missionaries"—who, through the efficient and expediting graces of the Dutch Reformed Church, responded from across the country to the clarion call for help in faraway Oklahoma.[21]

Hendrina Hospers, or Miss Hospers, as she came to be called by everyone, was one who responded to the plea for help. She had an especially warm and kindly way about her that drew the Apaches to her. She reminded some of the elders of Mother Alypius, the devoted nun who had taught the youngest children nearly two decades earlier at Fort Marion, Florida. Especially exciting to the orphaned children were the horseback rides with Miss Hospers, rewards for well-behaved students who also learned their lessons and showed through word and deed that they were becoming good Christians. Hospers and one child at a time often rode double on her horse to the separate Apache villages to visit, to teach the Euro-American ideas about good housekeeping, and especially to talk about the Lord. "Miss Hospers took my father with her wherever she went," said contemporary Chiricahua Apache Kathleen Kanseah. "He loved her."[22] Many other Apaches, children and adults, loved Miss Hospers as well, and she loved them. She is today held in high esteem by those adults who have heard about her from their parents and grandparents.

Hospers's and other young women's reasons for working among the Apache prisoners of war are curious, particularly since life at Fort Sill was often lonely and without promise of long-lasting companionship. Even though their motivations may have been altruistic, and they thought of themselves as missionaries, their work was restricted to routine, mundane duties that were often boring but freed the male ministers to devote their time to religious matters. The women workers served as children's caretakers, field matrons, and domestic workers although they informally sermonized and talked about the goodness and greatness of the Lord.

Fig. 41. Chiricahua Apache prisoners of war at the Dutch Reformed Mission, Fort Sill. Courtesy of Frisco Native American Museum, Frisco, North Carolina.

If the women workers were looking for husbands, there certainly was no shortage of single Apache males and widowers who needed wives to take care of them and their families. But many men were so sick with tuberculosis that any personal relationship with a woman from a different culture would have been too taxing; there were many differences to overcome, and that took energy, which was in short supply among ailing men. The exceptions, of course, were the young men who had attended Indian boarding schools. Sick or not, they would have had enough experience in the outside world to be able to sustain an intercultural relationship. At least two former students, both ill with tuberculosis, romanced the workers, and in time Jason Betzinez married Anna Heersma and Carlos Keanie married Martha Prince.[23]

Fig. 42. Four Dutch Reformed Church mission workers seated on porch of one of the mission buildings. From left: James Bell, Martha Prince, Hendrina Hospers, and an unidentified man. Courtesy of Fort Sill Museum.

Another answer to the question about why a young woman would want to spend a few years among the Chiricahua prisoners of war in Oklahoma was related to one of organized religion's goals at the time: indoctrinating indigenous peoples all over the country into Christianity. Women were active workers in both the eastern United States' organizations that supported missionary endeavors and the western field service itself. In addition, the academic and religious education of the Indians was a popular topic then in Congress around the turn of the century. It was so fashionable that the government supported select mission groups with a small stipend per annum, but with the proviso that the funds were to be applied to the physical well-being and the secular education of

Indian children. Coupled with contributions from church organizations and Indian advocacy groups, the domestic missionary field was well funded and well respected, and idealists of both genders were attracted to it.

There is one more, less selfless reason: an unmarried daughter might have been close in age to being considered an old maid, an unacceptable circumstance to many families in those days. Participating in the church's mission work among the Indians brought praise and glory to a family and, not incidentally, got the old maid out of the way and even might have found a husband for her. However, if he was an Indian, that would have been as unacceptable to most families as her spinsterhood.[24]

While the women's reasons for coming to Fort Sill were private, their actions among the children were open and loving, bringing happiness to their charges—some of whom were orphans from the wreckage left behind by federal and frontier policies that caused cultural devastation—and to themselves. To signal the benefits of Christianity—to send out a sign to the Apaches—the women dressed the children in the finest clothing available, whether the garments were previously worn and arrived in a box from a benevolent civic or church organization or were sewn by the women workers and former Carlisle students from donated bolts of cloth. Archival photographs show girls wearing pretty starched dresses and big cloth bows in their hair. The boys' shirts and trousers look tidy, and their caps are placed at rakish angles on their heads. The high button shoes that most of the youngsters are wearing look to be in good repair. Regardless of their current circumstances, all the children, including those from distant villages who were boarders and the affiliated adult Carlisle students, lived together in the school's dormitories. Thus, the women workers, the volunteers, and the ministers had total control over a large number of impressionable children, all of whom were the church's dependents in one way or another—similar to the Spanish colonial policy of reducción/congregación that had gathered the indigenes in order to control them, educate them, proselytize them, and indoctrinate them into Catholicism.

But what of the children who didn't live in the church compound or take part in church and school activities? Most of these youngsters remained in the villages and undoubtedly felt a hurt that tweaks everyone who at some time has been left out, who was not part of a group, who was "different." The simple solution, of course, was for the families to turn their children over to the missionaries, where they would join other youngsters and be taken care of in the same way. And that was what happened. Many parents temporarily surrendered their children to the church so that their youngsters would have the same opportunities as other Chiricahua children.[25]

If the situation had a familiar ring to some elders, they probably remembered with mixed feelings hearing stories about the Spanish frontier when their ancestors, those volunteer or captive Apaches, had a similar experience in the missions. Now, however, there was one colossal difference that overshadowed all the events of the past: most overt Apache resistance to the new ways was missing, helped along by decades of previous exposure to Christianity and by the current young adult generation, who did not consider it their duty to defend the ancient customs and lifeways. Being committed to the past would have been foolish for the young, educated future leaders; they had come too far into the surrounding culture to revert to a religion many never knew or could remember. Whether covert resistance remained at this moment can only be speculated, but an educated guess would lead one to believe that certainly some fidelity to the ancestors' ways was present, albeit well hidden.

Pragmatic parents were also an important component of this major cultural shift. These adults realized that to blindly defend and continue to observe the religion practiced by their ancestors would result without question in losing their children again, and that was too high a price for most. Consequently, at about the beginning of the twentieth century, observing Christianity's tenets and participating in Protestant religious services characterized many families, at least openly.

Joiners

Prayer meetings generally began with a hymn, after which a member gave a short prayer. Coppersmith has noted that during the meeting of February 4, 1900,

Benedict Johze, Sr. gave the invocation. Each member of the congregation read a scripture. The secretary noted that there were "quite many" absentees. Committees report that "they [were] doing well [and] improving in their work." The lesson for the evening was taken from Matthew, chapters twenty-one through twenty-seven [Matthew's account of the events surrounding Christ's entry into Jerusalem on Palm Sunday to his crucifixion and burial], in which many references were read by the members. The meeting closed with a song and benediction.

Notes from a meeting held on 19 August 1900 show that Asa Daklugie read the lesson after which the president took the chair and called a business meeting to order in which new officers were selected for the congregation. . . . Viola Chihuahua was elected President, Benedict Johze, Sr. vice president, Asa Daklugie, Secretary and Jason Betzinez, treasurer.

. . . Several different types of meetings were held weekly and activities included Consecration (communion) Meetings, business meetings, and activities for children in which games were played. All meetings were attended by mission staff. Membership seemed to hover between fifteen and twenty members of the Chiricahua and Warm Springs community.[26]

In time more and more adults attended the Sunday services, some with genuine commitment, some on the fence, and some simply to visit with their adult children. Several Apache women, wary, slowly became active in ladies' groups, and many men eventually assumed leadership roles in the congregation; it seemed that much overt resistance to Christianity was diminishing. By 1905–1906, the list of active church members included names of missionary women, Christian Comanches who had no church of their own, and Chiricahua Apache prisoners of war.[27]

James Kaywaykla	Eugene Chihuahua
Sam Haozous	Benedict Johze
Jason N. Betzinez	Miss Maud Adkisson
Clay Domeh	Miss McMillan
Nellie Carey	Miss Ewing
Carlos Keannie	Miss Lizzie Saunders
Howard White Wolf (Comanche)	Arthur Geydilkon

Marcellus Beazhun (Comanche)   Anice Simmons
Mrs. Sam Haozous (Blossom Wratten)   David Fatty
Banskli Naiche   Calvin Zhonne
Walter Louie   Duncan Balatche
James Russell   Harry Perico
Emma Toclanny   Mrs. Milliken
Miss Aspley   Miss Louis
Miss Bessie Cox   Bruce Kaahteney
Miss Amalie Clark   Dr. Baker
Mrs. Baker   Ramona Daklugie
Dorothy Kaywaykla (Naiche)   Viola Chihuahua
Mr. Saunders   Miss Mabel Navadohich

OFFICERS
President   Miss Adkisson
Vice President   Miss McMillan
Corresponding Secretary   Jason N. Betzinez
Treasurer   Benedict Johze

Several of the Apaches listed above had attended the Carlisle School: J. Kaywaykla, Betzinez, Johze, Zhonne, R. Daklugie, D. Kaywaykla, and Chihuahua. Keanie had been a student at another Indian boarding school, Chilocco. Educated, these young adults were sufficiently "Christianized" to take leadership roles within their community.

The Christian Endeavor Society (CES) was an organization of young people of various evangelical Protestant churches formed in 1881 to promote Christian principles and service. The Apache Mission CES of 1907–1908 at Fort Sill listed the following persons as active and associate members. However, it is important to note that not all of the Apaches listed below had been students at one of the Indian boarding schools.

James Kaywaykla   Benedict Johze
Jason N. Betzinez   Philip Pulis (a minister)
Miss Pugh   Miss Clover Mahan
Miss Heersma   Miss Lizzie Saunders
Miss Hospers   Miss Joan Saunders
Miss Aspley   Miss Ewing

Fig. 43. Chiricahua Apache prisoners of war Amy (on the left) and Blossom White, daughters of interpreter George Wratten and his Chiricahua Apache wife, Annie, n.d. Courtesy of Fort Sill Museum.

Mr. Will Pulis (a minister)
James Russell
Mr. Wicker

Rachel (Comanche)
Edward White Wolf (Comanche)
David Kenoi
Mrs. W. Pulis
Nellie Carey
David Banning
Dolly Mithlo
Blossom White (Wratten)

Eugene Chihuahua
Mr. Brady
Tocsi Chatahmeyerque
(a Comanche girl)
Isabel Perico
Bonalskli Naiche
Anna Vos
Amy Imach (Wratten)
George Martine
Mrs. Key
Miss Prince
Carlos Keannie

Maurice Chatto	Jeannette Russell
Watson Mithlo	Ramona Daklugie
Dorothy Kaywaykla	Viola Chihuahua
Mabel Johze	Jane Naiche
Tsisto Haozous	

Noticeably absent from this list is Asa Daklugie, who was a member of the CES at Carlisle, probably because it was practical for him to belong to the society at the time or possibly because his future wife, Ramona Chihuahua, was a member. It is well known that Daklugie adored her from their youth until their old age, especially including their years together at Carlisle, and that he truly wanted to please her. However, Daklugie's later statement, "My people have never liked to talk about our religion . . . because it is the only thing we possess of which the whites have not robbed us,"[28] indicates his fidelity to the ancestors' ways. His loyalty to tradition served as resistance to Christianity, one example being the omission of his name from the above roster. Although he eventually joined the RCA, Asa Daklugie is an excellent example of the Apache ability to retain tradition yet give the impression of cooperation with captors, a style of behavior that had characterized many of his ancestors on the Spanish colonial frontier.

Debo reported, "The strong-willed Asa Daklugie remained steadfast to the native religion, but [wife] Ramona [Chihuahua] was an earnest Christian, and Asa, whose love for her had begun in youth across the barriers of Apache etiquette and was to continue unchanged through a life extending beyond their golden wedding anniversary, accompanied her to all religious services."[29]

The commitment of the Chihuahua siblings, Eugene and Ramona, to Protestantism is interesting because of their father's expressed interest in Roman Catholicism at Mount Vernon, which may have been sincere or the leader's form of passive resistance. Ramona attended the Carlisle School and encountered Protestantism there, but Eugene, at the chief's request, was not removed from his family and did not enroll in any Indian boarding school. He apparently opted to join the Dutch Reformed Church and the Christian Endeavor Society on his own.[30]

An example of the business of Fort Sill's CES is clear in the minutes of the October 28, 1908, meeting, which opened with a

Fig. 44. Miss Anna Heersma, Dutch Reformed Church worker at Fort Sill, Oklahoma, ca. 1898. Courtesy of John Turcheneske, Jr.

prayer, followed by acceptance of the last meeting's minutes. Jason Betzinez presented the treasurer's report, which showed $0.48 in the treasury.[31]

Reports from the various committees were presented, and then the meeting was adjourned after a prayer by David Kenoi. The report of the proceedings was signed by Amy Imach, secretary.[32]

Publications

Along with periodic reports, several church publications have been preserved and further illuminate the missionaries' efforts in indoctrinating Chiricahuas into Protestantism. Keep in mind that the information is written from one perspective only—that of the Dutch Reformed personnel—and excludes much of the Apaches' true reactions and responses.

Fig. 45. Miss Maud Adkisson, Dutch Reformed Church worker at Fort Sill, Oklahoma, ca. 1898. Courtesy of John Turcheneske, Jr.

Reports of the Women's Executive Committee of the Board of Domestic Missions of the Reformed Church in America:[33]

1899—This year started the active effort to convince the Apaches to adopt, believe in, and become indoctrinated into Christianity. Wright described his first meeting with Lieutenant Beach:

> Driving across the Apache reservation and coming to a gate that opened on Nahwat's [a Christian Comanche] lands, I saw a cavalry officer with a white helmet, just closing it after passing through. He saw me coming and courteously opened the gate for me. I recognized Lieut. Beach, and he said, "In passing, preach to my people."[34]

Wright wrote that on Sunday mornings the young and old came together for Sunday school and participated, even though

Fig. 46. Dr. Frank Hall Wright, Dutch Reformed Church minister at Fort Sill, Oklahoma, ca. 1898. Courtesy of John Turcheneske, Jr.

many of the adults did not understand English, but the bright pictures on cards and charts appealed to them. This conclusion is reminiscent of Father Kino's efforts to indoctrinate the Pimas on the Spanish colonial frontier by showing them colored paintings of the saints, an action that was, then and now, an expression of perceived religious power, authority, and colonialism.

Wright also reported that the returning students found the mission to be a "refuge, a place where they receive encouragement and help in their hard fight to sustain the standard they have known in school."[35]

In taking the Comanche girl named Dorothy with her to the Apache villages, even though the girl didn't speak a word of the Apache language, Maud Adkisson was quite clever. From the Euro-American perspective, little Dorothy served as a living, breathing example of the obvious benefits of life with the missionaries. Archival photos published in later newsletters show Dorothy dressed immaculately in a starched white dress with a big bow holding back her hair. By her appearance, including the big smile on her face, she communicated one of the Euro-American values related to coming to Christ: cleanliness. However, a number of adult Chiricahuas of all ages probably didn't see anything worthwhile in imitating their captors and were content to observe their cultural customs and ignore the outsiders' ways. They saw no reason to associate with people so thoroughly unlike themselves. Yet the adult children were bringing change, and it could not be ignored,[36] even though at least some of the younger children might have carried feelings of resistance in imitation of their parents' reluctance. Still, the wish to "belong," to be like "everyone else," to be involved in what was happening was overwhelming to many children, and they wanted to be like their friends and cousins. Consequently, I believe that the appeal of Christianity was secondary to the children's wishes and that the RCA missionaries and workers knew this but had shrewdly planned to insidiously capture the youngsters for Christianity.

1901—A third house was added to the compound to accommodate the growing number of children attending the church school. "But," wrote an anonymous staffer,

> lately there has been an alarming amount of illness in the camps, and the people are uneasy and sorely distressed, feeling as though there were no secure foundation beneath them. They sent a message to the Christian Indians to meet them at a certain time and place. When they were gathered together, the people said, "We are blind. Give us the road. Help us to save our friends and children from so much sickness and death."
>
> They were told the plan of salvation, and also how they had disregarded the laws of health. They listened patiently, and it may be that this is the beginning of a great awakening.[37]

The matter of appealing to Christian Apaches for help in avoiding sickness and death could possibly have been the writer's exaggeration or imagination. The tribe's past experiences with contagion and the inability of Christianity's agents to immunize or protect them had long been established in oral testimony and tribal memory.

Fig. 47. Miss Martha Prince, Dutch Reformed Church worker at Fort Sill, Oklahoma, ca. 1898. Courtesy of John Turcheneske, Jr.

The Chiricahuas knew the "plan of salvation" was meaningless as a remedy for the immediate health problems, and the convoluted view of Apaches being responsible for their own ill health through careless neglect is ridiculous and reminiscent of Pratt's accusation about venereal taint rather than tuberculosis as the causative factor for the students' illnesses at Carlisle.

Also, the Apaches knew that practicing the Dutch Reformed religious ways didn't keep the flies away, and these pests were probably one of the worst disease-carrying vectors at Fort Sill. Recognizing the health problems that flies caused, the prisoners continually petitioned the military for eighteen-gauge screening for their windows and doors. Oddly, the military bureaucracy could not or would not fulfill this simple request. It wasn't until years later that a shipment of adequate screening was sent and installed in the homes in the twelve villages. By that time millions of flies had for years exacerbated the existing and pervasive unhealthy conditions in the villages.[38]

Monthly reports began to be published in June 1902 and reported that some of the Christian Apaches were drinking and gambling, but others were not. "To them and to the Reformed Church we owe our allegiance in the Master's work. May He cause His face to shine upon us."[39]

The report of January 1903 showed that "Geronimo came into camp on Sunday morning, but did not attend the afternoon meeting. However, he sent word that he was tired, had traveled all night and must sleep—he says that he is over eighty. Toward evening Mr. Wright walked over to Geronimo's tent and had a long, earnest talk with the old man, one of his family, nephew or grandson interpreting [this could have been Asa Daklugie]."

Geronimo sat with his head bowed during the upcoming sermon but began to mutter under his breath. Daklugie declared that Geronimo was saying, "The Jesus road is good and he told the people to go right into it." At one point, Geronimo leaped to his feet, clasped the minister by the hands, turned to the congregation, held his finger up toward heaven, and struck his breast with the other hand—an indication that they should accept the Jesus road.

The minister talked with Geronimo after the service and asked him to give some evidence of repentance.

> But this he did not give, nor did he ask for baptism, as did nine other Indians that day.[40] This is his confession as he gave it to me, requesting, at the same time, that the Christian people of American might pray for him. He says "that his heart is good toward the white people. Many of them who are in the Jesus road have told him that they love him, and he loves them. He says that his heart is good toward Jesus, that he wants to be in the Jesus road." As I lay that night in the mission at Medicine Bluff, and looked up into the starlit sky, so clear and pure, over the Oklahoma hills, I thought of the Holy Being who died for and saved me, and I must believe that the same sovereign grace will save Geronimo. (signed: J. T. Bergen)[41]

Geronimo's skill at manipulation is clear. Whenever he thought he was in danger of dying, either from an accident or from imbibing too much alcohol, he "got religion." *The Lawton Constitution*, a local newspaper, in a front-page item dated February 18, 1909, announced Geronimo's death and stated that he had professed religion in 1905 and joined the church.

> Later, however, he returned to his beloved habit of drink and, engaging also in gambling and horse racing, practically renounced his religion when lectured by his missionary, Rev. L. L. Legters. Shortly afterward he was suspended from the church. . . . Last fall, during a camp meeting among the Apaches, Geronimo talked with the missionaries as if he wanted to begin anew his religious life, but at the same time he was engaging in his old habits and was also telling his tribesmen that he held on to the old faith, the religion of his fathers, which knew no white man's God.[42]

Many of his fellow tribesmen held conflicting attitudes about Geronimo, still blaming him for their situation as prisoners of war. Had the congregation consisted of a majority of these Apaches, his conclusion that the "Jesus road" was good would have been humorous. On the other hand, if his supporters were numerous in the group, they would have believed him, but all Chiricahuas knew that he was a master manipulator, and that understanding would have colored everyone's opinion of his statement.

True to form, six or seven months later Geronimo revealed that he had not surrendered the traditional Apache ways and was not ready to accept Christianity. As a matter of fact, he demanded that a puberty ceremony be held, and because he was greatly respected as a medicine man, the family of a maiden followed his wishes, much to the chagrin and dissatisfaction of the church people.[43]

Many Chiricahuas viewed the puberty ceremony and its attendant drinking and gambling as essential observances of their sacred ways and not sins, as the missionaries claimed. An anonymous writer noted that the church people spent two whole days trying to break up the dance that accompanied the puberty ceremony, not due to the dancing alone, but because gambling and drinking were inseparable from the activities.[44] There is no indication in the publication of how many Chiricahuas participated in the age-old ritual and its attendant socializing, nor of their names, so it is impossible to tell if they were the "resisters" or not. However, it is probable that some of the attendees were learning how to compartmentalize their traditional religion and Christianity, a trait many of their ancestors on the Spanish colonial frontier had mastered.

In September 1903 a camp meeting held under a thirty-one-by-forty-five-foot tent brought the Chiricahua Apaches together with neighboring Comanches, who were also being evangelized by Dutch Reformed missionaries. More than 150 Comanches took part, but there is no count in the publication of the number of Apaches who attended. One usual feature of a camp meeting was mass baptism, and this session was no exception. Geronimo made his presence known by making a speech and submitting himself for baptism, as did the younger of Naiche's wives, Hao-zinne.[45]

The next month, October 1903, Wright provided information about one of the most loyal churchgoing Chiricahuas, reporting that Jason Betzinez stood up and confessed that

> "I have done three very wrong things. First, I have broken God's laws; second (and he would bear down the fingers of one hand and another with his other hand; you know he is a blacksmith by profession and a good one, and, as Mr. Roe said, he seemed to be hammering it out), I took one cigar and it grew on me until it was heavy; third (and again came down another finger) I have broken the Sabbath and played ball on Sunday—the very thing I have stood out against for three years." We blessed God for the prodigal's return who has sure solely tried our souls, our patience and our faith.[46]

Betzinez provides a rare insight into exactly what the Dutch Reformed missionaries required of the Christian Apaches. How he "broke God's laws" is not clear, but smoking a cigar and playing baseball on a Sunday would not be particularly offensive to many Apaches. By being afforded this look inside the church's attitude toward its Chiricahua members, it is not difficult to understand the hesitation many Apaches initially expressed regarding Protestantism.

August 1904—An Apache woman named Pauline, who was a member of the Christian Endeavor Society, died of pneumonia. Before her demise, the missionaries visited her and reported that "at the end she became nearly wild with the dirt and vermin and harsh words. We would gladly have taken her at the lodge or to the hospital, but her parents refused. We sent for a cot, for she had terrible bed sores, but they said it shook and quivered so (woven wire springs) that some one must have died on it and this was the spirit, so they discarded it and put her back on a pallet on the ground. One feels so helpless."[47]

Pauline's situation is a good example of the conflicts that occurred within families. She was a Christian, but her parents clearly held the traditional beliefs about spirits and death. Pauline's terminal illness rendered her incapable of making decisions for herself, and her family then took responsibility. From this example, one might conclude that she didn't have a Christian burial, but records reveal that a Pauline Bat-lat-chu, born in 1879, died in 1904 and was buried in the Apache prisoner of war cemetery at Fort Sill.[48] It probably was the same individual.

1905—Printed in the January issue were a review and a look backward to the previous September's most successful camp meeting. More women than ever had filled the seats (previously, women had been the most suspicious and mistrusting), eight persons committed themselves to the church, and "a husband and wife were reconciled." Apache women were beginning to take a more active church role on several levels, for some sold their beadwork and contributed the profits of more than a hundred dollars to the church. At the meeting Bonalskli Naiche, son of the chief and grandson of Cochise, stated publicly that he wanted to be a missionary to his people. He asked Roe for assistance in obtaining a higher education so he could study the Bible and return from his classes to help the Apaches become Christians. The young man left in early January 1905 to study in nearby Colony, Oklahoma, at a Dutch Reformed church.[49]

The February issue contained a statement by an Apache named Calvin (Zhonne?) that caused a controversy within the group. He stood up and criticized the Chiricahuas, saying, "When we hear anything that others tell us is right or wrong [referring to the Bible], we pay no attention. We think we can do big things. We don't care if it is right or wrong."[50]

This testimonial is the equivalent of shaking a finger at friends and relatives and admonishing them to pay attention to the church's guidance—a rare event in Chiricahua society. Apparently Calvin was so involved with the missionaries that he felt he had license enough to ignore the Apache cultural custom of respecting the way other Apaches conduct themselves. Prior to this unusual example of disregard for tradition, manners, and propriety, only leaders like Chief Naiche and Geronimo would have had the legitimacy to lecture the people. One can only imagine the responses that resulted from Calvin's lecture; reactions probably ranged from applause to shunning.

Former Carlisle student John Loco asked for the first Christian funeral. His four-year-old daughter, Ruth, died on the first Sunday in January 1905, New Year's Day, of unknown causes. But not until three months later was the funeral described.[51] About a hundred Christian Chiricahua Apaches and Comanches stood about the open grave and sang "Nearer My God to Thee." At the end of the service, a collection was taken in the amount of $10.00 in order to help the family defray expenses.[52]

John Loco's motivation to ask for a Christian funeral probably was an extension of his family's long-standing cooperation with the Americans. Chief Loco, John's father, was well known for his helpful attitude in years past. Then again, John could have been indoctrinated himself into the Dutch Reformed Church's ways without any influence from his father.[53]

May 1905—Chief Naiche and Maud Adkisson visited Bonalskli Naiche, still studying at the Dutch Reformed church in Colony. Chief Naiche was asked to say a few words, which were translated for the Cheyenne and Arapahoe Indian students also studying there. Bonalskli interpreted his father's words in English.

> I want to speak to all these Cheyennes and Arapahoes as Christian friends because we are all following Christ together. I didn't do it right at first but three years ago I started being a Christian and I have been trying to do right ever since. I didn't know I was living a bad life but now find I am living the right kind of a life. At first I didn't know God's road was a good way, but as soon as I found that it was, I started that way. I have learned what is bad and I am trying to keep away from it. I am learning the good and pushing on to it, and Jesus is teaching my heart all the time.[54]

That Naiche had become a Christian and a true believer in 1902 or thereabouts cannot be denied, for his actions while incarcerated and throughout the rest of his life support his beliefs. To show his sincerity and devotion, he took the first name "Christian" at his 1902 baptism and was known from then on by that name. Naiche's faith was so strong that when the Chiricahuas were released from confinement, the missionaries who accompanied the people to Mescalero lived at Whitetail with him and his family.[55]

June 1906—A leaflet published by The Women's Missionary Board of the RCA describing three of the students attending the day school was distributed nationwide throughout the church's vast connections and was an essential and successful component of fund-raising.[56]

One of the featured boys, Maurice Chato, was the son of the warrior Chato, whom the leaflet described as a "bright and interesting man, a member of the church, and a spokesman of the people." Maurice, on the other hand, was "very stoical, not bright or quick at his school work, very quiet, even about his play." Lauding themselves, the anonymous writer of the leaflet noted the change for the better in Maurice during the three years he was in the church school and especially commented about his "real love for his books that is remarkable in an Indian boy. . . . As yet he has not openly confessed Christ."[57] Actually, what is remarkable is the condescending attitude that such a comment about loving books reveals, to say nothing of the fact that the child had not yet "openly confessed Christ."

Another of the featured boys was David Reno, whose parents, according to the publication, "are two of the worst old gamblers and Sabbath breakers there are in the tribe." Calling the father lazy and the mother shiftless, the anonymous writer lamented that the burden of work, caring for siblings, cooking, and looking after the stock fell to little David. Surprisingly, the writer stated that when the parents returned home, they would stone David if they were displeased at what he had accomplished.

David had apparently survived the "stoning" to reach the age of sixteen and become an "earnest Christian."[58]

The third boy who was featured, Harry Perico, was the son of a scout who was a "member of our church, but is inclined to cling to the old Indian customs." This statement is likely correct, for

Harry's father was closely related to Geronimo and was a member of his group at the time of surrender. Perico would have taken quite a while to incorporate the views of an outside culture into his behavior. Ergo, he was a resister.

His son Harry was described as the most promising and progressive grown-up boy in the tribe; he was twenty-one years old. Once again the condescension was apparent—this time in the form of calling him a boy—and was indicative of the missionaries' superior attitude, one that was reminiscent of the imperious views that the Jesuits held of the Chiricahua ancestors on the Spanish colonial frontier.

The writer portrayed Harry's mother as being a gambler and the home as neglected. The concluding remark was, "It is almost impossible to believe that he came out of this degraded home only a few years ago."[59]

These examples are incorrect, for no Apache relative or leader would have allowed the mistreatment of children, such as reported in the examples, to occur or to go on without stepping in to remedy the situation. Unfortunately, no documentation exists to contrast these views. With that in mind, it is possible that leaflets like this were deliberately designed to evoke sympathy and funding from the readers.

A year later, 1907, the missionary workers' enthusiasm had faded somewhat. Wrote an anonymous member of the church's Committee on Indian Work in its report:

> The [camp] meeting at Fort Sill proved to be different [than the Comanche meeting] in the nature of the work accomplished. It was found necessary to ferret out wrong doing, bring inconsistent Christians back to confession and a fresh start, and in one case, even to inflict Church discipline. Thus the work goes forward with a time to plough, a time to plant, and a time to reap.
>
> During the winter a remarkable outpouring of God's Spirit stirred the mission and tribe most powerfully, resulting in the conversion of many, and the reclaiming of a number of Christians who had "lost the Jesus trail."

The following extract from the same 1907 article speaks for itself:

It is wonderful, it is beautiful to see how willing the new members are to pray and help in any way they can and of course they are growing stronger each day. The services are most impressive and soul cheering.

The children are developing into little missionaries, helpful in every way.

If our dear friends will continue to pray believing, we can well expect the Apache tribe to be a power for good, and our friends will fully realize that they have not labored in vain. Let us in God's name and for His glory, convince the doubting ones of God's power to save the most benighted.[60]

Note carefully that this writer believed the children were developing into "little missionaries," an accomplishment of great worth to the church people. However, one wonders about perspective. From the point of view of the missionaries, the conclusion was fair, but no doubt there were Chiricahua children who were simply paying lip service to the Dutch Reformed personnel. On the other hand, varying degrees of fidelity to both the traditional ways and Christianity was also a factor in the hearts of the children and could not be detected openly.

In 1909, probably through their adult children's urging, 14 more Apaches decided to take religious lessons, and 5 infants and 10 adults were baptized, adding up to a total of 94 in full church membership. About 70 persons of all ages were separately enrolled in the Sunday school, two Christian Endeavor Societies—one for the adults and one for the youngsters—were active, and the Missionary and Sewing Society had been organized for the elderly women. Fifty-seven children attended the parochial school, but 4 dropped out the following year, 1910. At that time, 29 children lived in the orphanage. By 1912, the year before the prisoners' release from incarceration, 115 Apaches attended Sunday school.

The Day Star, a monthly publication, was issued by the Mission Board and sold in bulk quantities to Sunday schools and church mission sites at the rate of eight cents a copy. It too was designed to provide information about the RCA's activities among the Chiricahua Apaches in an attempt to solicit funds. Highlights from selected issues are below.[61]

In a column called "Housekeeping in the Tepees," the unidentified writer told about a meeting in Kah-ah-tenny's village with the women to talk to them about Jesus. When asked if they knew Jesus and prayed to him, they all answered, "Yes. They all know *of* him but do not dwell *in* him; therefore they follow none of His teachings, making their religion in vain."

The women were listening only halfheartedly and chatted while the writer read the Bible to them, so she finally stopped and asked the young interpreter Dorothy to intervene and restore order. When the women were quiet, "we continued the Bible study, which they all listened to very attentively." The writer and Dorothy next went to Mangus's village to teach the women how to cook and found, in one home, that dishes were in the bedroom. "I never use them," said the lady of the house. "I have plenty of flour, coffee and meat, but that is all."[62]

In the prisoner of war villages, this kind of passive resistance was not uncommon, despite Sunday appearances at church to the contrary. In their hearts, many Chiricahuas remained uncomfortable with Christian ways, despite becoming more familiar with the principles. On the other hand, some parents saw no conflict in observing the religion of their ancestors and simultaneously attending church, much as their ancestors had done at the peace establishments in Spanish colonial times. Accommodation or resistance was an individual matter, but Christianity was becoming increasingly "popular" among many families with adult children.

As an expression of Euro-American ethnocentrism, teaching the women how to cook didn't take into account that Apache women had been well versed in the art—their way—since time began. Overlooked by the missionaries and church workers was the fact that the women might not have wanted to learn other ways of preparing food, possibly worrying that the new way would make them sick. Ignoring or discounting the Chiricahuas' cultural experiences had also been a failing of the Spanish colonists, and it must have seemed to some Apaches—those who had heard stories about the past—that nothing had changed more than two centuries later.

Some Indian children at the Colony, Oklahoma, mission had written letters that were published in previous issues of *The Day Star* and read to the Apache children at Fort Sill. Being kids, the students wanted to write back, so two children were selected to write on April

2, 1900. Their unedited letters were printed in the June edition[63] and distributed nationwide to demonstrate how successful the children had become in learning and writing English; in turn, this information could generate funds for the Fort Sill Mission.

Dear Friend: I am fourteen years old, and my name is Bruce J. Ka-a-ht-eny. We have a nice time in Apache Mission School. We have our C.E. [Christian Endeavor] Society every Friday afternoon.

Our schoolhouse is near the creek, and we have nice flowers. We saw a letter from some Indian girls at Colony, Okla., and we were very glad to see that letter, and we want them to see our letter. My home is near the schoolhouse. Well, I must close my letter. Your friend, Bruce J. Ka-a-ht-eny.[64]

The second letter was from Arthur Geydilkon (also spelled Guydelkon). He wrote:

Dear Friend. I am an Indian boy just nearly fourteen years old. I am in fourth reader. The schoolhouse is near the creek and the trees are getting leaves.

I am head of all the class. I have two sisters and one brother. My home is far from school; I think it is a mile and a half. I come to school on foot and some time I never be late, and be in time.

All the boys are glad to go to school every day. Our teachee name is Miss Moseley, she is very good teachee. It is time for fishing. I close my letter this time and I say Goodby. Arthur Gey-dil-kon.[65]

A published letter from a boy named Uncas Benedick (probably Uncas Noche)[66] described a

good time on Sunday, and we run after jack-rabbits and little calf and everything we see going, and some boys are going to church every Sunday and sometime I go to . . . and sometimes on Sunday big boys play with soldier. . . . And on Sunday I come to church and some times I don't come to church. And do you love your friend Uncas Benedick.[67]

In that same issue, Maud Adkisson described the events of the previous Christmas, during which similar gifts as on earlier holidays were distributed to happy Apache children. However, she noted, "The Christian Indians were particularly remembered." The meaning of her comment is chilling if taken literally, but one hopes that all the children were treated equally and that the missionaries didn't show any favoritism.

Nine-year-old Osceola Chihuahua, son of Chief Chihuahua, was taken ill just before Christmas of 1900. Maud Adkisson wrote about him, stating that after six days in the Apache hospital at Fort Sill, while everyone thought the boy had pneumonia, it was actually diagnosed as tuberculosis. "Osceola had not given his heart to Jesus," wrote Adkisson, "but one day Miss McMillan [a teacher] went to see him and spoke of this matter so deeply resting in our hearts. She said, 'Osceola, don't you *know* Jesus can save you?' 'Yes, I know,' he said, 'but sometimes I forget.'"

Osceola later expressed a wish to be baptized, and a nearby Methodist minister performed the baptism in good time. When nothing more could be done, his parents took him to a medicine man who unsuccessfully treated him; Osceola died in 1901.

Adkisson wrote, "We particularly wanted him to unite with the Church and receive baptism for the strong effect it will have over boys of his age."[68]

That the missionaries were already looking to Osceola—dead or alive—to be a good example for the living is exemplified by their comment. It was a rather harsh decision at an especially poignant time.

At the request of the missionaries, thirteen-year-old Vincent Binday[69] wrote the following Bible story, "The Story of Water," as he called it, from memory. The text has not been edited and appears exactly as the boy wrote it.

When it was many people they were sin, and many too many wifes. But Noah just have one wife, and Noah walk with God. And God to Noah to make an art, and so did Noah. And God told Noah that it would be flood of water all over the world. And all the men would die. But Noah and his wife and his three sons and wifes, not going to die. And he told him make room for the animals, and all of it, two of a kind of animals. And God said to

Noah, just 7 days and it will be great flood of water all over the world. And the animals, two by two they go in. And Noah and his wife and his three sons and his son's wifes would go in the art. And God shut them up. And the windows open up above and it rain 40 days and 40 nights. All the men in the world die, but Noah and his wife and his three sons and his sons' wifes save in the art. And it was ten months and Noah send out a raisin [raven] and it did come in again. And he sent out a dove and it came again. And he was waiting four days and sent out dove again, and it brought a leaves; and Noah know that the water going down. And he send out dove again and it did not come in again. And God told Noah that he was not going to send flood of water on world again. And he build an altar. And God told Noah that he put rainbow in clouds.[70]

It is tempting to comment that Vincent Binday's comprehension of the story of Noah and the ark was remarkable, but to do that would be complicit in evaluating the boy's understanding from a Euro-American point of view. Suffice to say that Vincent sounds like he was a good student and the missionaries must have been proud of him.

An article by an anonymous writer stated that the RCA missionaries now had "an excellent day school and kindergarten, a Sunday school and Christian Endeavor Society, as well as the Orphanage where over twenty children are cared for, and the Babies' Home where six poor little Indian children, under five years old, live with the nurse or matron, who gives them the care and love they have never known in their own homes."[71] The last statement was obviously written to impress readers everywhere. Most Apache children had been unconditionally loved and well cared for in their homes; exceptions were few.

Hendrina Hospers reflected on Christmas 1908 and wrote about the joys and wonderment the children expressed. On the Sunday prior to Christmas,

one of our school girls gave herself to Jesus, the gift that pleases Him most of all. It is harder for these boys and girls to live for Jesus than for you, who have Christian homes and parents. They have so many temptations around them and all so much that is evil right in their homes. . . . Think of how some of them live, their parents and those around them drinking and gambling. Pray that the influences they have here in our mission home may help them to be shining lights to their people. . . . We have some very faithful little Christians.[72]

A Few Words . . .

The years away at the Carlisle School had groomed many Apache youngsters to act like and look like Euro-Americans, had turned them under pressure[73]—temporarily or permanently—away from their families' ancient religious ways, and convinced many, but not all, of them that there was a better life waiting for them in Jesus. They were the Chiricahuas' new firebrands, Christian adult children blazing the way to a future that was unimaginable to most of their parents. The children were now participants in the vanguard of a new life, one that impressed and satisfied most of them. Astute parents recognized that if they didn't follow their educated children's ways, they ran the risk of being left behind.

Some of these Chiricahua/Warm Springs Apaches were youthful leaders, for example, James Kaywaykla, Jason Betzinez, Carlos Keanie, Benedict Johze, Mabel Johze, Ramona Chihuahua Daklugie, Asa Daklugie, Dorothy Naiche Kaywaykla, and Viola Chihuahua. Others, such as Sam Haozous, Blossom Haozous, Amy Imach, and Eugene Chihuahua, seemed to have a natural ability to lead without a boarding school education. Several were related to chiefs: Jason Betzinez was the great-grandson of Chief Mahko of the Bedonkohe Apaches, as were Benedict Johze and Sam Haozous; Mabel Johze was the granddaughter of Warm Springs Chief Loco; Asa Daklugie was the son of Juh, a Nednhi chief; Ramona Chihuahua Daklugie, Asa's wife, was the daughter of Chiricahua chief Chihuahua, as was her brother Eugene; Dorothy Naiche Kaywaykla was the daughter of Chiricahua chief Naiche and the granddaughter of Cochise; Sam Haozous was the grandson of Warm Springs Apache chief Mangas Coloradas; Blossom Haozous and her sister, Amy Imach, were the daughters of interpreter George Wratten and his Chiricahua wife, Annie.

It appears that these young adults had inherited leadership qualities and directly applied them in the religious arena. More and more mothers and fathers, grandmothers and grandfathers, older brothers and sisters, uncles and aunts and cousins followed, trying to understand and grasp for themselves the appeal of the Protestant Word of God. To some of the prisoners, Protestantism wasn't much different from Catholicism, which, in turn, had some resemblance to the traditional religion of their ancestors, and so it wasn't difficult to accept. Others supported both religions, walked a "middle ground," so to speak.

As time passed, a few adults haltingly came forward off the hard chairs for baptism when beckoned by the minister, first hesitating a second or two to look around at their proud children for approval. When prompted or prodded, many men and women rose and mouthed the Apostles' Creed in halting, stumbling English, trying so hard to imitate their sons and daughters, who were, by now, comfortable with the English language. They sang strange words to unfamiliar melodies: "Jesus loves me, this I know, for the Bible tells me so." They held the Book in their hands, hefting it now and then to gauge its weight as they imagined all the sacred stories that their children said were inside. Something like our tales about White Painted Woman and Child-of-the-Water, a few probably thought. And they looked to the left and they looked to the right at the young adults of the tribe, confidently standing up with beaming faces, willing warriors for Christ now, ready to carry their people into a world full of the hope and promise of Jesus and Christianity.

Some adults still were paying lip service to Christianity, though, speaking and acting as if they accepted the principles of their captors' religion but harboring a few reservations. These resisters were not unlike their tribal ancestors on the Spanish colonial frontier, those Chiricahua Apaches who were responsible for retaining the religion of the ancients in their hearts and minds. These twentieth-century adults—and some children—would form a nucleus of preservation that bridged the centuries so that today several ancient rituals still remain.

A few Chiricahua Apaches wondered what was unique and better about the new ways. After all, they thought, we have always worshiped one God, as the Christians do. We have always prayed to the Creator, as the missionaries and other white people do. Our hero, Child-of-the-Water, is like Jesus, and both their mothers are highly respected and cherished. When that priest or minister stands at the altar and gives out the wafer and the wine, he is just like our medicine men and medicine women who bless us with hoddentin. Our ancestral religion too acknowledges the invisible world, and we have special spirits like the Holy Ghost. We have always taught our youngsters the ways of our ancestral deities. We have always sung sacred songs, and we have always told sacred stories about the beginning of time, even though ours are from memory and not written down in a book. And at the end of life, we have always had ceremonies that send our people off to a new world, just as the Christians do.

So, if there is only very little difference in all of this, why do we have to change?

CHAPTER SEVEN

Trails and Trials

Geronimo's death in 1909 prompted a long, tortuous bureaucratic process in Washington that culminated in early April 1913, when more than 180 newly freed Chiricahua Apaches left Fort Sill on trains bound for the Mescalero Apache Reservation in New Mexico.[1] Eager to start over unencumbered by prisoner of war status and restrictions, they were accompanied by the Reverend Henry Sluyter of the Fort Sill Mission and workers Hendrina Hospers and Martha Prince. A Dutch Reformed minister, Richard Harper, had already been at Mescalero for a few days when the special train arrived at about two-thirty in the morning on Friday, April 4, at the nearby Tularosa depot. The following Sunday each Protestant Christian family proudly presented their church membership letters of transfer to Harper. Already serving a small number of Mescalero Apaches, the congregation was strengthened by 89 Chiricahuas and their families.

The Roman Catholic families among the Chiricahuas worshiped at first in various Mescalero homes under the guidance of a traveling priest until Franciscan Albert Braun was assigned to the reservation in 1916; he would become a legend among the Chiricahuas. At the beginning of his religious efforts among them, however, "he soon learned that, since few [of the Apaches] came to him, he must go to them," wrote Eve Ball. "Beside his rifle, he

Fig. 48. St. Joseph's Mission, Mescalero Apache Reservation, New Mexico. Photo by author.

carried the equipment for saying mass, and when he performed the rite, they listened with respect."[2] Even though he had little knowledge of the Indians, his determination, sense of humor, and keen understanding of human nature helped him adapt quickly to his role as missionary among the three different groups of Apaches at Mescalero—the Chiricahua, Mescalero, and Lipan. While his greatest asset was his ability to connect Catholic religious teachings to the Indians' own culture, this talent was helped along by some of the Chiricahuas' long-standing fidelity to Catholicism. One example of his relations with the Apaches is told in a tale that has remained part of the tribal lore.

> Occasionally a few of the Chiricahua men took Father Braun with them as they went hunting. Braun took advantage of these occasions to talk about religion. For example, the priest once

asked, "Before the coming of the missionaries, how did your people know there is a God?" An unnamed Apache answered, "You see the [turkey] tracks and you don't ask if there is a turkey ahead; you know there is. In the same way, we see evidence of a God. We see it in the mountains, in the trees, and in the grass. We see it in the sky and the clouds and we know that all are his work, for to us his name means 'Creator of Life.'"[3]

The Chiricahua Apaches who remained in Oklahoma—fewer than ninety men, women, and children—lived at Fort Sill another year while Congress debated and then passed a bill allotting lands outside the military post.[4] Most of these former prisoners of war eventually joined the RCA at a small church in Apache, Oklahoma, about nineteen miles north of Fort Sill.[5] They were now on their own and would struggle for a livelihood, having been dropped in the middle of an agrarian society of white farmers and ranchers who regarded them suspiciously. And many of their loved ones, on whom they should have been able to count for cultural, physical, and emotional support, were far away in New Mexico, having their own difficulties.

Through all the discussions prior to release, the issue that most distressed the prisoners was the government's unilateral selection of individuals whom they would allow to remain in Oklahoma. Members of the Board of Indian Commissioners, sitting in Washington, D.C., had identified only fourteen Chiricahuas who were "qualified" through intelligence, industriousness, and physical fitness to be thrust into the American mainstream of rural life as it existed in Oklahoma. The evaluation was apparently dependent on the assessor's subjectivity, much like the assessments of ancestors made by the priests in the Spanish colonial era.

At first no consideration was given to Apaches who failed to meet the standards but who nonetheless had their hearts set on living in Oklahoma. Most of these men and women became so upset when told they would be transferred to Mescalero that they turned to their longtime favorite missionary worker, Hendrina Hospers, for counsel and guidance. She quickly sent a letter describing the situation to Reverend Walter C. Roe, now RCA's Superintendent of Missions for the Oklahoma field. As a superb communicator with a national reputation and one of the Chiricahuas' staunchest allies,

Roe wrote a nasty letter to the Board of Indian Commissioners threatening legal action and another public scandal about the government's ongoing abuse of the Apache prisoners unless reconsideration was made immediately.

Official documents offer some insight into the army's choices. On October 16, 1911, military officials had held a conference at Fort Sill with sixty-four Apache men regarding their transfer. Representing the government were Colonel Hugh L. Scott, Colonel Edwin St. John Greble, and Major George W. Goode. James Kaywaykla interpreted, and Henry E. Russell, a reporter from the nearby town of Lawton, recorded the proceedings. Notable by their absence—they were not invited—were any of the Chiricahuas' missionary advisers and advocates.

Scott opened the meeting by stating he had been to Mescalero and met with the Mescalero Apaches regarding the transfer of the Chiricahuas.

> They said they wanted you Apaches to come there and live with them, that you are Apaches like they are, that you used to visit them, that your older people visited them and that they were always friends, and that if you come there and live with them that you can inter-marry. . . . They believe if they got new blood in their tribe that their health will be much better, that they would not disappear as they are doing now, having nobody else to inter-marry with. . . . In other words, if everyone goes there, and there is 240 of you, and added to the 400 of them, would make 640 persons and you would have an equal share in that $1,300,000. worth of timber [being harvested and processed in the reservation's sawmill] and have the same right of settlement on any part of the ground not occupied that any Mescalero Apache has got.[6]

Unknown to Scott, intermarrying with the Mescaleros was a meaningless inducement. The years of incarceration hadn't diminished the Chiricahuas' high opinion of themselves. They were still ethnocentric, still believed they were a superior people—intelligent, independent, and self-sufficient—so they couldn't imagine themselves needing marriage partners or even any assistance from the dispirited Mescaleros. And while the prospect of sharing in a huge amount of money from tree harvesting might tempt others,

Scott's offer didn't change many minds among the Chiricahuas. His understanding of them didn't include the fact that financial wealth—as comprehended by Euro-Americans—was irrelevant. Despite nearly three decades of interacting with those values, most Apaches still measured riches in terms of kinship and what individuals and families could give away, not accumulate. Not surprisingly, then, Scott's presentation fell on deaf ears.

Life at Whitetail

A month after the Chiricahuas arrived in New Mexico, Major George W. Goode, who had been the officer in charge of Apaches at Fort Sill, traveled to Mescalero for a six-day tour of inspection to see for himself how much progress had been made in settling the former prisoners at Whitetail, a remote and natural valley about seven thousand feet in altitude.

Whitetail is breathtaking in its beauty. In spring, purple and yellow wildflowers line the sides of the gravel road up to the location, and an abundance of dandelions colors the gentle slopes. Very tall lodgepole pines and ponderosa pines grow profusely. After a rain or heavy winter or spring snow, the land remains wet for a long time, and the forest cover holds the moisture as well. It is cooler than one might imagine. The hot sun that warms different regions of the reservation takes its time finding a way through the tall evergreens. The air is always crystal clear. Wild turkeys cross the road, white-tailed deer nervously stare at interlopers through the safety of the trees, and occasionally a wild horse appears. It was an ideal location for the former prisoners to begin their new lives.

To Goode's chagrin, however, he found quite a few families encamped in tents around the agency, still waiting to permanently relocate. His official report urged that quick action be taken to fulfill the government's promise of adequate housing, but five months later only thirty families had been assigned and construction on twenty-five more houses had not yet begun.

With a harsh winter just around the corner, many Apaches—some ailing with tuberculosis—had been issued only new shoes and blankets to help them through a long, cold season in the mountains. Concerned, the RCA missionaries "believed the Chiricahuas'

Fig. 49. Early photo of Dutch Reformed Church on the Mescalero Apache Reservation, New Mexico, n.d. Courtesy of Mrs. William Cleghorn collection.

future at Mescalero was uncertain since provisions for their permanent establishment were either slow or 'constantly deferred,'" wrote John Turcheneske, Jr., quoting an item from the RCA's publication titled "The Mission Field."

> Furthermore, altitude, unaccustomed cold, living in tents, hardship and want are making heavy drains on the health and strength of the newcomers. Were conditions not improved immediately, missionaries foresaw the time when, out of desperation [the Chiricahuas] . . . would return to former religious practices.[7]

This warning was designed to influence policy makers who were unfamiliar with the Chiricahuas' "former religious practices" but who subscribed to the sensational myths that had always, it seemed, swirled around the people. In truth, and the missionaries

Fig. 50. Students attending the Whitetail Day School on the Mescalero Apache Reservation, New Mexico, ca. 1948–1950. Courtesy of Rev. Robert S. Ove.

knew this, the Apaches would never have been able to resume most of their traditional practices for many reasons, but especially since the situations on which the ancient religion depended, for example, warfare, no longer existed.

In January 1914, William H. Ketchum, a Jesuit and member of the Board of Indian Commissioners, talked with the Chiricahua leaders and later urged Congress to appropriate approximately $200,000 to both the Mescaleros and Chiricahuas to start a business—breeding and raising cattle. Ultimately, a $75,000 lump sum was awarded, not enough to substantially begin a herd, but the Chiricahuas—no strangers to challenge—dug in their heels once again. This time, however, they were prepared to manage their fate. Farming and running a cattle herd were good opportunities for self-sufficiency, so with the appropriated federal money they bought livestock and prayed with the missionaries to accomplish their goal of profitable cattle management. By this time, families

Fig. 51. Mr. and Mrs. Eugene Chihuahua and grandson Vernon Simmons on the Mescalero Apache Reservation, New Mexico, ca. 1943. Courtesy of Rev. Robert S. Ove.

had started to grow as they had in days of freedom. All ages and sizes lived together at Whitetail, shared a little or a lot, but were pleased to be with each other. Most everyone kept their eyes on the future and worked toward the day when they hoped the tribe would be reconstituted in population and be much more than a shadow of its once mighty self.

The Chiricahuas handled the housing situation at Whitetail with some aplomb, despite poor construction by government-hired employees that caused the homes—uninsulated two- or four-room log cabins with porches—to resemble shacks more than living quarters. The government's lumber was so green that the sap oozed out each time a nail was driven. When the wood dried, it cracked and the knots dropped out. Insulation consisted of mud smeared between planks; the floors were either mud or bare boards. In most

Fig. 52. Chiricahua Apache home at Whitetail, on the Mescalero Apache Reservation. Courtesy of Frisco Native American Museum, Frisco, North Carolina.

cases, the government-supplied furnishings were also in sad condition—torn couches, battered tables, and wobbly chairs. While women hung curtains in some windows and put down throw rugs to make the home look attractive, the men shored up the sagging lumber and reinforced the walls and ceilings. Still, James O. Arthur, the RCA's minister on the reservation at the time, observed that "when the high winds from the west [come] sweeping down the canyon, every crack and knot-hole is discovered to admit the cooling breeze."[8]

Fueled by abundant wood from the surrounding forest, potbelly stoves provided heat; only a very few homes had propane. Most houses had an indoor sink in the kitchen, but pipes froze routinely during cold weather, and then the people walked to the schoolhouse to fill buckets and cans with water from the only protected tap.

Fig. 53. Remains of a barn at Whitetail, ca. 1993. Courtesy of the author.

Kitchens contained only a few pots and pans, but that wasn't a problem. Reflecting traditional practices, the Apaches preferred cooking outdoors around an open fire and eating on dishes that often were only tin pie plates; empty jelly jars and old cans, accumulated from church sales, served as glasses. A few elders ate with hunting knives, wiped clean on pants or sleeves, as they had done in days long gone.

Outhouses were prominent and permanent fixtures across the landscape. Personal cleanliness required heating water on the stove or over an outdoor fire and pouring it into a large metal tub. To conserve precious water and fuel, bathing was often a family affair, with children using the same water, one after another, until everyone was clean.

Regardless of the poor conditions, though, the housing at Whitetail offered more protection than what was available to relatives and friends still living in the tents surrounding the Mescalero Agency buildings. Several families were still there five years after they arrived on the reservation.[9]

In remembering her early years at Whitetail, Chiricahua Apache Elbys Hugar, the great-granddaughter of Cochise, recalled that her father, Christian Naiche, Jr., attended the Dutch Reformed church at Whitetail and then talked about Jesus at home. Hugar occasionally sings in the Apache choir today, and when she's in church, she prays in the old language. "We can pray in Apache . . . if that's what we want, or we can pray in English. We pray to one person. . . . When an Indian prays, they pray for everything and everyone . . . not only themselves [but] for the poor, the sick, and for what we have here."[10]

The late Dorcie Kazhe, another Whitetail resident, also remembered days gone by.

> A church was established by the Reformed Church of America. I was a Presbyterian and it was a very similar form of worship, so I joined. The church had a little white chapel and we would gather there for ladies' aid [activities], sewing, and potlucks. We came to church as a place to see and meet one another, because it was steady, a good thing. The missionaries came on Sunday afternoons.[11]

During the week healthy Apache men dug wells and cisterns and laid pipes all across the landscape. Since rural electrification wouldn't reach Whitetail for another thirty years or so, candles, coal lamps, and the moon provided light at night. The federal government built the two-room schoolhouse, and the missionaries, aided by Chiricahua men, constructed the small mission church on a slight rise just at the bend of the road toward the cow camp; many of the Apaches happily attended Sunday services, and the church became a social center. Others considered the church to be a strictly religious setting. For example, Wheeler Tissnolthos was a superb orator who never missed a chance to speak favorably about the teachings of the church, either within its four walls or on other occasions. He droned on and on, long after most of his audience was exhausted from the effort of listening to him. And during Sunday services, Eugene Chihuahua, son of Chief Chihuahua, often raised his magnificent operatic voice in song and praise, as did Asa Daklugie and Jasper Kanseah, Sr.

Several other men and women also became leaders in the church congregation at Whitetail. Among them were

Duncan Balatchu—elected member of the first Business Committee

Alfred Chato—former warrior

Hugh Chee—great-nephew of Cochise

William Coonie—former U.S. Army scout

Azul Geronimo—Geronimo's last wife

Robert Geronimo—son of Geronimo and cattle rancher on the reservation

Charles Istee—son of Chief Victorio

Jasper Kanseah—former scout with the Seventh Cavalry at Fort Sill

Charles Martine—scout who convinced Geronimo to surrender

Rogers Toclanny—former U.S. Army scout

Edwin Yahnosha—helped build the Whitetail RCA church[12]

Despite the obvious devotion of these people, certain ministers had doubts as to their sincerity. In later years, Reverend Reuben Ten Haken worried aloud that the Gospel had penetrated too few hearts and that some Apaches had come to church only because a relative pushed them. "These people honor me with their lips, but their hearts are far from me," he said. "The whole Apache nation would have been won over . . . if it hadn't been for the un-Christian activities of certain white people in their dealings with the Indians and with each other."[13]

One wishes he had been more courageous and identified the persons in his reference. His comment about lip service implies that resistance to Christianity was just beneath the surface among many Chiricahuas, as it had been in various forms dating back to the days of early contact.

Reverend Robert Ove, a teacher at Whitetail before he became a Lutheran minister, hypothesized that many Chiricahuas' willingness to accept Christian teachings may have been the result of a story told long before recorded time. Oral testimony has preserved a legend that tells about a white man carrying a Bible who would come to visit the Apache people. This tale was told to Ove in correspondence with Ten Haken's wife, Bernice, who quoted Belle Kazhe, a Chiricahua. Said Kazhe to Ten Haken years ago at a Thanksgiving celebration, "Our ancestors told us about a higher power—God—and said that someday a man with yellow hair, blue eyes, and a book under his arm would come and he would have the truth and we should hear and listen to his words, and that came true when the first white man (missionaries) came to our Apaches."[14]

While many Whitetail residents were Protestants, several families attended St. Joseph's Catholic Mission, near the center of Mescalero. One reason Catholicism was attractive to Apaches, according to Sister Juanita Little, a contemporary nun with a Chiricahua heritage, was its practice of permitting the Mountain Spirit dance on its grounds. "The Apaches were never asked to surrender or compromise their ancient religious heritage in order to belong to Saint Joseph's," she said. "As a matter of fact, when the church was being built, the Apaches conducted a ritual inside the unfinished walls."[15]

Here is a good example of what is currently defined as "compartmentalism" but is actually a form of continuing resistance, however subtle, to Christianity. By permitting this traditional activity within its walls, though, St. Joseph's Mission wisely acknowledged and respected an ancient, spiritually powerful heritage—one that still lives today.

Another tradition that remains strong at Mescalero is the dance of the Mountain Spirits. Today it is performed publicly and privately. Coppersmith, writing about the Oklahoma Chiricahuas, believes that the dance "has lost much of its spiritual significance for most members of the tribe [but] it still projects a powerful political and cultural symbolism which personifies the survival of Chiricahua . . . identity."[16] Some tribal members would take offense at this remark and shrug it off as just another outsider's point of view. To many Apaches, particularly those who annually travel the five hundred miles from Mescalero to Apache, Oklahoma, to participate in the festivities, the dance will never lose its significance at all and will continue to be thought of as one of the bulwarks of the religion of their ancestors.[17]

Seven years after the transfer from Fort Sill to Whitetail, the Apaches' continuing distress and impoverishment came to the attention of an old soldier-friend, Hugh L. Scott, in 1920 a major general and new member of the Board of Indian Commissioners. In late spring he paid a visit to see for himself if the rumors and nationwide publicity about destitute Apaches were true. Assessing the situation firsthand, Scott apologized. "I am sorry. I am responsible for your people moving here," he said.[18] He offered to personally escort anyone who wanted to return to Oklahoma; only a few people took him up on his offer because the friends and relatives living around Fort Sill were doing no better.[19]

Yet most of the Whitetail Apaches were content with their difficult lives despite the hardships. Families were growing, and government teachers at the school and the Dutch Reformed missionaries and workers were helping the people become comfortable with the ways of the dominant white culture. Contagious diseases, especially tuberculosis, were waning, and good companionship usually filled the rarefied air.

During the 1950s one or two families at a time left Whitetail and moved toward the center of the reservation. The church building was moved intact to another part of the reservation, where it was used as housing; it no longer stands. Most of the government-built drafty homes at Whitetail have also fallen to the earth like wounded warriors of old. Living at Whitetail or closer to modern facilities on the reservation had slowly accustomed these Chiricahuas to being a free people, and they had remained a tight-knit group. They preserved their language, some of their ceremonies, several of their sacred stories, and most of their history, even though many former prisoners of war were loathe to discuss or pass on to their descendants their experiences while confined.

The grandchildren of the incarcerated Chiricahuas are now in their seventies and early eighties and have seen and felt the impact of American society on old Apache ways. They worry that their ancestors' customs, experiences, and lifestyles will soon be unimportant memories to the current generation or will be lost altogether when their children and grandchildren become completely acculturated into the anonymity of the American melting pot.

In the face of that fear, the puberty ceremony is still held every year during the July 4 week. Claire Farrer and Bernard Second have reported that despite pressure to acculturate to the Anglo way of life, many young women on the reservation today choose a ceremonial even though it places restrictions on them and makes requirements of them and their extended families. . . . It is not necessary, however, to have a ceremonial to become a proper woman. And it is even possible to have a ceremony several years after menstruation, although such events are usually private. . . . The meaning of the ceremonial [today] is complex. Like any good celebration it speaks to individuals on many levels. Some celebrate as homecoming, seeing friends and relatives, and renewing ties. Others celebrate in a religious fashion, believing that as long as the religion is intact, the Apaches will survive. For some it is a time of license, while for many it is a time to rejoice in being Indian, specifically Apaches, and to show Anglos what hospitality and generosity really mean.[20]

Celebrating this age-old rite year after year is a form of resisting total acceptance of Christianity. The puberty ceremony continues an indestructible loyalty to the rich Chiricahua Apache heritage, a well-deserved pride in the ability of the human spirit to persevere in its religious beliefs despite the evidence that reveals the recurrent attempts of European and American governments and their agents, the Catholic and Protestant churches, to the contrary. One other major historical custom also remains: the ancestors' language.

The Chiricahua Apache tongue is still spoken freely at Mescalero among three hundred tribal members. The younger generation may also understand and speak it, but today English is the main language of communication across the reservation. However, elders are part of the school's instruction program and speak in their native language to children in the early grades in order to keep the language alive. A dictionary of the Chiricahua/Mescalero vocabulary has been compiled and published, but an outsider would need an accompanying audiotape to learn how to pronounce the multisyllabic words.

Certain cultural customs are also observed, such as consultation and participation in healing ceremonies, but nowadays there is no need for hunting and gathering to provide sustenance, and so the many prayers that accompanied that activity, as well as the prayers before and after warfare, are no longer said as they had been in the past. And contemporary Apache women usually give birth in the Indian Health Service Hospital on the reservation or nearby hospitals, so the services of a medicine woman/midwife, including her traditional prayers at birth, only infrequently are used.

Intermarriages among the Chiricahua, Mescalero, and Lipan Apaches are a fact of life, and young men and women also look to Hispanic peoples or to Anglos as partners. Many single mothers with children live on the reservation. In some ways, the situation resembles the days of old when the Chiricahua Apache roaming bands on the Spanish colonial frontier eagerly welcomed individuals of all ethnic backgrounds into their local units so that the children of these affiliations could be raised as Apaches.

The majority of Chiricahuas today are practicing Christians. On Sundays the pews at the Mescalero Reformed Church and St. Joseph's Mission are full; youth and elder activities at both churches are well attended. Also, baptism, confirmation, and first holy communion are events looked forward to in families' spiritual lives. The attraction of powwows, once an essential social-political-religious ingredient in most Indian societies, is growing among Chiricahua Apache young men and women but not in terms of a spiritual exercise; it is an excuse for socializing, which is also important.

The Chiricahua community within the borders of the Mescalero Apache Reservation has managed to retain a degree of cultural identity while simultaneously participating in the dominant society's activities and religions as well. For example, during his lifetime Eugene Chihuahua saw no conflict in observing the Christian ways and continuing his ancestors' traditions. Remembering the days at Whitetail with Eugene, his grandson Vernon Simmons said:

> Eugene used to get up about four or five in the morning, maybe earlier than that. I'd ask Grandma where he was going. She said he was going to pray. But I know he didn't go to church that early in the day. Once I asked him about it. He said he prayed because we needed rain. . . . On the porch he told me, "There's something you do as a duty when you're in the city or somewhere else. If you want help, call to your father in heaven. Get out of the city, go find some trees, mountains, birds. Get up early in the morning. Go out there and pray like you're really praying for

something. The churches are coming into Mescalero. It's a different way they teach, but it's all the same God, all the same father. You could go to all of them, but it's meant for us to go into the woods." I asked Eugene, "When you go out to the woods and pray to God the Father, do you pray in English?" He said he didn't because God understands everybody.[21]

Life in Oklahoma

The modern Fort Sill Chiricahua/Warm Springs Apache tribal complex is north of the town of Apache on an allotment of land that once belonged to Dorothy Naiche Kaywaykla. The tribe purchased the property from her descendants, built its administrative offices on it, and then added several outbuildings over time, including a gymnasium and a facility that now houses social programs. Nearby are dance grounds where the Mountain Spirit dancers dance. An annual celebration is held each September to honor and commemorate the tribe's heritage.

Those Chiricahua Apaches who, from 1913 through 1914, remained in Oklahoma, chose to live in these pastoral surroundings. Although the government promised each Apache 160 acres, the late chairperson Mildred Cleghorn stated:

> No one got 160 acres. The closest they got was 158 acres and the least amount they got was 23. A majority received 80 acres apiece. My father got 80 acres, my mother got 80 acres, and [because I was a child] I got 50 acres. Yes, we were promised 160 acres apiece, but Uncle Sam doesn't follow through. . . . We in Oklahoma stayed [at Fort Sill] one year longer [than those who went to Mescalero]. Because we had to find a place to live. It was about 1923 that the last Apache got an allotment.[22]

The former prisoners of war who farmed in towns around Fort Sill experienced life quite differently from their friends and relatives at Mescalero. While the Whitetail Chiricahuas kept their cultural and religious traditions and language alive, in Oklahoma the people really had no choice but to blend in, to become part of the mainstream community, to interact with everyone else. As a consequence, those activities that fostered Chiricahua identity, cultural loyalties, and allegiance to one another and to the ways of the ancestors began to weaken.

For example, the puberty ceremony is almost never held in Oklahoma. Coppersmith reports that Michael Darrow, the tribal historian, informed him that the

> tribal elders made a conscious decision not to practice this rite for a number of reasons. First, to be practiced correctly and in its entirety, the Coming Out ceremony is expensive. It could become a significant burden for a people struggling to survive . . . in the decades after their release from Fort Sill. Second, to be practiced correctly, elements of the ceremony require commodities such as lodge poles which were not available, again without a great deal of expense, from the local area. For the ceremony conducted . . . in 1994 cedar poles and mescal leaves were trucked in from New Mexico. In essence the tribal elders from the early post-allotment period decided not to practice the Coming Out ceremony. Therefore, it receded from its preeminent place in Chiricahua . . . Apache life.[23]

The dance of the Mountain Spirits is performed by Oklahoma Chiricahua/Warm Springs men and is a highlight of the annual September festival. Mescalero friends and relatives are always invited, as are some of the reservation dance groups; many make the five-hundred-mile trip to renew tribal and family connections. During these visits one may occasionally hear snippets of the ancestral language, but today many Oklahomans are unable to speak as their ancestors did. As young marrieds, the former Carlisle students spoke English at home, their children learned English, and the ancestors' tongue gradually became the families' second language.

A similarity of both Oklahoma and New Mexico Chiricahua Apaches is intermarriage with those outside the culture. The Fort Sill Apaches in the 1920s and 1930s were significantly affected by outside unions as a younger generation left home to seek fortunes elsewhere; these relocations affected cultural identity and cultural allegiance. Some of the Chiricahuas chose Comanches, Kiowas, or spouses from any of the other Oklahoma tribes, as well as Anglo wives and husbands. Each of these choices eroded what it meant in

Fig. 54. Apache Reformed Church, Apache, Oklahoma, ca. 1990. Photo by author.

the old days to be "Apache," particularly the ancestors' loyalty to each other and to the tribe.

The Apache Reformed Church, religious home to many of the Fort Sill Apaches, was built some years after the Chiricahuas were settled in the area around Fort Sill. Today it is near its original site, amid a grove of old, leafy trees. Rows of polished wooden pews fill the room. Behind and to the side of the church, Hospers Hall is utilized for activities such as quilting and youth group interests.

Mildred Cleghorn was a faithful parishioner, and on Sundays and Wednesday nights, during Bible study and hymn singing, she raised her soprano voice to sing in praise of her Christian God. On at least one Sunday each September, her feet must have been uncomfortable, still sore from dancing the previous night around a blazing bonfire in the same steps her ancestors used to honor and respect their ancient heritage. In her mind, there was never a conflict between Christianity and the religion of her heritage.

I don't want to give the wrong impression, but the symbolism we have in the Apache tribe is the same symbolism that Christ has in the Bible. For example, fire. In our way, fire is very important. You notice the fire when we dance, when the Mountain Spirit dancers dance around the fire. Well, the Holy Spirit came down to the fire too. [The people] went up into the high places to fast and pray, and they got a message. Moses got a message. That's why I say it's amazing how our people relate to the Biblical standards of Christian religion, the symbolism I was mentioning before. Like the fire and the pollen. You can't get a flower or growth without pollen. Pollen to us represents fertility, and we color our clothes with yellow. That's why yellow is such a predominant color among our Apache people. There are so many beautiful things about our Indian people, our Indian way, that I hope we shall never lose.

Also, we're taught to share in the Apache way. Well, there in the book of Matthew it tells you. The birds and the bees don't worry about what they're going to eat tomorrow, and that's the way our Indian people are. Today is when you live. So, you do what you can today to help other people, to share.

I guess I have accepted [the loss of culture and religion] to a certain extent, but then again I haven't. I still feel a personal loss. I can't speak my language today. I can understand it, yes, but we've lost it here in Oklahoma and we've lost a lot of the good things. . . . We never have puberty ceremonies. We didn't have anyone here to do the ceremony. I definitely feel I lost something. And I don't think it will ever come back. It's gone for good.[24]

A Few Words . . .

If the Euro-American assumption that Christianity and civilization were synonymous was correct, when the Chiricahua Apaches were released from confinement, they were considered by the government to be sufficiently civilized because most appeared to have accepted Jesus as their savior.

But what of those Apaches who, like Eugene Chihuahua, went into the woods and prayed to Ussen and then prayed and sang hymns in the Dutch Reformed church on Sundays? Would he have been considered "civilized" even though he still prayed outside the church walls? More questions than answers are raised, for who could really know what was in the deepest part of the Chiricahuas' hearts—that sacred circle where spirit meets flesh? Only Ussen.

CHAPTER EIGHT

Speaking Out

Voices of the Chiricahua Apaches and others—echoes from some now in the invisible world and direct communications from several others still full of lively spirit—talk about the Apache religion, culture, history, and heritage. Added for more flavor are the voices of a few non-Apaches—one mission worker and the clergy. Several of the statements have been taken out of context, so readers should keep that in mind, but many of these speakers believe there is no conflict between the old and the new—traditional and Christianity. The lack of dissonance is understandable given certain fundamental similarities: one god, a female lesser deity who gives birth to a son conceived by nonmale, nonhuman sources, and the son as savior of the people. Not to be overlooked is the appeal of the principle of strong male leadership both in Christianity and on the tribal level, where the chief, like Jesus, was compassionate, kind, generous, and understanding as well as being a leader and a guide.

The Chiricahua Apaches

COCHISE

This highly respected Chiricahua leader met with U.S. general Gordon Granger in September 1866 at Cañada Alamosa, in New

Fig. 55. Bronze bust of Cochise entered into the American Indian Hall of Fame, Anadarko, Oklahoma, in 1989. Photo by author.

Mexico. The discussion addressed removing Cochise and his people from the area around Cañada Alamosa and placing them on a reservation.

> I speak straight and do not wish to deceive or be deceived. I want a good, strong and lasting peace. When God made the world He gave one part to the white man and another to the Apache. Why was it? Why did they come together? God made us not as you; we were born like the animals, in the dry grass, not on beds like you. I came here because God told me to do so. I was going around the world with the clouds, and air, when God spoke to my thought and told me to come in here and be at peace with all.[1]

Fig. 56. Chiricahua Apache Toos-Day-Zay, daughter of Mangas Coloradas, wife of Cochise, mother of Naiche. Postcard photo, n.d.

In this statement, Cochise reiterates the age-old cultural belief that God (Ussen) wanted the Chiricahuas to live in the Southwest. This is a significant reiteration and transfer of a spiritual concept that remained intact through at least two centuries of exposure to Christianity, forced or voluntary, on the Spanish colonial frontier, in the American Southwest, in prisoner of war camps, or in freedom.

Cochise's reference to "God" should not be taken as a literal utterance. He undoubtedly referred to "Ussen" in his discussion and the translator inserted the word "God" into Cochise's remarks. At the time he met with Granger, Christianity had not influenced Cochise to the degree that he would substitute one way for the other, although he certainly was aware of the missions and activities in Bacoachi and Janos in centuries past.

NAICHE

Son of Cochise, Naiche assumed leadership of the Chiricahuas at age twenty, when his older brother, Taza, died in 1876, two years after Cochise's death.[2] Naiche's mother was the daughter of Mangas Coloradas, a most revered chief. Naiche was father to eight sons and six daughters, of whom six sons and two daughters died at Fort Sill. He himself died of influenza at the Mescalero Apache Reservation Hospital on March 16, 1919. Below are excerpts from a speech he gave in September 1911 at a camp meeting at Fort Sill:

> You—Kiowa, Comanche, and white people back here—through your help my whole band of people give themselves to the Lord. This makes me glad, and I feel like talking about this. I am thankful to you all for what you have done for us; your songs and your testimonies. You will all be remembered, I am sure. I have finished.[3]

> Every Sunday we have a meeting and Sunday School so that we learn more. I am glad that people teach me about Jesus and I am very glad to do what Jesus tells me to do. Here we live in White Tail, a few Christians of us. About four or five of us work hard with our own people. All of our people have heard the good teaching but not all try to live that way. Five of us—Duncan, Stephen, Cooney, Jasper and myself—try to help our people and keep them from going back in the old way. When we have no missionary here we have meetings in the same way. One who can read, reads to us and we sing Indian songs and pray in the same way on Sunday.[4]

Naiche spoke frequently at the Whitetail church and always urged his friends and relatives to walk the Christian road:

> The Christian road is not an easy road. There are hard things sometimes. But we all understand there is work we have to do.

Fig. 57. Chiricahua Apache chief Naiche and wife Ha-o-zinne. Postcard photo, n.d.

We cannot understand all at once. We learn slowly but after a while we will understand. I think God sent us here [to Mescalero] to help our Mescalero Indians on to the Jesus road. We must be thinking God sent us here for that, and we must work.[5]

Naiche's fidelity to Protestantism appears to have been sincere, and I can find no documentary evidence of resistance to Christian teachings. Once again, one of the enduring traits of the historical Chiricahua Apaches was their pragmatism, and Naiche, being an astute, intelligent leader and having learned from his father's example, likely concluded that resistance would be futile. When he was convinced of that, he took an active role in convincing tribal members

Fig. 58. Chiricahua Apache chief Naiche at Fort Sill. Frisco Native American Museum, Frisco, North Carolina.

to accept Christianity, although as will be shown below, many had doubts but were able to respect both religions without difficulty.

GERONIMO

As one of the most powerful medicine men of the Apache people and a deeply spiritual holy man, Geronimo was well regarded by most friends and relatives for his many unique abilities in the traditional religious realm. With that in mind, below are excerpts of a conversation, translated by Asa Daklugie:

As to the future state, the teachings of our tribe were not specific. . . . We believed that there is a life after this one, but no one ever told me as to what part of man lived after death. I have seen many men die; I have seen many human bodies decayed, but I have never seen that part that is called the spirit; I do not know what it is; nor have I yet been able to understand that part of the Christian religion. Since my life as a prisoner has begun I have heard the teachings of the white man's religion, and in many respects believe it to be better than the religion of my fathers. However, I have always prayed, and I believe that the Almighty has always protected me. Believing that in a wise way it is good to go to church, and that associating with Christians would improve my character, I have adopted the Christian religion. I believe that the church has helped me much during the short time I have been a member. . . . I have advised all of my people who are not Christians to study that religion because it seems to me the best religion in enabling one to live right.[6]

Geronimo had never actively participated in the Dutch Reformed Church's activities until one day in the summer of 1902, when he sat in the front row of a camp meeting, listened intently, and suddenly jumped to his feet, declaring, "Now we begin to think that the Christian white people love us."[7] Despite this declaration, Debo believes that Geronimo did not discard his primitive beliefs but supplemented them with Christianity, thus resisting in his own way through compartmentalizing both religions. But did he truly incorporate some of the Protestant dogma, or was he just pretending? His consummate skill at manipulation should have been taken into consideration by the missionaries after the immediate flurry of good feeling produced by his statement. When the excitement abated, his remarks should have been evaluated objectively rather than subjectively. If that had been done, Geronimo's seeming acceptance of Christianity and its expected consequences would be seen with a bit more clarity. As it was, from the missionaries' point of view—what a feather in their cap! What an impression they would make on their superiors if they could declare that Geronimo, the former terror of the Southwest, became a Christian under their tutelage. That notwithstanding, I believe that Geronimo wholeheartedly practiced the religion of his ancestors until the end of his life and that he told the Dutch Reformed missionaries what they wanted to hear. He was no longer in a position to resist with guns and ammunition, so he used the next-best thing—the missionaries' needs as demonstrated by their vulnerabilities to flattery—as a form of protection for his most cherished ancestral beliefs.

It must also be recognized that Geronimo was aging and his influence and standing among tribal members were waning. Joining the church and professing Christianity, as many Chiricahua Apaches were doing at the turn of the century, would have returned status to him and elevated him once again in the eyes of the people.

ASA DAKLUGIE

Son of noted Ncdnhi Apache chief Juh and nephew of Geronimo, young Asa Daklugie surrendered with Mangus's small group in October of 1886. He was a youthful prisoner of war at Fort Pickens for a short time until he was sent to the Carlisle School. When his education was complete, Asa returned to his family at Fort Sill and later became one of his generation's leaders, a position of status that he held for the rest of his life. In his older years, Daklugie talked extensively with author Eve Ball.

> So long as one of the old Apaches lives, he will continue to [practice our religion]. There are some things in the New Testament that I doubt many Apaches understand—like your queer three-headed God.
>
> We make no pretensions of brotherhood with white people, for we are a religious and moral folk. In times of death or other tragedy, our people, regardless of church affiliation, usually revert to the solace of our old religion. It comforts us and we see no reason why we should not. Many Apaches, both young and old, are active members of some Christian church. They can do this because they see no conflicts in the two faiths. I have often acted as interpreter to ministers, and I have attended churches for many years, partly because [wife] Ramona wanted to go and partly because of my love and respect for Father Albert [the much-beloved priest at St. Joseph's Mission]. Much of his teachings were, so far as I could see, just what we had believed before

Fig. 59. Asa Daklugie. Source unknown. Photo acquired through eBay, 2000.

the coming of the Black Robes. I have much gratitude, too, for the churches that have, I think, done more to bring about an acceptance of the ways of civilization than has the government. At Fort Sill the Dutch Reformed Church provided both a school and a little hospital long before the government did either. Apaches are sincere in their acceptance of Christianity because in it they see nothing in conflict with their old religion.[8]

Daklugie's mention of the belief system that existed before the "coming of the Black Robes" refers to the traditional religion of the ancestors, which was quite remarkably like Christianity. And his conclusion that the "Apaches are sincere . . . because . . . they see nothing in conflict with their old religion" raises questions. For example, if the similarity hadn't existed, would there have been a conflict? And if the conflict existed, would resistance have taken a much more aggressive form? In other words, would the people not have been as welcoming toward the Dutch Reformed missionaries?

An important point that Daklugie didn't address concerned the Chiricahua Apaches on the Spanish colonial frontier. They too saw similarities between their traditional religion and Catholicism, but their resistance was dramatic: they burned the churches and killed the priests, unlike their descendants at Fort Sill, whose resistance has to be either imagined or challenged.

Daklugie is a prime example of the Chiricahuas' ability to divide their loyalties between the traditional religion and Christianity. While a student at the Carlisle School, he participated actively in at least one student religious organization—the Christian Endeavor Society—but never completely accepted Christianity. As a married adult, he went with his wife, Ramona, at her insistence, to the Dutch Reformed church at Whitetail and later at Mescalero and was quite fond of the Catholic priest, Father Albert Braun.

One must believe that while at boarding school, he practiced Chiricahua Apache pragmatism in participating in the religious activity. However, when freed from imposed obligations, he resisted the white ways and always professed fidelity to the religion of his ancestors.

COONIE (KUNI)

Born in 1856, Coonie was a scout against the Chiricahuas during the Apache campaigns of the 1880s. His first wife died at Fort Sill, and he then married the woman warrior Dahteste. They lived at Whitetail with two children from Coonie's first marriage and took two orphans into their home—the Johlsanny children Richard and Samuel, both nephews of Chief Chihuahua. Coonie is the "Cooney" referred to in Naiche's statement above.

> I thank our Father in Heaven that He has put this thought in our heart, to get together here and worship Him. The Bible has taught us that we have one Father above, and that is how we can call ourselves brothers and sisters. . . . I am thankful for these missionaries here. They think so much about us, and put us

together here to worship our Father in Heaven. We can prove this thing by these children down here [pointing to the orphanage children]. How the missionaries take care of our children! You can all look at them and see how clean they are, and what the missionaries think of us. I joined the church about 12 years ago [1899]. I was bad man myself before I joined in this Christian life. I used to act that way because I thought that was the way to act in this world, but since I find these Bible words I look at it different. Now, when I was living in that old life, I used to suffer more. I used to always be hungry, sleepy, thirsty, and I don't get enough of anything in that life. Now, ever since I choose the Jesus road, I never suffer like I used to. I am very glad to say these words to you. . . . It is different and my heart is happy. That is all.[9]

Coonie showed no evidence of resistance to Christianity. On the contrary, he and Naiche became the first two Chiricahua Apache elders in the Whitetail church. The cause of his whole-hearted acceptance is not clear, and no documentary evidence exists that explains it.

LAWRENCE MITHLO

Mithlo was born in 1864, a member of a large extended family, and lived until 1938. Sometime in the early 1930s he spoke with linguist Harry Hoijer, who recorded his comments. Fort Sill Chiricahua/Warm Springs Apache tribal historian Leland Michael Darrow passed on Mithlo's thoughts:

Pray to God [and] Child of the Water. We live because of those two. They made the earth and the sky. Though hardship, hunger, cold, heat, poverty all overmastered them, they talked to their children about God and Child of the Water. They thought by means of them. All of this is true.[10]

Here Mithlo equates Child-of-the-Water with God, an unusual relationship because the latter is ordinarily likened to Jesus. In any case, Mithlo has expressed the duality—Christianity and the traditional religion—with no evidence of competition between the two. It is significant, however, that in his mind both shared equal status.

MILDRED IMACH CLEGHORN

Mildred Cleghorn, a Fort Sill Apache chairperson for nearly twenty years and a nationally known spokesperson for her tribe, was born a prisoner of war on December 11, 1910. She has appeared in documentary films, was active in several local Oklahoma and national Indian organizations, gave innumerable speeches across the country, and represented the Reformed Church of Apache, Oklahoma, for years at religious gatherings.

> I try to live a Christian life. I'm an elder in the church and I study the Bible like you do as a Christian each day. The symbolism we have in our tribe is the same symbolism that Christ has in the Bible.
>
> I have been an elder in the church for about fifteen years. I represent our church at the American Indian Council Committee, a church organization. Then I had the privilege of being on the General Program Council, one of the top organizations of the church where the programs of the church are reported.
>
> When I was growing up, my mother, father, and the older folks used to say, "Well, look around you. There's not an Indian who lives nearby. You have nothing but white people all over. You've got to go to school." That's all I ever heard. "You've got to learn the white man's way, and you've got to do a little bit more if you can because you have to fight all the time for whatever you get, whatever you want." Loving and sharing is not the white man's way. The white man competes. Among most of our Indian people, love and sharing are the thing. We have extended family clear down to the umpteenth or seventeenth cousin, you might say, and they still have the same blood I have. It might be a drop, but it's there.
>
> If I could have one wish for the Apache people, it would be for them to be Apaches throughout eternity. Forever.[11]

Fig. 60. Mildred Imach Cleghorn, August 1989. Photo by author.

Cleghorn's parents, Amy and Richard Imach, were among the first Chiricahua Apaches to support the work of the Dutch Reformed Church while prisoners of war at Fort Sill. Both parents held positions of authority in the church and were leaders in the missionaries' efforts to recruit other Apaches. Upon release from incarceration, her parents continued their involvement with the church.

Mildred Cleghorn was a practicing Protestant who held deeply religious Christian beliefs, but the last sentence in the interview above demonstrates that she has retained a significant interest in the traditional ways. This was also evident every time she danced during the Mountain Spirit dances at puberty ceremonies. Without hesitating, she wrapped herself in her shawl, stepped into the circle, and danced a step that began among Apache women in the time before time. As she danced, she often closed her eyes and prayed but never said which of the two ways of worship she was observing in her prayers. However, if the next morning was a Sunday, she attended the Protestant church services, as she did every Wednesday evening to sing hymns.

Cleghorn exemplified the modern Chiricahua Apache in that she was able to accept both religious ways and saw no conflict in doing that. But to the end of her days—she died in 1997—she thought of herself as an Apache prisoner of war and expressed a wish to be buried at Fort Sill in the prisoner of war cemetery. Does this last desire indicate a final resistance to the white ways, including their religion? I believe so.

BENEDICT JOHZE, JR.

Born a prisoner of war at Fort Sill on April 18, 1908, Johze is the son of Benedict, Sr., who himself was the maternal great-grandson of Chief Mahko of the Bedonkohe Apaches and brother of three of the warriors—Fun, Tsisnah, and Perico—on whom Geronimo depended the most. Johze, Jr.'s, mother, the granddaughter of Chief Loco of the Warm Springs Apaches, was called Mabel, although her Apache name was Nah-do-yah, which means "getting-down-from-something-one-has-climbed," as from a horse. Both Benedict, Sr., and Mabel attended the Carlisle School.[12] Johze, Jr., first attended school at the Reformed Church's mission on Fort Sill. As an adult, he held many official positions in the Fort Sill Apache tribe from 1930 to 1973.

> I knew [the missionary worker] Miss Ewing. She would go around to the villages in the buggy. She would come over to our house quite frequently at that time. I guess she rode horseback too. I have seen her picture on a horse. She just talked to my mother and father whenever he was there. I guess she talked about the church and the Bible. She probably helped them along with sewing, cooking, or something like that. Looking back on

my father and mother today, I don't know whether to call them "devout Christians" or something like that because they were at church all the time. I used to smell the ladies' cooking in the building there. Of course, I played around the mission all the time. My mother would drive a buggy over there on Sundays. Seemed like that was our place to go all the time. I guess my father was on the consistory when it started. He was always right there with the missionaries and the preacher and James Kaywaykla. I think one of those buildings was a little church. I think I heard one time that they had a curtain right down through the middle because of the tradition.[13] The people who remained here after they left didn't do that. Those farther back—that went to Mescalero—did.

I attended school at the mission school, the last three months or so [that we were incarcerated]. My birthday is in April and so the mission was still teaching the kids there—those that remained—so my mother used to take me over there on a buggy.

We came to church [in Apache] on the wagon, which was something like fourteen miles to the church when they had afternoon services only. Every other Sunday. The minister, Mr. Harper, would come up on the train on Saturday evening and then stay overnight in a little room at the church. They had a little bed for him to sleep on. A little kitchenette. Back then cars were just coming in. Not many people had them. They traveled mostly in wagon, buggy, or horseback, or train. I think there were a lot of Indians who turned out for Sunday services.

At first the Indians used the Presbyterian Church in Apache for Sunday service. They went along like that for two or three years. That's where we used to go to church—in Apache. After that they built a little church south of town. Still standing. My mother was always at the church and the missionaries was always coming to our home to visit and stay around. That's the way I remember it. I always went to church, even when we were in Fletcher and had to come all the way over here in a wagon, but that's what my father did. Every Sunday we would come maybe three or four hours before church and he would visit one family on one Sunday and the other family the next time. I guess he was still an elder. I guess he felt that was his job among the families around here.

Of course, my mother went along with him in the church work. In all that time, after he died in 1918, she just went right along with them in church. I don't guess she ever joined any other church. She stayed there in that church all the time. I was always in church. We sang our Indian songs and they still had an interpreter. Maybe they didn't need one, but anyway they had one. James Kaywaykla. People like John Loco were always speaking Apache. They would always get up and testify to one thing or another. As well as some of the other members.

[Protestantism] was probably what they needed. When these preachers came along, some of them began to talk about it. I guess they could kind of relate to it. Respected it too. [Most of the missionaries] always had nice things to say. Seemed like they all had regard for other people. They wanted to have their people do the right thing to other people. I guess it was the same way among the Apaches.

I was a little surprised when the Father over there [in Mescalero] allowed the Mountain Spirit Dancers in the Catholic Church. I have been over there several times and the elder Fathers there didn't do that. It seems that this Father who came there said the people felt depressed and that they didn't have any pride. The older Apaches. He said in fact the young people didn't know anything about their history or where they came from. He saw that among his congregation. So, I think he got James Kaywaykla's and Eve Ball's book [*In the Days of Victorio*] and started teaching them about their history so that they might have the knowledge. I think what he did there by doing that he thought he would get the Indians to have more pride, to think better of themselves and to improve themselves. I don't know if it worked. I don't go to Mescalero very much, just once in a while. So, I wouldn't know if it worked. I guess he was trying to encourage them in some way. By doing that he thought he might get them interested.

I think the missionaries did the best job they could for the people. I remember a woman who used to be at the Comanche Mission. She came out here in a Model T Ford and would visit all the Apaches and some other Indians. Sometime we would be picking cotton with James Kaywaykla and she would come out into the cotton field and talk to us about the Bible and so on. Yes, I remember her doing that.

Back when I was at Fletcher, about ten years old, I remember getting a book from the church. It was about the only Christmas present I would get. It seemed like our church here was under the Comanche church. Maybe not, but I felt it. I remember when Reverend Harper left. Mr. Reid became the preacher there and he stayed until about 1925 or 1927. Reverend Robert Chaat also preached there, about 1935 or something like that. The preachers to the Comanches would always come over here. We didn't have one here. That went on until about 1954 or 1955. By that time there was only a few of us—maybe four or five—going to church.

As years went by—right after the war or during the war— some of the members were in the armed services, others went into defense work at other places, other towns. My wife and I, we stayed around here during all of that time, so Reverend Robert Chaat finally elected my age group at that time as church officers. They elected me Deacon at first and then later on I became an Elder. I thought I had to look after the church so my brother-in-law and I mowed the lawn and swept out the church for meetings.

After the meeting one time around 1955 a Miss Marcus from the church's headquarters in Michigan came down and said that she thought we had to close up the church because there weren't very many members. She said she would come back later, but in the meantime we were to tell the members the church would consider closing our church. And so we told the people and of course they said, "No, they can't do that. It's our church." And so they talked among themselves. At that time I didn't know who owned the building, whether the Apaches owned that piece of land or what. So, on the Sunday Miss Marcus came back, the whole church was full. They were all in there and I think she brought Reverend Andy Kamphuis and his wife along. They just sat there and observed. Right after that she didn't speak to that anymore. Finally she got Andy to come here. At that time it was just that little church building there, nothing else. Andy brought his trailer house and parked it where the pastor lives now. I began to notice that after Andy came as our regular minister, the different churches and organizations would send other materials and things to the church. When Andy took full charge he began bringing in little kids—didn't matter what they were—Indians or whites—he brought them all in. Gradually he got other people to come to church there. Now, there's mostly Comanches in there and some of my people and one colored lady goes there now. All of the older Apaches died off. So, Andy had to go out and get other people to come there. The times are changing. So, that's the way it went.

My wife used to take care of the books, collections and things. She kept records. Treasurer. From the 1930s on up until Andy came and then she retired. She just turned it over to another person. She also used to work with the kids and put on the Christmas program. She could play the piano and sing and so she had a choir there. I guess she went along about twenty some years doing that. As I said, I was kind of like the caretaker. Once I told my brother-in-law that I thought I wasn't very faithful to the church and I didn't think the folks should put me up as a church officer anymore. And he got mad and said, "Who else?"[14]

As one of only two surviving prisoners of war in the summer of 2002, Johze, Jr., is in an excellent position to describe the events of the past as they concerned Protestantism. It is clear from the above interview that he was resolute in his acceptance of Christianity. His parents, Benedict, Sr., and Mabel, were leaders in the early church at Fort Sill, and so Benedict, Jr., as a child, became indoctrinated at an early age and showed no wish to resist.

MABEL RUTH KEANIE SPEARMAN

Named for Mabel, Benedict Johze, Jr.'s, mother, Ruth Spearman (she doesn't use her first name) was born in the Johze, Sr., home near Fletcher, Oklahoma, on March 10, 1917, four years after her father, a Warm Springs Chiricahua Apache named Carlos Keanie, was released from imprisonment. Keanie's mother was Ban-gi-gah, the widow of Nonithian, a Warm Springs Apache warrior whose

Fig. 61. Contemporary Chiricahua Apache woman Ruth Keanie Spearman sitting on Jason Betzinez's lap, ca. 1919. Courtesy of Ruth Spearman.

father was the noted leader Delgadito. Ruth's mother, the missionary worker Martha Prince, met her future husband, Carlos Keanie, while she worked at the Dutch Reformed Church's mission at Fort Sill.

Spearman attended a one-room country schoolhouse until she was six years old, when her father died of tuberculosis. After a further short stay on the farm, she and her mother returned to the mother's relatives in Illinois. As an adult, Spearman attended business college in El Paso, Texas, and took accounting courses at the University of Texas. She worked in the business field and married a doctor, enjoying twenty-two years with him until he died in June 1991. She is today a sprightly eighty-something who is active in Presbyterian church work in El Paso.

Fig. 62. Contemporary Chiricahua Apache woman Ruth Keanie Spearman, 1997. Photo by author.

One photo in her collection depicts her missionary-worker mother standing beside Medicine Bluff Creek at Fort Sill. A note on the back, written by Mildred Imach Cleghorn, states,

I asked Miss Prince how she made up her mind to come to the mission. [She said] Miss Hospers wrote a letter to her home church asking for someone to come and help her. The pastor asked Miss Prince and after much hesitation she finally decided to go. After she got there she said they were having camp meetings and Mom and Pop [Amy and Richard Imach] were the first people she met. She became terribly lonesome and wrote home begging to go back to Chicago—but they asked her to stay one month, which she did—and she said by that time she loved the place and her work.

For personal reasons, Martha Prince Keanie shared very little information about her marriage and the years working among the Chiricahuas at Fort Sill. Ruth never pressed her mother and grew up "white," as she says. It has only been in the last few years that Ruth has fully acknowledged her Apache blood. Even though our two interviews brought out only a smattering of information, the results allow a glimpse into a lost way of life:

My mother always wanted to be a nurse, but her family said, "Oh, no." They didn't want her to take care of men, so perhaps letting her go to Oklahoma was the alternative.

My mother was not a missionary, per se. She was a worker at the missions, more like a matron in the orphanage. She and Anna Heersma [another worker] lived together—the woman who married Jason Betzinez. My mother was just a general worker. I know she wasn't trained in a seminary like some people are nowadays at least. She was needed as a worker out there and the Mission Board sent her.

My mother was homesick at first, as any young person would be, but eventually she became accustomed to the ways of the Apaches and learned to ride horseback. She just loved the freedom of the country. Eventually she married my father so she must have liked the whole situation. I think they probably met at the church. I have often wondered what the attraction was. She never said one bad thing about my father. Of course, when people die, you forget the bad. But apparently she loved him. She didn't have to marry him. He was always kind and gentle and generous and this and that. My mother wasn't generous. She wasn't stingy, but she held on to that nickel for fear that it would get away from her. That's the Dutch in her. They always say the Dutch are so thrifty and so on.

Many of the children [she cared for] were orphans. Their parents had died from tuberculosis. There was a little girl named Margaret—I don't know her last name or who she belonged to— but one time Mom went home on vacation and she took that little girl with her to Chicago. She was a small girl. Maybe eight years old. I'm sure she was a curiosity back up there in those days.

My mother and father must have been married before that group went to Mescalero because they lived at Whitetail. He worked at the Reservation hospital [as a carpenter], but whether he commuted from Whitetail every day, I don't know. Mother never mentioned living at Mescalero itself. How he got back and forth, I don't know, because he didn't have a car.

I think the reason I was born on the Johzes' property was that our home wasn't built yet. The barn was built first. Mama told me we lived in the barn part while the house was being finished. Maybe I was born in Mabel's house because it was closer to Fletcher, where the doctor was.

My father had tuberculosis and I'm sure he had it before they were married because I have seen a picture of him in his Army scout uniform and he looks thin, emaciated, and sickly. He was confined in the Indian Hospital in Lawton for a time— weeks, months, or a year—but when they knew he wasn't going to recover, he wanted to go home. So they let him come home. We had a sleeping porch on the side of the house and I was not allowed to go on that porch but I remember that I could stand at the door and we could talk back and forth. I don't remember anything we said. He passed away in 1923 and my mother took me back to Illinois. and that was the last time I had any contact with the Indian part of my life.

I remember my father as a figure walking around, but I couldn't say what he looked like. All I have is the picture I mentioned. I think he was of slight build. Even if he hadn't been ill, I don't think he would have been a big, tall man. He wasn't short and squatty, either.

Instead of going to town and playing dominoes or billiards, he was busy in his barn keeping his harness oiled and keeping things neat. The barn had a loft with hay and we had chickens. Our hen used to have a nest under the barn and she would hide there. I reached under there to get eggs and there was this big old bull snake. I have been afraid of snakes ever since.

On Sundays, they hitched up the buggy and the old sorrel horse. I can just see that buggy whip waving around. At the time nothing was paved, of course, around the farm. We had that deep red sand. As the wheels went around, the sand would fly. Yes, we went to church regularly as far as I can remember. I have vivid memories of that church.

I also remember going to camp meetings in Lawton on the ground of the Reformed Church's complex. A Reverend Harper baptized me. How he came there, I don't remember. Part of me remembers going to Sunday School at the Methodist church in Apache, Oklahoma, because I remember a little Easter play we had. I remember saying, "If I were a flower, I'd like to wear a little red rose bud in my hair." I must have been about three years old. That's the only thing I remember about ever going to church in Oklahoma. That was my first and only church performance in my whole life, so it stayed with me.

I remember Miss Ewing. Now, she was a real missionary. She is mentioned in Jason Betzinez's book. Then there was a Miss Dublink. I don't think she's mentioned in his book. I remember Mama talking about all the workers that were there. They had a jolly good time after they got acclimated. They went on picnics with the Indian fellows and did things like that.

Geronimo wasn't one of my mother's favorite people, but she did attend his funeral. I have a photo of his burial site with ladies wearing old-fashioned hats. One of them could have been my mother.[15]

The next interview took place six years later. In the interim, Ruth had had a devastating medical experience that nearly took her life. She very slowly had come back to being herself and was happy to celebrate her eighty-third birthday on March 10, 2000. The next day we began talking.

Too bad I don't remember much about my [Apache] grandmother, Ban-gi-gah. My mother told me she had been shot in the foot, swimming across the Rio Grande either to Mexico or from Mexico. I don't know if she was fleeing the Mexicans or the U.S. cavalry, but she survived. When my father was dying of tuberculosis, my grandmother came from Mescalero to see him. She wouldn't come into the house at Whitetail but slept outside in her bedroll. I don't think that my mother forbade her to come in; I don't think she wanted to, either, because my father was so sick and she didn't want to catch tuberculosis, or she didn't like my mother, or she felt uncomfortable. Probably a little bit of all of the above.

Jason Betzinez was my father's cousin. I called him Uncle Jason although he was not an uncle; perhaps he told me or wanted me to. I called his wife [missionary worker Anna Heersma] Aunt Anna. His mother lived in a little house nearby. I don't think Anna wanted her in the house. They built her a little one-room place. I don't know if she did her own cooking. She was a nice old lady who gave me presents. She always had a sack of piñon nuts which she shared with me.

I have always lived in the white environment and so I think of that as my heritage. But I am reminded of my Indian heritage all the time because I have inherited my father's farm and it's integrated into my life but I don't go around thinking about it. But I do think about Indian people. Most feel their ancestors were taken advantage of—which they were—and run off their native lands and the government took it over. But they're still howling about that. Forget it. It's over. You can't do anything about it. Pro-gress. There are at least two examples of progressive women in our tribe. Mildred and Ruey.[16]

Each has white blood, though. Did that make a difference? Was their white blood an impetus for them or was it in their nature? Maybe the real difference is that some children are not pushable into education and some are.

Religion is very important to some Indians. I think you are right when you say the old Apaches became Protestants for the sake of their children and to be with their children. It stands to reason and I think that would be the only reason. I really don't think they had much incentive on their own to change, but if they were to continue to have any communication with their children, that was the way to do it. They really had no choice. Think of this: the children were little missionaries on their own, weren't they? I wonder if my mother thought of that.[17]

Ruth Spearman's memories were limited by her mother's reluctance to say very much about her experience among the Chiricahuas at Fort Sill. Whether Ruth's father, Carlos Keanie, ever resisted the Christian teachings is now lost to history, but an educated guess is that he, being romantically involved with a Dutch Reformed matron, accepted the tenets without question. Ruth's allegiance to Protestantism has been lifelong, and she knows very little about the traditional religion of her Chiricahua Apache ancestors.

RUEY HAOZOUS DARROW

The daughter of two Chiricahua Apache prisoners of war, Blossom Wratten and Sam Haozous, Ruey Darrow was chairperson of the Fort Sill Apache/Warm Springs Chiricahua Tribe. Blossom Haozous's father was George Wratten, the white interpreter who remained with the Apaches all through the years of imprisonment. Sam Haozous was the great-grandson of Chief Mahko of the Bedonkohe Apaches and the son of Nah-ke-de-sah, the daughter of Mangas Coloradas. During an interview in late 1989 Ruey Darrow talked about the puberty ceremony:

> If the girl believes it's going to mean something to her, then I believe in it . . . for her. I think she can go in and out of that world and be the better for it. There are a lot of things that Apaches teach their girls in those ceremonies. It's eight days of concentrated teaching. Some of the women my age [in her sixties when the interview was conducted] who had the ceremonies have profited, I think, not only because they learned something of how to present themselves to the world, but also it's just a way of life. A girl needs some help getting through the ceremony, even though she's been prepared from the time she was born. I don't know how the girls are doing as far as learning the Apache language is concerned. Kathleen [Kanseah] says her girls [granddaughters] understand some of it because she really talks a lot to them in the old language. But other folks have not done the same. It's kind of like you have to get far enough away from the puberty ceremony to be able to go back. And then you've developed a greater appreciation for it. Some of these people have not gone far enough away.[18]

Every year Ruey Darrow attended the puberty ceremony at Mescalero, driving from her home in Fort Cobb, Oklahoma. Her mother and father, Sam and Blossom Haozous, were among the first Chiricahua Apaches to take an active role in church activities at Fort Sill and showed no resistance. Upon release from incarceration, Ruey's parents continued their sincere involvement with the church. Ruey Darrow practiced no formal organized religion.

LELAND MICHAEL DARROW

In undated, typed notes sent out to tribal members, Michael Darrow, as he is called, the son of Ruey and Robert Darrow and the Fort Sill Apache/Warm Springs Chiricahua Tribe's historian, commented on the education received by his ancestors:

> After the Apaches were made prisoners of war, most of the children were taken away to boarding school. The purpose was to erase all traces of their Indian culture. They were taught that Indians were primitive, ignorant, superstitious savages whose only salvation was to abandon their old ways and become hardworking Christians like the white people. The effects of this indoctrination are still being felt through several generations.[19]

The Missionary Workers and Clergy

HENDRINA HOSPERS

Known far and wide as a friend to the Chiricahuas, Hendrina Hospers worked with the ministers and other personnel at Fort Sill. After the Apaches' release from Fort Sill, Hospers lived with them at Whitetail on the Mescalero Apache Reservation, later spending time in Apache, Oklahoma, Albuquerque, New Mexico, and on the Jicarilla Apache Reservation in Dulce, New Mexico.

> We have to get used to doing everything here [Fort Sill], even conducting a little funeral service, which I have had to do at the grave of Bonalskli [Naiche's son]. He was sick for a long time,

just the result of his hard life. Such a place for that boy to be—dirty and no care whatever. A few weeks ago I was there; he looked so dirty. I mustered up courage—I was afraid I might incur the wrath of old medicine man Tahnitoo and Mrs. Tom—and asked if it would not cool his fevered face to bathe it in cold water. I had taken towel and soap with me. His face lighted up; he said he had not been washed since he was sick, and I believed it; he was so dirty, his hands I really could not wash clean. I put a pillow-case on his pillow and left sheets for his bed.[20]

It is difficult to imagine that the Naiche boy was so dirty that Hospers couldn't wash him clean. Readers must keep in mind that she included the above observations in an article she wrote for a publication that was circulated by the church. Consequently, as had been done in the past by writers for church communiqués and by Superintendent Pratt at the Carlisle School, this description may have been embellished in order to evoke sympathy and its results among subscribers.

FATHER CHARLES POLZER, S.J.

Charlie, as he is informally called by many colleagues, was formerly the curator of ethnohistory at the Arizona State Museum and has served as director of the Documentary Relations of the Southwest, a project focused on the Spanish colonial Southwest. He is an author and expert on Padre Eusebio Francisco Kino and the historical Jesuit missions of northern New Spain.

No missionary, whoever he was, ever got on a horse and rode off into Indian country to preach. What always happened was that the missionary was in consort usually with a military escort and they made a reconnaissance into this area. With the military—four or five mounted soldiers—the missionary was present at an Indian rancheria or a complex of rancherias. They usually had some other Indians with them who were conversant in the other Indian language. Nobody used sign language. Words went back and forth. Usually the Indian interpreters were also knowledgeable of some form of Spanish, not necessarily of the highest.

They would ride into an Indian area and make contact with the natives and then tell them what the benefits were if they were to become vassals of the king. Then the missionary and the military would leave and go back to wherever they were situated. It usually wasn't terribly far away, maybe a hundred miles or so. Then they would wait and see what the Indians decided. Almost invariably, the Indians they visited would tell the Jesuits they would like to have a missionary. The missionary was always waiting to be invited up into Indian territory. The Jesuits were not really in contact with the Apache groups. They were aware of the Apaches, they knew them, they felt the effects of them in terms of the hostilities that they experienced, but they never really made an evangelical move toward them. Some of the Apache groups thought the missions had a good deal going on, some bands of Apaches would come in and make contact with the Spanish settlements, be they haciendas, presidios, or missions, or mission-controlled areas.

When you look at the missionaries and ask the question, "What was their attempt at contact with the Apaches?" the fact of the matter is that we know that some of the missionaries did attempt it, but they either didn't last or they got killed or run out. Of course, they didn't always have the benefit of the Spanish military in trying to reach them because the Apaches saw the soldiers as an immediate threat. The missionaries were willing to work with the Apache if they could and thought maybe they could create peace among the Apaches, but it just didn't happen.

A typical day on the frontier wasn't very much different for the Jesuits or anyone else in terms of missionaries. The basic distinction is that the early Franciscan groups tended always to put a sufficient amount of stress on their monastic life. So there would be communal prayer and two or three people would live together in a tiny community. The Jesuits, on the other hand, never did that. We were always alone. Every man was a single man wherever he was and he kept in contact by correspondence and other forms of communication but not by living together. So, you find a networking among the Jesuits, but you don't find them living together on the frontier. It's a significant difference between the Jesuits and the Franciscans.

The frontier Jesuit's day started with rising fairly early and following the old traditions—no longer followed in the Catholic Church—and that is that Mass was said in the morning because he had to fast. He couldn't eat or drink anything if he was going to celebrate Mass. He had to approach that with full fast and abstinence. After Mass he could break his fast, have breakfast, and move about doing the other tasks. Indians were always invited in to pray and celebrate at that morning Mass. Not everybody came. A lot of women were there, but the men would go out to work in the fields or tend their horses. Sometimes they came on feast days, but other than that they were not expected to be there. For the most part, kids in the mission village would come in and they would be given lessons, sometimes by the priest, depending on the catechism, exercises, and so forth. There would be a stress on music, a lot of emphasis on musical instrument training. They had a pretty good orchestra at some of the missions, full blown. Then there was mathematics and then the Spanish language was taught. Music, math, and Spanish were largely the curriculum that they had.

The day had a kind of a prayer-life to it. The missionary directed community prayers, he did the education, and he did other work as well. At night he usually wrote letters, books, or kept up the mission books. The only thing that would vary the routine would be a feast day. Sometimes they would carry on a fiesta for three days. These were almost all centered on liturgical days on the calendar. The feast of the saints, the feast of the patron, or Corpus Christi. In preparation for some of these days they did a lot of teaching through morality plays. There was a lot of what we would consider entertainment. They were very, very strong on music and dance. They didn't go much for the Indian dances because they looked upon those as being pagan, but of course it makes very little difference.[21]

FATHER KIERAN MCCARTY, O.F.M.

A native of Iowa, Father Kieran moved to Santa Barbara, California, as a youth. There he learned to read, write, and speak Spanish and also developed a love for the Spanish colonial architecture prevalent in the ocean-side city. His interest in Latin American history and the conquest of the New World took him to the Catholic University of America in Washington, D.C., where he received a master's degree and a doctorate in history. He is a Franciscan priest by calling, a historian by education, and a researcher by passion. Father Kieran spent most of the early 1960s in Mexico researching and working as a consultant for the Mexican National Institute of Anthropology and History. He collected records and documents from Spanish colonial times and microfilmed them for permanent records. In 1966 he was part of a team of researchers who uncovered the grave of Jesuit father Eusebio Kino, the founder of many missions in the Sonoran Desert. Later that year he was assigned as pastor at San Xavier del Bac, just south of Tucson. In 1980, Father Kieran took a position as research historian for the University of Arizona Library. At the time of this writing, he is receiving treatment for Parkinson's disease.

Most historians, in writing up the Apache reactions to the Mexican government's cutting down on the rations they had been promised back in 1786, don't mention their faithfulness. I like to mention the fidelity. It was one of the Apache characteristics.

The Apache ethos is not generally peaceful, but the Apaches at the Tucson presidio [not the Chiricahuas] were content with the arrangement of getting rations, at least to the extent of staying at the presidio and not finding any cause to behave differently.

If I were a Franciscan on the frontier trying to convert the Apaches, I would try to first learn what they thought, their own beliefs. As I got to know them, I would hold formal classes in the Christian beliefs.

Christian lessons on the frontier included morality. It's part of our ethos. Love and peace. Bernardo Galvez's policy started feeding the Apaches in 1786. It was successful, which has always been a mystery to me. The number of Apaches who deserted the presidios [to return to their homelands] was exaggerated. They were very loyal. We are talking about fidelity and the fact that this free lunch started in 1786. The Apaches couldn't help but enjoy it. The common opinion about the Apaches was that they raided and killed for no reason at all, but I think they had a plan.

The Jesuits operated in the age of power. They came like visiting wise men to northern New Spain. They had a very religious ethos and still do, but some of the Spanish Jesuits had a strict, domineering attitude. On the other hand, there were delightful Bavarian Jesuits. The Jesuit approach to introducing religion to the natives was very different than the Franciscan approach. The Franciscans had a tradition of hospitality, kindness. The Franciscans were the good guys. St. Francis is universally loved. A kinder man there never was.[22]

FATHER PAUL BOTENHAGEN, O.F.M.

At the time of our conversation in March of 2000, Father Paul had been on the Mescalero Apache Reservation at St. Joseph's Mission for three and a half years. He talked easily and openly of his experiences, remarking that everything he had learned during his religious training did not apply to life and work among the reservation's peoples. He said he has put his academic lessons on the shelf and is letting the people teach him. In response to my recitation of the legend about Calaxtrain and the glass box containing the carved wooden image of the Virgin, Father Paul said the tale was "awesome." Then he read a printed prayer by Archbishop Oscar Romero:

> It helps, now and then, to step back and take the long view.
> The Kingdom is not only beyond our efforts,
> it is even beyond our vision.
> We accomplish in our lifetime only a tiny fraction of
> the magnificent enterprise that is God's work.
> Nothing we do is complete,
> which is another way of saying that
> the Kingdom always lies beyond us.
>
>
> No statement says all that should be said.
> No prayer fully expresses our faith.
> No confession brings perfection,
> no pastoral visit brings wholeness.
> No program accomplishes the church's mission.
> No set of goals and objectives included everything.

This is what we are about.
We plant the seeds that one day will grow.
We water seeds already planted,
knowing that they hold future promise.
We lay foundations that will need further development.
We provide yeast that produces effects far beyond our capabilities.

We cannot do everything,
and there is a sense of liberation in realizing that.
This enables us to do something
and to do it very well.
It may be incomplete,
but it is a beginning,
a step along the way,
an opportunity for the Lord's grace to enter and do the rest.

We may never see the end results,
but that is the difference
between the master builder and the worker.

We are workers, not master builders,
ministers, not messiahs.
We are prophets of a future that is not our own.
Amen.[23]

REVEREND ROBERT SCHUT

Bob, as he likes to be called, has been the pastor at the Mescalero Reformed Church for nearly two decades. Having first met him in 1989 and then visited with him again in March of 2000, I saw that he had the same commitment, the same energy, and the same spirit. He was still just as enthusiastic about his ministry and happy to be working among the three groups of Apaches—the Chiricahua, the Mescalero, and the Lipan—living together on the reservation.

I think if there's anything we as white dominant society people need to learn from the American Indian is the fact of what spirituality is all about. You hear some of our people pray, and even though I don't understand the language, there is beauty, there's authenticity. You know that it's a communion between themselves and God. They just tie all of life together. They'll pray for every member of their family by name and a prayer of from five to ten minutes long is nothing.[24]

REVEREND ROBERT S. OVE

Now a retired Lutheran minister, Robert Ove's first aim in life had been to study drama and become an actor and director. He had methodically stepped toward that goal by acting in high school plays and by starring in the senior class play. At Carthage College he majored in English and minored in psychology and music, eventually switching his minor to education. He qualified for a secondary school credential and did practice teaching at a local high school. After college he worked for two years as a teacher in the two-room schoolhouse at Whitetail on the Mescalero Apache Reservation. In 1955 he seriously examined his Christian faith and entered a seminary. (In April of 2000 he said, "I hope to examine my faith as long as I live. That is the only way to keep it alive.") There he set his sights on the mission field. During his religious internship he found many other areas of church work that he enjoyed as well. He entered the regular ordained ministry and "never regretted my choice."[25]

> Christ loved to get away into the desert to be alone with the Father, but people kept following him. The first time he tried was immediately after his baptism by John. He managed to stay away for forty days. I can see many parallels with the Apache practice of the young boys going off into the wilderness to "prove" themselves. It was their rite of passage. It was where they found their faith firsthand. I can see differences also, but I recall reading about Geronimo's venture into the wilderness when his sister was dying.
>
> I think we have to keep in mind that (1) missionaries and pastors are still human (sometimes more human than others) and

(2) with totally different traditions and backgrounds (much depending on where in Europe they came from and what denominations they were attached to over there), their approaches to mission work among the Apaches were also totally different. When you add personality differences to denominational differences, it makes it very hard to say what the missionaries have done to the Apaches. The response of the Apaches to these missionaries is also very different and involves many factors. There were some good and some bad apples in both the early Spanish and later Protestant basket. Both learned something along the way. Some were genuine and some were misguided. Some were deeply spiritual, caring missionaries who had the good of the people in mind, while others were establishing power bases or building financial empires at the expense of the poor natives. I have read the history of Christianity from the earliest days, and the same is true wherever the missionaries traveled. Some were sensitive, some blundered in like the proverbial bull. But this is true of politicians and professors as well as pastors.

Even non-natives like us who are concerned about native rights can prove to be poor friends whose misplaced enthusiasm has done more harm than good. This is why I tread very lightly. All I have to offer is my love for these people who have become my dear friends and not just objects of my battle for justice. If justice comes as a result of what we write, then I am happy. If our writings only result in better understanding and a feeling of brotherhood with these friends, then I'm content with that.

I remember that Asa [Daklugie] didn't have any trouble with the Old Testament, but he didn't like the Jesus idea of loving your enemies. If the missionaries had more of the love of Jesus, there might have been more Apaches left![26]

Chiricahua Apache Clergy

SISTER JUANITA LITTLE, O.S.F.

Sister Juanita is a Franciscan Sister enrolled in the Mescalero Apache Tribe through her paternal grandfather, who was captured by a band of Apaches near Chihuahua, Mexico, more than a century ago. He was then six years old and was reared according to Apache ways. Today she lives on the reservation.

Our people are a wandering people. Their history is one of wandering all over the southwest and into Mexico. So the Chief, the Leader, the Guide, is a very important person among the people. This Guide has to clear the way. I see Jesus as One who has, first of all, won us a freedom through His suffering and death. He has cleared the way for us but He still walks with us on this journey. He walks with us as guide, as provider, as protector, and healer.

For a long time I thought I was a Catholic Indian, but I'm beginning to see myself more as an Indian Catholic. I was baptized in the Catholic Church. I made my first confession and first communion and was confirmed.

My family really didn't go to church that often. My father was too busy making a living for all of us. Churchgoing wasn't that important. Our prayer life was. My mother [a San Juan Pueblo, New Mexico, native] taught us to pray. A Spanish priest used to come and teach us catechism. I was ten years old before I made my first communion [older than many others] because of the language problem.

It never bothered me to be Catholic and Indian. I guess I never gave it much thought until I was thirteen years old. I asked my father if I could go through the puberty rite. My father said, "You're a Catholic. If you go through the puberty rite, that's not just a social activity. You have to believe what they tell you in the Indian way. You have to take it seriously." So I thought that I'd better think about this. Going on to school in St. Louis and becoming a Sister just took this opportunity away from me.

In my years in Catholic school, the sacramental life of the Catholic Church became very important to me. The Eucharist, the confession. This is what I want to share with my people at home. The Father image is very strong. We understand that. We need much healing. We need nourishment. We will find it in the Church. In the encounter with Jesus, the Healer, the Nourisher, the Protector, the Conqueror of Evil. The Church demands to give all. If you really love God and Jesus, you have to respond in service. When I make that response, when any of us Indians make that response, we make it with all our Indianness. This is the only way we know how to express ourselves. In our Indianness, our language, our prayer form, and our art.

That is why now, through this process, I'm beginning to see that I am an Indian Catholic. I want to tell my people, "You can be Indian and you can be Catholic. They are both the same." Except that in the Catholic Church, we are members, not just of the tribe, but of the worldwide family. We meet the same Jesus. We are healed in the same way. We are nourished in the same way as everybody else. If we can see ourselves in that way, we can see that we are made equal. We are all brothers and sisters with all other nations. That is what it means for me to be an Indian Catholic.[27]

A Few Words . . .

Resistance had many expressions among the Chiricahua Apaches at Fort Sill. True, a small number of prisoners of war accepted the teachings of the Dutch Reformed missionaries without question and became intimately involved in spreading the Word among their friends and relatives. Others, however, painted a thin veneer of Christianity over their traditional religious beliefs and continued to practice, in their hearts, the ways of the ancestors. Still more were able to sincerely divide their loyalties between both ways of worship. All in all, the statements and opinions expressed in the interviews describe the powerful impact and meaning of Christianity over time to diverse Chiricahua Apaches. The thorn in all of this is that the degree of Christianity's general impact within the tribe as a whole, from Spanish colonial days to the time of release from confinement during 1913 to 1914, cannot be determined because of its varying importance in each life.

CHAPTER NINE

Interlude

The twenty-first century will see more and more Indian writers speaking out about their traditions from a stance that rejects western academic interpretation and relies on cultural knowledge to assess the events that affected their peoples. Those circumstances will ultimately pit the continuing credibility of Euro-American constructs against understanding experiences through a cultural lens rather than a higher education. In essence, the knotty matter will become the veracity and applicability of non-Indian, academic analyses to Indian experiences, including those related to religion. Now, though, we are in an interlude and should take advantage of this moment to reflect on where interpretive history and interpretive anthropology has been and try to predict where it will be in the future.

Forcing events that impacted Indian peoples into theoretical frameworks so that they meet western academic standards of interpretation perpetuates colonization. Today's alternative is to encourage readers to make up their own minds rather than interpret for them. And that is what I have done in many instances throughout this book, for I sincerely believe that Kidwell, Noley, and Tinker are absolutely correct—absent a written Chiricahua Apache interpretation of their history, there is no way to adequately and correctly evaluate and convey their experience with Christianity through non-Indian interpretation. Yet until a common usage of language is agreed upon by all parties, the western model must remain.

Certain truths about the Chiricahua Apache experience with Christianity are obvious. Missionaries working among these indigenes, from the Jesuits and Franciscans on the Spanish colonial frontier to the Dutch Reformed at Fort Sill, were partners with their governments in deculturation. Although genocide was also a possibility, this accusation should not be made haphazardly and demands to be proved without a doubt. Still, along with exhibiting the best intentions, the Christian religious personnel in contact with the Apaches attempted to destroy the very culture and people they were committed to save.

Everyone will agree that the Chiricahua Apaches' encounter with ethnocentric Spaniards who believed in the Aristotelian doctrine of superior and inferior races profoundly changed their traditional society. However, it would be nonsense to assert that religious syncretism—blending of dissimilar symbols, acts, and beliefs to produce a new form—characterized this entire experience. Instead, Christianity slowly crept into individual Chiricahua hearts in varying degrees, remained there to take root and blossom, or was discarded in time. Of course, Apache resistance to evangelizing done by the Jesuits and Franciscans also occurred, but again inconsistently, depending on external conditions. Other Chiricahuas walked the "middle ground," maintaining a relationship between the past and present, honoring the ancestors' ways and at the same time respecting the aspects of Christianity that appealed to them. A small number accepted Christian dogma totally.

It is fair to question whether Apache adaptations to Christianity made on the Spanish colonial frontier were sincere or were simply lip-service pronouncements—pragmatic submission—that negotiated and facilitated food, shelter, and survival. James Axtell noted the possibility of deceptive behavior, stating, "The Indians ensured the survival of the native culture by taking on the protective coloration of the invaders' religion. . . . This brand of Christianity often lay very lightly on the surface of their lives."[1] And William Griffen, writing about the Chiricahuas at Janos, added, "Their attitude toward Christianity was one of aloofness and indifference."[2]

Another example of the Chiricahuas' pragmatic and cooperative attitude is clear when one examines the Apaches' interactions with

Catholic religious personnel while confined as prisoners of war in Florida and Alabama. Several Chiricahua men, just a few months off the warpath, sang patriotic and religious songs with the sisters of St. Joseph, an almost absurd situation. And not to be overlooked as well is the fact that while imprisoned at Mount Vernon, Chief Chihuahua asked a priest to baptize his newborn child. Interestingly, it appears that some Apaches accepted Catholicism but, according to the army's Alabama minister, resisted Protestantism—an aspect of the incarceration that needs further investigation and understanding from the academic and Indian points of view.

When the educated young Chiricahuas returned to their imprisoned families from the Carlisle School, the Dutch Reformed missionaries' daily presence at Fort Sill reinforced the tenets of Protestantism most of the young people had accepted. These new leaders then appealed to their elders by word and deed—some would say coercion and blackmail—and eventually, many of the older Apaches, pragmatic still and worried about losing their children once again, followed them into Protestantism.

Today, religious dimorphism is the norm among some descendants of the historical Chiricahua Apaches: both traditional and Christian ways exist side by side. For example, the annual festival held at the tribal complex in Apache, Oklahoma, is also an extended family reunion during which relatives and friends dance, celebrate their heritage, and renew cultural ties. Because the Chiricahuas are still a kinship-based culture, the gathering especially serves as a vehicle to transfer their culture to the next generation. On the Sunday after the event some of the same participants who danced with the Mountain Spirits the night before can be seen attending the Apache Reformed Church, walking along the church's hallway—a narrow passage that is lined with framed old photographs of the first congregants, former Apache prisoners of war.

On the Mescalero Apache Reservation the ancestral paths are also connected to the present time mainly by the annual July puberty ceremony, by the Mountain Spirit dancers, and through singing hymns in the ancestral language during Protestant and Catholic church services. The Mescalero Apache Reformed Church, like its counterpart in Oklahoma, has posted publicly many framed old photos of the first Apaches to join its congregation. Across the highway, at St. Joseph's Mission Church, photos and sketches of Victorio, Geronimo, Naiche, and Cochise look down at the congregation from their positions over the inside exit door leading from the nave to the vestibule. But most significantly, and undeniably characteristic of the long-lasting impact of Christianity on these Chiricahua Apaches at Mescalero, is a magnificent oil painting of Christ as an Apache hanging behind the altar. Nothing more need be said.

NOTES

AUTHOR'S NOTE

1. Opler, *Myths and Tales*, 1. Opler translates *Ussen* as "Life Giver" and states that Ussen "is a nebulous divinity existing for logical completeness rather than because of the functional importance of the concept in Chiricahua Apache religion. . . . This . . . may be a result of Western European influence."
2. A cultural icon, the giver of the puberty ceremony, and mother of Child-of-the-Water.
3. Opler, *Myths and Tales*, 1–2. One of Opler's informants attributed this tale also to the influence of Christianity but without identifying the time and place the story was adopted.
4. Coppersmith, "Cultural Survival," 32–35.
5. Kidwell, Noley, and Tinker. *A Native American Theology*, 185, n. 13.
6. Ball, *Indeh*, 56.

PREFACE

1. Guy and Sheridan, *Contested Ground*, 7–9. A frontier is also a geographical area where power is contested and negotiated, and "in both Latin American historiography and popular culture the frontier was a place to be feared, a spawning ground of barbarism and despotism rather than democracy" (7–9).
2. Kidwell, Noley, and Tinker, *A Native American Theology*, 39.
3. Father Kieran McCarty, interview, 12 January 1999.
4. For more information, see Michael Yellowbird, "What We Want to Be Called," *American Indian Quarterly* 23, no. 2 (spring 1999): 1–21.
5. Shoemaker, *Clearing a Path*, 4.
6. Kidwell, Noley, and Tinker, *A Native American Theology*, 53.

7. For more information about "inculturation," see ibid., 9, especially as they state that the "Catholic Church has asserted domination over Indian belief systems through the doctrine of inculturation, which asserts that God is essential to all cultural experiences because culture is based in experiences of nature, and God is the creator of nature. . . . In the model of inculturation, conversion entails a modification of cultural experience rather than a complete denial of it." This sounds similar to deculturation.

8. Ibid., 56.

9. Ibid., 67.

INTRODUCTION

1. Favata and Fernandez, *The Account*. Forbes states that there are "good reasons for holding that the Athapascans were [in the area] in the 1200s or 1300s" (*Apache, Navaho and Spaniard*, xix).

2. Sweeney, *Cochise*, 339.

3. Stockel, *Survival of the Spirit*, 255.

4. Ussen, the Giver of Life, is the One acknowledged to be all powerful and the One to whom all honor and reference as the ultimate deity is given. Ussen is thought of as the Creator, the maker of world and people, and the source of all supernatural power. Since the creation, however, this Giver of Life has had little direct contact with humankind. Morris Opler reports, "One might say that this deity has been invoked to lend conceptual wholeness to the supernatural world of the Apache." Stockel, *Chiricahua Apache Women and Children*, 4.

5. Hoijer, *Chiricahua and Mescalero Apache Texts*, 1. Chiricahua Apache informant Lawrence Mithlo stated, "At the beginning the Creator existed. Everyone knows about him. And White Painted Woman also existed. Afterwards Child of the Water was born. Killer of Enemies was also born."

6. Weaver, *Unforgotten Gods*, xi.

7. Ibid.

8. Kidwell, Noley, and Tinker. *A Native Theology*, 7.

9. Ibid., 11.

10. Viewing priests as powerful shamans is similar to Gutiérrez's thesis in *When Jesus Came, the Corn Mothers Went Away*.

11. Ancient midwifery practices call for a medicine woman to wash and bless a newborn with tepid water immediately after birth. If circumstances are such that no water is available, the healer's sputum is an accepted substitute. As she runs water over the newborn's body, the medicine woman utters prayers for the child, a practice similar to that conducted by Christian clergy when they baptize.

12. Although a complete description of the unsanitary conditions on the Spanish colonial frontier as they existed in the missions has yet to be developed, it is fair to assume that living and working amid various degrees of squalor were part of the entire mission experience. In view of those unwholesome conditions, the possibility exists that the contaminated water used during baptismal ceremonies could have been the vector responsible for some of the infants' ailments.

13. This information comes from personal experience when, exploring the former Warm Springs Apache Reservation north of Truth or Consequences, New Mexico, in 1991 with a group of the Chiricahua Apaches, I asked a medicine woman to accompany me to a hidden site where I hoped to find relief for a full bladder. Surprised, she commented that one of her duties as a medicine woman was to help women locate these types of sites, far from the eyes of the men, and said that in days long gone, special women in the tribe had similar obligations.

14. For an excellent description of the mission setting, see Spicer, *Cycles of Conquest*, 288–98.

15. Weber, *The Spanish Frontier in North America*, 20.

16. Faulk, "The Presidio: Fortress or Farce?" In *New Spain's Far Northern Frontier*, ed. Weber, 69.

17. Thrapp, *The Conquest of Apacheria*, x–xii.

18. Kidwell, Noley, and Tinker, *A Native American Theology*, 131.

CHAPTER 1

1. Jacobs, "The Meeting of the Two Ways," in *Native and Christian: Indigenous Voices*, ed. James Treat, 187–88. This Cayuga Indian writer believes that syncretism is "the most dangerous response to Indian culture. . . . Even Indian Christians in a search to be relevant . . . have been caught up in the dangerous deception of syncretism."

2. Matson and Schroeder, "Cordero's Description of the Apache—1796," 337. See also Cortés, *Views from the Apache Frontier*, 53.

3. Ball, *Indeh*, 56–57.

4. Boyer, "Folk Psychiatry of the Apaches of the Mescalero Indian Reservation," in *Magic, Faith, and Healing*, ed. Ari Kiev, 417, n. 43.

5. Opler, *Myths and Tales*, 97, n 2.

6. Ibid., 97–98. In many cases it is difficult to ascertain where traditional Chiricahua Apache tales become blended with Christian doctrine.

7. A striking similarity occurs in John 3:5 in the Bible, where Jesus says, "Except a man be born of water and of the Spirit, he cannot enter into the kingdom of God."

8. Barrett, *Geronimo*, 59–64.

9. Hoijer, *Chiricahua and Mescalero Apache Texts*, quotes Chiricahua Apache Lawrence Mithlo saying that after the Menace ate White Painted Woman's small children named Child-of-the-Water and Killer-of-Enemies, "White Painted Woman went about weeping. 'How can people be created on the surface of the earth!' she said. Then White Painted Woman prayed. And it rained. She lay face upward for the water. And her child was born of the water" (1–2). There is a mix-up in chronology here, for if, as Mithlo asserts, in the beginning the Creator and White Painted Woman existed, along with her two children, Child-of-the-Water and Killer-of-Enemies, then the two children were eaten by Menace (see below), and next she was fertilized by rain and gave birth to Child-of-the-Water, he was her third birth but named after the first child, now deceased. However, remember that these creation myths and cultural tales do not have to be logical or even accurate. But they must be believed.

In his notes, Opler adds that the Menace was a huge monster, looking like a man, carrying a knife and a large burden basket in which to put his victims. "There is an independent body of stories about the monster," wrote Opler, "who is probably to be identified with the 'big owl' of other Southern Athabascan myths" (95). With regard to White Painted Woman becoming fertilized by rain, Opler wrote, "Some versions have it that she lay under a waterfall, others that she exposed herself to rain on a mountain top. According to some of Opler's informants, impregnation occurred when the water entered her vagina, others say this occurred when water fell upon her navel or upon her head" (95).

10. Farrer, *Thunder Rides a Black Horse*, 53. White Painted Woman is the symbol of the regenerating, always changing earth and possibly even the manifestation of Mother Earth herself. The eternality of this cultural icon is testimony to her enduring quality and ageless, exalted position. In this way she reminds many Roman Catholic Apaches of the Virgin Mary. However, this is not an example of syncretism because the two impressions remain separate from each other, neither blended in Christian nor Apache thought and practice.

11. Farrer, *Living Life's Circle*, 23. For a different version of the creation myth, see Bourke, "Notes on Apache Mythology," 290.

12. Farrer, *Living Life's Circle*, 27.

13. Ibid., 22–24.

14. Opler, "The Concept of Supernatural Power among the Chiricahua and Mescalero Apaches," 70. This classic article is an essential ingredient to any research on Apache spirituality.

15. Bourke, "Notes upon the Religion of the Apache Indians," 436.

16. The Hebrew and Aramaic term for the Holy Spirit is *ruach*, a feminine noun.

17. Ove, e-mail, 17 June 1999. Ove has deliberately or inadvertently blended conventional Christian belief with traditional Apache religion—a powerful admixture and a good example of syncretism.

18. Opler, *Myths and Tales*, 7.

19. Ibid., 12.

20. Farrer, *Living Life's Circle*, 30–31.

21. In *Living Life's Circle*, Farrer's informant, a Mescalero Apache medicine man named Bernard Second, told her, "To us a cross is the four directions of the universe, coming together, converging; that's the cross to us" (31).

22. Bourke, *The Medicine Men of the Apache*, 479, 499–507.

23. Crossen, *Jesus*, 23.

24. Opler, *An Apache Life-Way*, 197–98. Opler states that for most Apache people, other than the Chiricahuas, Killer-of-Enemies is the culture hero and Child-of-the-Water is a subordinate brother or companion. The Chiricahuas have reversed these positions, and some have eliminated Killer-of-Enemies altogether from their mythology.

25. In *Chiricahua and Mescalero Apache Texts*, Opler states that although Navajo, Western Apache, Lipan, and Jicarilla Apaches consider Killer-of-Enemies to be the principal cultural hero,

By the Chiricahua and Mescalero . . . Killer of Enemies is relegated to a subordinate position, an unenviable position, or is forgotten altogether. In some
versions he figures as an older but more timid brother of Child of the Water,
again as a maternal uncle, or as the step-father of Child of the Water. Some
Chiricahua informants have said that the term Killer of Enemies is synonymous with "enemy" or "white man" and cases have been noted where parents and grandparents will not allow children to utter the name of Killer of
Enemies, giving the children the explanation that it is the name of the "devil"
or an "evil one." (94–95)

26. Opler, *Myths and Tales*, 15–18.
27. Ibid., 66.
28. Debo, *Geronimo*, 434.
29. Kluckholn and Leighton, *The Navajo*, 180. A Navajo origin myth tells of a great
    flood that drove Holy People to ascend to the present world through a reed. At
    about this time, their female lesser deity, called Changing Woman instead of
    White Painted Woman, was created. In time she was impregnated by the sun and
    water from a waterfall. She gave birth to twin sons. Kluckholn writes, "Changing
    Woman is the favored figure among Holy People. She had much to do with the
    creation of the Earth Surface People [ordinary human beings, Navajos]" (181).
30. Opler, *Myths and Tales*, 1–2. The biblical flood is described in Genesis 7–9. Many
    North American Indian tribes have folkloric legends about a great flood.
31. Opler, *An Apache Life-Way*, 195.
32. Ibid.
33. Stockel, *Survival of the Spirit*, 14.
34. Opler, *An Apache Life-Way*, 196.
35. Bruce Chilton explained, "In the epochs before scientific 'laws,' people were more
    apt to see the whole of natural experience interpenetrated with forces that were
    invisible but powerful. A sign was a moment in which that interpenetration
    became tangible; human experience became a transparent lens for the divine, and
    the sign promised irreversible change." Chilton, *Rabbi Jesus*, 152.
36. In *Chiricahua and Mescalero Apache Texts*, Hoijer and Opler state that hoddentin
    represented "growth and vitality" (112). It is also used ceremonially, particularly
    in rites of infancy, healing, and locating an enemy. In *An Apache Life-way*, Opler
    states, "A shaman who got his power from a star could locate the enemy by making
    a cross of ashes on his left hand and holding it up to the star, the morning star.
    This was much used in war. Sometimes the cross was traced in pollen, or abalone
    shell was held aloft in the hand. Then a flash of lightning in the direction of the
    enemy appeared" (215). In the transfer of ceremonies from father to son, one rel-
    ative to another, or mentor to pupil, hoddentin seals the transmission. In *An
    Apache Life-way*, Opler's informant told him, "Then the last night, the last thing
    he will do is to put pollen in our mouths four times, and the fourth time the power
    will come to us" (211).
37. Bourke, *Apache Medicine Men*, 51.
38. Bourke, "Notes upon the Religion of the Apache Indians," 449–52.

39. For more information, see Opler, "Reaction to Death Among the Mescalero Apache," 454–67.
40. Stockel, *Women of the Apache Nation*, 65.
41. Stockel, "A Good Day to Die," 36–41.
42. Opler, *An Apache Life-Way*, 472–77. Several years ago a very powerful Chiricahua Apache medicine man died in New Mexico. He was held in such high regard that one family canceled their daughter's puberty ceremony to wait through the year-long period of mourning.
43. Stockel, *Survival of the Spirit*, 15.
44. Opler, *An Apache Life-Way*, 229–37.
45. The symbolism of ashes to keep evil away is different from the ashes used to bless Catholics on Ash Wednesday, but their common denominator is the religion-related use of ashes.
46. Opler, *An Apache Life-way*, 242–48.
47. For more information on witches and witchcraft, see Opler, *An Apache Life-Way*.
48. In *Chiricahua and Mescalero Apache Texts*, Hoijer and Opler state that most curative ceremonies are rites "performed by shamans who have obtained supernatural power from one of a great number of sources. These sources include natural phenomena such as lightning, morningstar, plants, animals and supernaturals. . . . A ceremony is acquired by an Apache as a result of a personal encounter with these Mountain Spirits." After an experience guided by the Mountain Spirits, an Apache medicine man or medicine woman, "when hired for the purpose, may conduct his ceremony to cure the sick and keep away or drive away epidemics and diseases" (111–12).
49. A story that has recently surfaced among Mescalero Apaches concerns the rock art purportedly etched by Mescaleros into rocks near El Paso, Texas. Teresa Pijoan's informant told her that medicine people would take their patients to these rocks, perform their ceremonies, and then etch the offending ailment into the rocks to give it some substance and to show the patient that the disease had been removed and was now on the rock.
50. In an article, Boyer stated that only thirteen of twelve hundred individuals on the Mescalero Apache Reservation were believed to have the power of a shaman when he explored their culture. Boyer, "Further Remarks Concerning Shamans and Shamanism," 235–57.
51. For more information, see Opler, *An Apache Life-Way*.
52. Anonymous, interview with Pijoan, October 1989.
53. In *An Apache Life-Way*, Opler devotes many pages throughout the book to Apache power. Opler's work in this area has never been matched.
54. Bourke, *The Medicine Men of the Apache*, 550–54.
55. Bourke, *Apache Medicine Men*, 106–7.
56. Ibid., 503.
57. Stockel, *Women of the Apache Nation*, 6. See also Opler, *Myths and Tales*, 15.
58. In *Chiricahua and Mescalero Apache Texts*, Hoijer and Opler note that the puberty rite is also a social function. During the time the Apaches depended on hunting and gathering,

no large section of a tribe could be together for a long period of time. The Girl's Puberty Rite acted as the social occasion. . . . It became the focal point around which the natural desire for tribesmen of a locality to meet, exchange views and property, greet old friends and make new ones, become crystallized. And so the custom arose of expressing thanks and delight that a daughter or close relative had grown to womanhood by playing host and providing food and entertainment for all who cared to come. (104)

Opler devotes several pages to commenting on this ancient ceremony.
59. Davis, "Apache Debs," 10.
60. Esdzanadeha is White Painted Woman's name among the Western Apache. It translates to "Changing Woman."
61. Nicholas, "Mescalero Apache Girls' Puberty Ceremony," 194–204.
62. Basso, "The Gift of Changing Woman," 119–72.
63. The Chiricahuas were often in flight from their enemies during the 1700s and 1800s, and the ceremony then had to be held in an abbreviated form, ranging from a two-hour ritual to the full four days when possible. Regardless of how close the pursuit, the ceremony was never interrupted by the enemy, but there were some close calls.
64. Reverend Robert Schut, interview, 21 March 1989. D. C. Cole, who claims some Chiricahua Apache identity, states that the puberty ceremony was once a reason for raiding; that is, the attendees needed to be fed. *The Chiricahua Apache 1846–1876*, 20.
65. Blossom Haozous, interview with O'Brien, 22 July 1976. A copy of the entire interview is available at the Fort Sill Museum.
66. In *Chiricahua and Mescalero Apache Texts*, Hoijer and Opler state that the

Mountain Spirits are a race of supernaturals who dwell within the interiors of many mountains, according to Chiricahua Apache belief. There they are said to live and conduct their affairs much as the Apache used to do in aboriginal times. The Mountain Spirits conduct a dance and ceremony in which some of their men are masked and appear with their bodies painted in various patterns. Occasionally an Apache is fortunate enough to have a supernatural experience with the Mountain Spirits of a particular mountain, to witness the performances of these masked supernaturals, and to be instructed in the songs, designs, and prayers which belong to the rite. After this Apache returns to the world outside, and to his own people, he masks and paints Apache men in imitation of the supernaturals he has seen, and sends them out to dance at times of widespread sickness or impending disaster. This procedure or rite is expected to establish rapport between the shaman and the original supernaturals from whom he gained his power, and to enlist the aid of the Mountain Spirits in the emergency which confronts the encampment. (6)

67. Opler, *Myths and Tales*, 74–75.
68. Paul Ortega, interview, 16 January 1995.

CHAPTER 2

1. New Mexico Highlands University's historians and paleographers Richard Flint and Shirley Cushing Flint state there were "basically 100 major expeditions during the 16th century. They were led by Spaniards to explore the Americas. But these were not undertakings of the Spanish crown. All but a handful were funded by private individuals, so the leaders of these expeditions had to finance themselves. A person had to get a permit or a license from the king, but the funding was up to them" (*Albuquerque Journal*, 8 October 2001).

2. The Pimeria Alta was the northern part of the province of Sonora, Mexico, and comprised all of the Indians who lived north of a conventional line running from east to west from Cucurpe to Caborca and to the western sea, in all, the extent of the land that is embraced by the line and the rivers Gila and Colorado. See also the preface.

3. Kessell, *Spain in the Southwest*, 79, wrote, "By terms of the *patronato real*, . . . the Spanish crown administered the Roman Catholic church in Spanish America."

4. McCarty, "Franciscan Beginnings," 12.

5. Liss, "Jesuit Contributions to the Ideology of Spanish Empire in Mexico: Part I," 316–18. Canonists of the day asserted that temporal sovereignty came to an emperor, a king, or a prince through God's representative on earth—the pope.

6. Hall, *Social Change in the Southwest*, 29.

7. Griffiths, *Spiritual Encounters*, 22.

8. Weber, *The Spanish Frontier in North America*, 304–6.

9. A group of researchers at the University of Arkansas who study tree ring records have found evidence of a "mega-drought" in the sixteenth century that wreaked havoc for decades and extended from the Sierra Madre Occidental in Mexico and the Southwest to the Rocky Mountains and Mississippi Valley ("Researchers Find Evidence of 16th Century Epic Drought Over North America," U. Arkansas, Fayetteville, press release, 7 February 2000). See also *Dallas Morning News*, 8 January 2001.

10. Clendinnen, *Ambivalent Conquests*, xi.

11. Reff, "Critical Introduction," 30.

12. Ibid., 25.

13. Deeds, "Rendering Unto Caesar," 17.

14. Ures is in central Sonora, about twenty miles northeast of Hermosillo. In 1636 Francisco Paris, S.J., founded the mission San Miguel de Ures on the Rio Sonora. Four years later the church was built.

15. Reff, "Critical Introduction, 35.

16. Ibid., 12, 17.

17. Father Charles Polzer, a noted Tucson, Arizona, Jesuit, differs on the intent of the missionaries. He believes they did not want to destroy the native cultures but wanted to "uplift" the Indians into a more complex world than they had known without denying their antecedents (Polzer, lecture, 14 February 2001).

18. Todorov, *The Conquest of America*, 147.

19 Reff, "Critical Introduction," 1.

20. Constructing an adobe church and quarters for a priest caused a site to be known as a "town" (Kessell, *Friars, Soldiers, and Reformers*, 3–11). The presidios were closer in definition to a garrison than a fort.

21. Kino was born in the north of Italy and became a Jesuit in 1655. He sailed for Mexico in 1670 and was sent to the Pimeria Alta in 1687. Kino was an energetic man, an iconoclast, best suited to the extremes of the civilized world when there were no bureaucrats to hold him back. While baptizing Indians was his mission, during twenty-four years in northern Sonora he also mapped the area, started ranches, and made fifty exploratory forays across the Sonoran Desert toward the Colorado River in search of souls to save and an overland passage to the west. He brought a telescope with him to New Spain and used it, along with his storytelling abilities, to introduce Christian thought to the indigenes. Literature on Kino is abundant. For a brief biography, see Thrapp, *Encyclopedia of Frontier Biography*, vol. II, 786–87.

22. Caywood, "The Spanish Missions of Northwestern New Spain: Jesuit Period," 6.

23. Liss, "Jesuit Contributions to the Ideology of Spanish Empire in Mexico: Part I," 326.

24. Griffiths, *Spiritual Encounters*, 20–21.

25. Kessell, *Friars, Soldiers, and Reformers*, 69.

26. Reff, "Critical Introduction," 41.

27. Kino founded many missions himself and was instrumental in establishing others. Examples are available at www.southwestfrontiers.org.

San Ignacio de Caborica was visited by Kino in 1687, the year he arrived. A Father Pinelli was assigned in 1690 and Father Campos in 1693, probably evangelizing under a ramada until a church was built in 1702.

Imuris was visited by Kino as early as 1687, and a chapel, San José de Imuris, was built by a Father Sandoval in 1691. By 1797 a church was no longer apparent.

Cocospera was visited by Kino as early as 1687, and three years later a resident priest was there. A church, Nuestra Senora del Pilar y Santiago de Cocospera, was built by 1698 but destroyed in Indian attacks. A new church was dedicated in 1704, fell into disrepair by 1730, and was further damaged by Apaches in 1746. A Franciscan, Father Santiesteban, constructed a new church in 1784.

Magdalena was established by Kino as a visita in 1689 or 1690, and Father Campos from nearby San Ignacio built a church beginning in 1705. Kino died here in 1711.

San Antonio Paduano del Oquitoa, a visita in 1690, waited until 1730 for its first church. After 1767 the Franciscans made some additions. The church is still in use and is a rare example of the flat-roofed early Jesuit churches of Sonora.

San Pedro y San Pablo de Tubutama was founded on the Rio Altar by Kino or his fellow Jesuits in 1691. After several churches were destroyed by continuing raids, the Jesuits built a large one in 1764, and the Franciscans added to it after 1768.

Santa Gertrudis de Saric received supplies from Kino in 1698, but the first resident missionary arrived in 1732.

Santa Maria Suamca was a visita established by Kino in about 1701 but didn't have a resident priest until 1732. Suamca was abandoned shortly after the Jesuits were withdrawn in 1767 due to Apache attacks.

Established by Kino at the Pima village of Guevavi on the Santa Cruz River in 1691, Guevavi became a cabecera twice—once in 1701 and again in 1771. Guevavi was abandoned by 1776.

La Purisima Concepción de Nuestra Señora de Caborca was founded by Kino or his fellow Jesuits in 1694 or 1695. Francisco Zavier Saeta, S.J., was the first priest but was murdered. Three churches were built, destroyed, and rebuilt. The last one, constructed in the late 1740s, was destroyed in the Pima revolt of 1751. The present church was begun after 1803.

San Xavier del Bac was originally an O'Odham village. The church, begun by Kino in Bac, became a visita of San Ignacio. The first real church was built between 1756 and 1763. The present magnificent edifice was begun by 1783 and completed by 1797.

San Diego de Pitiquito was a visita of Caborca, probably established by Kino in 1706. The church disappeared by 1730, as did a subsequent church built in the 1760s. The present church was built in the late 1770s.

Atil was a visita of Tubutama in 1747. The ruins are still visible at the small community of Atil.

San Cayetano de Calabazas was a visita of Tumacacori or Guevavi until the 1780s, when it became a Jesuit ranch. A flat-roofed adobe church was completed in 1772 or 1773 and was burned at least once in Apache raids but rebuilt as a church and a residence.

28. Reff, "Critical Introduction," 23, 37, 42.
29. Griffen, in "Problems in the Study of Apaches," 142, discusses the difference in concepts of leadership, influence, and authority among Europeans who selected whom they believed to be native "headmen" to deal with. Relying on the Eurocentric concept of "leaders" to inform their selection, the Spaniards were often surprised when those who were chosen were not looked upon similarly by the Indian population. Citing as an example Juan Jose Compa, a well-known frontier Chiricahua Apache leader, Griffen states, "Mexican officials had labeled him both 'General' and 'Chief' although he does not seem to have been the leader of an important rancheria."
30. Note the difference between deculturation and genocide. The Spaniards initially had no desire to kill the Indians, only to indoctrinate them into Christianity and assimilate them into Spanish society as taxpayers.
31. Bolton, "The Black Robes of New Spain," 264.
32. Griffiths, *Spiritual Encounters*, 23.
33. Polzer, *Rules and Precepts*, 123–24.
34. Cutter and Engstrand, *Quest for Empire*, 114.
35. Weber, *The Spanish Frontier in North America*, 126.
36. Polzer, lecture, 14 February 2001.
37. Weber, *The Spanish Frontier in North America*, 126.
38. Manje, *Luz de Tierra Incognita*, 6, 35, 46.
39. Opler, *Myths and Tales*, 28–71.

40. A number of Indians from diverse bands may have been in this group.
41. Reff, "Critical Introduction," 11.
42. Nentvig, *Rudo Ensayo*, 27, 82. This account is a classic.
43. Arbelaez, "The Sonoran Missions and Indian Raids of the Eighteenth Century," 368. Arbelaez's evaluation of certain Jesuit documents shows that the missionaries often incorrectly listed (exaggerated) the number of livestock stolen or killed during the Indian raids and that total destruction of the mission's property, as frequently claimed in the documents, did not actually occur.
44. Opler, *An Apache Life-Way*, 246–48. Opler identifies the characteristics; I applied them to the Jesuits.
45. The Spaniards may have been relieved to have the Apaches steal their warhorses because they were so heavy that it was difficult for them to navigate the rough terrain. Light cavalry horses eventually replaced the animals, which the Apaches no doubt stole as well.
46. Ricard in *The Spiritual Conquest of Mexico*, 83, states that "conversion took place . . . in three stages: acceptance in principle of the most important dogmas, briefly explained; baptism; and catechism. . . . Haste was at times excessive."
47. Clendinnen, *Ambivalent Conquests*, 36–37.
48. An excellent article describing the missionaries' efforts to cope with the continuing epidemics is Treutlein's "The Jesuit Missionary in the Role of Physician," 120–41.
49. Reff, "Critical Introduction," 42.
50. Ibid., 45.
51. Todorov, *The Conquest of America*, 135–36. Whether the Jesuits tried to combat disease is open to speculation.
52. Reff, "Old World Diseases," 92.
53. Jackson, *Indian Population Decline*, 109.
54. Reff, "Critical Introduction," 23.
55. Park, "Spanish Indian Policy in Northern Mexico," 330. Rubi also praised the "zeal, patience, gentleness of character and the industry with which [the missionaries] instructed the Indians" (Pfefferkorn, *Sonora*, 253).
56. Opler, *An Apache Life-Way*, 5. An entire chapter, pp. 5–76, describes this trait.
57. Taken from a sign in an exhibit at San Xavier de Bac's museum.
58. Deeds, "Render Unto Caesar," 4. The surviving Jesuit documents today are housed at the Archivo General de la Nación (AGN) in Mexico City.

CHAPTER 3

1. Clendinnen has written an excellent article titled "Disciplining the Indians: Franciscan Ideology and Missionary Violence in Sixteenth-Century Yucatan," in which she graphically describes the methods used by the Franciscans to restore and continue order when the natives had caused chaos. *Past and Present* 94: 27–48.
2. Clendinnen, *Ambivalent Conquests*, 46–49.
3. South of Tucson, Tubac is now a well-known Arizona site favored by artists and craftspeople. Several of the historic buildings have been re-created.

4. Kessell, "Friars versus Bureaucrats," 151. See also Elizabeth A. H. John, *Storms Brewed in Other Men's Worlds*, 440, where she states that Anza "saw no hope of true pacification of the Apaches." John also stated that "Rubi suggested that the Spaniards abandon all commitments to the Apaches, which only invited the hostility of their enemies in the interior, and ally instead with the Comanches and Norteños, either to subdue or to exterminate the Apaches." Kessell has also written "Anza Damns the Missions," 53–63.

5. Weber, *The Spanish Frontier in North America*, 229.

6. Michael Stevenson reports in his database (www.southwestfrontiers.org) that Bacoachi was established at the site of an Opata village on the upper Rio Sonora below Cananea. It was first missionized by New Mexican Franciscans in the 1640s and shortly after that by the Jesuits. The first church was built in 1678.

7. Kessell, "Friars versus Bureaucrats," 151. See also John, *Storms Brewed in Other Men's Worlds*, 440.

8. Father Kieran McCarty, interview, 12 January 1999.

9. An excellent study of the mission economy is in an article by Cynthia Radding de Murrieta titled "The Function of the Market in Changing Economic Structures in the Mission Communities of Pimeria Alta, 1768–1821," 155–69.

10. Fontana, "Biography of a Desert Church," 20.

11. Kidwell, *Choctaws and Missionaries in Mississippi*, 85.

12. Murray, "Spreading the Word," 47.

13. Whiting, ed., "The Tumacacori Census of 1796," 2–3.

14. Moorhead, *The Apache Frontier*, 183.

15. Ibid., 183–85.

16. McCarty, interview, 26 January 1999.

17. Griffen reports in *Indian Assimilation in the Franciscan Area of Nueva Vizcaya*, 92–93, that "children of unknown parents [were] listed [in the records] as Apaches" and that "the term 'Apache' was being employed somewhat loosely, whereas other tribe names were applied more specifically." While marriage records were generally incomplete, scattered throughout are references to Apache women marrying men from other tribes in the early to mid-1700s.

18. The number of deaths from dysentery or other gastrointestinal disorders was not recorded.

19. Although the word *egalitarian* is commonly used to describe the Apaches' sociopolitical organization, it may be inaccurate. Leaders always existed, but often informally, without election or appointment. Individuals well known within the group for their specific talents were called upon when appropriate. If it can be said that one leader had more stature than others, it would be the medicine man, considered to be most powerful.

20. Weber, *The Spanish Frontier in North America*, 233. Weber states that by 1793 some two thousand Apaches had settled into eight peace establishments.

21. Kidwell, Noley, and Tinker, *A Native American Theology*, 10.

22. Flores to Ugarte y Loyola and Ugalde, Documentary Relations of the Southwest [hereafter DRSW], Master Bibliography #041-02962. Most letters in the packet

of 102 pages address the viceroy's animosity toward the Mescalero Apaches and his desire to exterminate them.

23. Sauer, "A Spanish Expedition into the Arizona *Apacheria*," 11. Sauer quotes from a journal, but the identity of the writer is missing because the material lacks a front page. This information is the first I have discovered that mentions baptism prior to decapitation.

24. Ugarte y Loyola may have adopted this practice from the Apaches themselves. In DRSW, Master Bibliography #041-3248, letters from military officers dated from February 12 to July 10, 1778, describe the Apache practice of cutting ears off corpses to prove death. Eleven years later, letters between Ugarte y Loyola, the viceroy, and others regarding the successes of military ventures against the Apaches list the number of ears collected from dead Apaches (Ugarte y Loyola to Flores, DRSW, Master Bibliography #041-04336).

25. Chiricahua Apache cultural memories proclaimed that the way one appears at the moment of death is the way that person will look throughout eternity.

26. Weber, *The Spanish Frontier in North America*, 232.

27. Matson and Fontana, *Friar Bringas Reports to the King*, 121–22.

28. Ibid., 122.

29. These days those differences are thought of as left-brain and right brain functions.

30. Matson and Fontana, *Friar Bringas Reports to the King*, 121–22.

31. Ibid., 125–29.

32. Ibid., 127.

33. Michael Stevenson, in his database at www.southwestfrontiers.org, reports that Janos was initially established as a presidio shortly after the Indian uprising of 1684 to defend the settlements in the region. The presidio's full name was San Felipe y Santiago de Janos.

34. The act of exchange itself as an Apache ritual needs further study.

35. Och, *Missionary in Sonora*, 179–80.

36. For a detailed description of later trading and raiding activities, see Hatfield, *Chasing Shadows*.

37. More research is needed to fully comprehend this complex set of interactions.

38. More research is needed to fully understand this situation.

39. Archer, "The Deportation of Barbarian Indians," 377.

40. Ibid., 380.

41. Ibid., 379. Cuba was a dumping ground for many outcasts other than Indians. Vagabonds, army deserters, gamblers, and others considered corrupt or vice ridden were put on the ships to Havana.

42. Ibid., 384.

43. Ibid., 385. With Mexico's independence from Spain, policies of exiling Indians ended for a time before being reinstated against the Yaqui and Maya Indians.

44. Ugarte y Loyola, Denojeant, Grimarest, DRSW, Master Bibliography #041-04318. Also Ugarte y Loyola and Tovar, DRSW, Master Bibliography #041-04319, and Ugarte y Loyola, Grimarest and Denojeant, DRSW, Master Bibliography #041-04321.

45. Deeds, "Indigenous Responses to Mission Settlement in Nueva Vizcaya," 300.

46. In later years this military tactic was expanded to eventually include Chiricahuas as scouts against their own people. For example, U.S. General George Crook used Apaches against each other and explained, "Nothing breaks them up like turning their own people against them" (McDermott, *A Guide to the Indian Wars*, 61).

47. Matson and Fontana, *Friar Bringas Reports to the King*, 67, 74–75.

48. Officer, *Hispanic Arizona*, 76.

49. Griffen, *Apaches at War and Peace*, 106.

50. Park, "Spanish Indian Policy," 231.

51. McCarty, ed., *A Frontier Documentary*, 17. "Peninsular Spaniards" were those born in Spain.

52. Ibid., 20–21. McCarty believes that the Apaches mentioned in this letter were the Pinal Apaches.

53. Stevens, "The Apache Menace in Sonora," 219.

54. Griffen, *Apaches at War and Peace*, 208.

55. Cruikshank, "Oral History, Narrative Strategies, and Native American Historiography," 10.

CHAPTER 4

1. Weber, *The Mexican Frontier*, 45–46.

2. Ibid., 51.

3. Ibid., 207.

4. Ibid., 52.

5. Hall, *Social Change in the Southwest*, 238.

6. Weber, *The Mexican Frontier*, 274. This is the oldest treaty still in force between the two countries.

7. Hatfield, *Chasing Shadows*, 14.

8. Ibid., 217.

9. Ibid., 1.

10. Ibid., 15.

11. Ibid., 2.

12. Prucha, *American Indian Policy in Crisis*, 30–72.

13. A record of the testimonies is found in *Memorials and Affidavits*.

14. Prucha, *American Indian Policy in Crisis*, 31–32.

15. A list of the denominations and their assignments to reservations can be found in Prucha, *Documents of United States Indian Policy*, 142–43.

16. For an excellent discussion of this subject, see Keller, "Christian Indian Missions" and "Church Joins State to Civilize Indians."

17. While many agents had filled their positions with honor and labored selflessly for the welfare of the Indians, others abused their trust and brought discredit to the office. In 1868–1869, President Grant first sought to correct the situation by appointing army officers as agents, but in 1870 Congress prohibited the action. Grant then appealed to the religious denominations.

18. McDermott, *A Guide to the Indians Wars of the West*, 4–7.

19. Illick, "Some of Our Best Indians Are Friends . . . ," 284.
20. Clum was born on September 1, 1851, on a farm in New York State. He completed one year at Rutgers College in New Brunswick, New Jersey, and then became a weather observer at Santa Fe, New Mexico. A member of the Dutch Reformed Church, with which Rutgers College was then affiliated. He arrived there on August 8, 1874. Thrapp describes him as being "brash, impudent, contentious and nearly impossible to get on with . . . but he was also brave, intelligent, reliable in action, probably honest and, in sum, a fine agent." Thrapp, *Encyclopedia of Frontier Biography*, vol. I, 287.
21. Fritz, *The Movement for Indian Assimilation*, 135–67.
22. For a full depiction of the events, see Hatfield, *Chasing Shadows*.
23. For an informative discussion of the warpath language, see Opler, "Chiricahua Social Organization," 231.
24. Bourke, *On the Border with Crook*, 485.
25. Known originally as the Castillo de San Marcos, the fort is the oldest masonry fortress in North America. The Castillo has served not only Spanish but also British and American forces as the key defense of early Florida and its capital city, St. Augustine.
26. Numbers are not firm.
27. Barrett, *Geronimo*, 79–80.
28. Stockel, *Survival of the Spirit*, 289, n. 10.
29. Ibid. While several descriptions of the Mountain Spirit dance have been documented, none is better than John Bourke's "The Medicine Men of the Apache," 582–85.
30. Sister Mary Albert, telephone conversation with author, 5 July 1991.
31. Stockel, *Survival of the Spirit*, 117.
32. Ball, *In the Days of Victorio*, 195, 197. Kaywaykla was later sent to the Carlisle School as well.
33. The Apache men were Naiche, Geronimo, Mangus, Perico, Fun, Ah-nan-dia, Na-pi, Motsos, Chappo (Geronimo's son), Yahnozha, Tissnolthos, La-zie-yah, Kilth-se-ga-ah, Zhonne, Pae-she, Hunlona, and Goso.
34. Plans to fortify the Pensacola, Florida, harbor were prepared in 1822, in anticipation of the selection of Pensacola as the site of the principal navy depot on the Gulf of Mexico. To secure the approaches to the navy yard from foreign invasion, the U.S. Army Corps of Engineers constructed Fort Pickens in 1829–1834.
35. Woody Skinner, conversation with author, 21 June 1991.
36. Bearss, *Historical Structure Report: Fort Pickens*, 769, 772. Two other train cars with the women and children aboard proceeded eastward to Fort Marion.
37. *Pensacola Commercial*, 5 April 1887.
38. *The Pensacolian*, 11 June 1887, quoted in *Historical Structure Report*, 780–81. Woodward B. Skinner's booklet, *Geronimo at Fort Pickens* (Pensacola, Fla.: Skinner Publications, 1981), tells almost the same story but increases the number of spectators to five hundred and cites an advertisement in the local newspaper about the excursion. Skinner's description does not include the date.

39. Wheatley, "The Caged Tigers of Santa Rosa," n.p. Quoted in Skinner, *The Apache Rock Crumbles*, 214.

40. Opler, *An Apache Life-Way*, 224–29.

41. Ibid., 227–28.

42. Radding, "Cultural Boundaries," 120–21.

43. The location of the Alabama prisoner of war camp is today called Searcy Hospital, a State of Alabama mental institution. In the early 1700s, when the territory was Spanish, it was a fort on the Mobile River that served as a port of entry and separated the Spanish from the American landholdings in that area of North America. The fort was subsequently abandoned because of drinking water problems and the medical peril from omnipresent mosquitoes, but the land continued to be utilized by the military. In 1811, the grounds contained a former military cantonment, arsenal, and barracks and were home to soldiers fighting wars with local Indians. In 1824, Congress authorized the construction of arsenal buildings, and when these were completed, U.S. soldiers were stationed there until 1861, when Confederate Alabama troops took possession. After the Civil War, the property reverted to the United States and was occupied as a barracks until 1900. Eleven original buildings of the arsenal, erected in the 1830s, were still standing in 1992 and had been under continuous maintenance for more than 160 years.

44. Ball, *Indeh*, 138–39, 152–53.

45. For a complete description of this tragedy, see Stockel, *Survival of the Spirit*.

46. Arthur Capell, interview, 24 June 1991.

47. Belinda Jones, interview, 24 June 1991.

48. Turcheneske, Jr., *The Chiricahua Apache Prisoners of War*, 21.

49. Letter from Eustis to Hemenway, 5 January 1888. No further identity of the "little interpreter" is available. George Wratten usually served in that position at Mount Vernon, but he could never be described as "little," so there must have been a second interpreter, possibly a child. Letter is in file at the Frisco Native American Museum, Frisco, N.C. (hereafter FNAM).

50. Patric Howley, conversation with author, 27 August 1999. Howley had strong feelings about the nation's treatment of all Indians, not only the Apaches, in the 1800s. He said, "What occurred was a tragedy. What has been done to them is similar to the horror that was done to the Jews by Hitler."

51. Skinner, *The Apache Rock Crumbles*, 295.

52. FNAM, Shapard, "Prison Life Continues in Alabama," 171, unpublished manuscript.

53. The actual identity of these two females remains cloudy. They could have been wife Zi-yeh and daughter Eva, but it is also possible—as rumor has it—that Geronimo took a young wife while at Mount Vernon and the child was the product of that 1888 marriage.

54. Skinner, *The Apache Rock Crumbles*, 295–96.

55. Ibid., 294. Go-kliz was Chief Naiche's brother-in-law, having married Naiche's half sister. He had been one of the U.S. scouts working against the Chiricahuas. He died at Fort Sill in 1901.

56. FNAM, report by Bourke appended to letter to adjutant general, 5 July 1889.

57. Marion Stephens's memoirs are housed at the Manuscripts Division, Sterling Memorial Library, Yale University, New Haven, Conn.

58. Articles written by Sophie Shepard about her experiences at Mount Vernon can be found in *Lend a Hand*, January 1890, 37–42; March 1890, 163–66; and May 1890, 333–37.

59. FNAM, letter from Kellogg to adjutant general, 17 November 1889.

60. Searcy Hospital Christmas card, 1989.

CHAPTER 5

1. Stockel, *Chiricahua Apache Women and Children*, 20.

2. Ibid.

3. Ibid., 20–21.

4. Ibid., 21.

5. Ibid., 21.

6. Ibid., 23.

7. Opler, *An Apache Life-Way*, 15–17.

8. Ibid., 25.

9. Stockel, *Women of the Apache Nation*, 31.

10. In an interview with the author, the late Mildred Imach Cleghorn, born a prisoner of war and later chairperson of the Fort Sill Chiricahua/Warm Springs Apache Tribe, told me that her mother had punished her and her cousin because they had set the barn on fire. "We were so small," she said, "that we could fit into a gunny sack. I remember [my cousin] sitting looking at me and we were crying [inside the gunny sack]. . . . Later I could never get her to admit that she did that. . . . She just said, 'Oh, I wouldn't do that'" (Stockel, *Women of the Apache Nation*, 130).

11. Pratt's papers are at Yale University's Beinecke Library, WA MSS S-1174.

12. These Indian prisoners left in 1878, and eight years later the Chiricahua Apaches arrived.

13. The Hampton Normal and Agricultural Institute was founded in 1868 as a private, nonsectarian, coeducational institution of higher education to prepare promising young African American men and women to lead and teach their newly freed people. The school was on the banks of the Hampton River in Hampton, Virginia, near Chesapeake Bay. It was later renamed Hampton Institute and, still later, in 1984, became Hampton University.

14. Landis, "Carlisle Indian Industrial School History," 3.

15. In 1882 Congress authorized $67,500 as that year's total appropriation for Indian education.

16. Adams, *Education for Extinction*, 12.

17. "Manifest Destiny" was a slogan under which American expansion westward was legitimized. Historian Robert Utley wrote in *The Encyclopedia of the American West*, "Manifest Destiny provided a comforting justification for what in reality was self-serving gain" (272).

18. I am grateful to David Wallace Adams for writing *Education for Extinction:*

American Indians and the Boarding School Experience, 1875–1928, from which these four Indian education experiences have been borrowed. However, the conclusions are mine.

19. Betzinez, *I Fought with Geronimo*, 153.

20. Tatum, *Our Red Brothers*, 361. The "King's Daughters' Circle" was a group for young Protestant women.

21. Adams, *Education for Extinction*, 167.

22. Ibid., 171.

23. Ibid., 168.

24. Ibid., 168–69.

25. Ruey Darrow, conversation with author, May 1991.

26. Mildred Imach Cleghorn, conversation with author, September 1993.

27. Ball, *In the Days of Victorio*, 199–200. James Kaywaykla entered the school on April 30, 1887, and remained until 1898, when he returned to his imprisoned people at Fort Sill, Oklahoma. James later married Dorothy Naiche, the daughter of Chief Naiche, who himself was the son of Cochise.

28. Contemporary Chiricahua Apache woman Kathleen Kanseah's family name was Cheez-lay-teed-lay, but this obviously was too much for anyone to record, and so her male ancestor was arbitrarily named Smith.

29. Terry, "Naming the Indians," 304. Members of the military also had problems with the Apache names and reacted similarly. When a name was too difficult for a soldier to record in an official ledger, he simply substituted an Anglicized name. As time passed, the original names faded into oblivion unless they were kept alive by oral history and oral tradition.

30. The late Mildred Imach Cleghorn told me that her father's Apache name was Enohm, but he took the name of a farmer, Imach, with whom he worked as part of the outing system at Carlisle.

31. Stockel, *Survival of the Spirit*, 119.

32. Ibid., 119–20.

33. Jason Betzinez was the coauthor of a well-known book, *I Fought with Geronimo*. It must be noted that all of the information in the book is subjective and Betzinez's opinion only. Too many readers have, in the past, taken his words quite literally and have assumed that his point of view was shared by all Apaches. That was and is still not the case.

34. Pratt to Commissioner, 24 May 1889. FNAM, Frisco, N.C. Oddly, Pratt's reference to 106 students having been brought to Carlisle from Mount Vernon Barracks was incorrect. Most, if not all, were actually taken from their parents at Fort Marion in St. Augustine, Florida. Also, his reference to "venereal taint" was a transparent attempt to lay blame for the illness among Chiricahua Apache children on conditions beyond his control. There is no evidence that his statement was taken seriously. Finally, his statement about "sifting" the Chiricahuas and "the unhealthy ones disposed of" is chilling and reminiscent of the attitudes of those responsible for the Holocaust in Europe.

35. Allegedly, this vast unmarked graveyard is the same one that contained adults who died at Mount Vernon. If the site is truly as identified, it is inaccessible today due

to thick brush and undergrowth.

36. *Carlisle Arrow*, 9 March 1905, as quoted in Landis, "Carlisle Indian School History," 11–12.

37. Eustis to Hemenway, 5 January 1888, FNAM.

38. Pratt, *Battlefield and Classroom*, 297. Each publication contained a certain amount of information designed to put the best-possible face on the activities at Carlisle.

39. Landis, e-mail communication, 17 June 1998. I have been unable to find documentary proof of this assertion.

40. Prucha, ed. *Documents of United States Indian Policy*, 143. Catholic agents were assigned to the following reservations: Tulalip and Colville in Washington Territory, Grande Ronde and Umatilla in Oregon, Flathead in Montana Territory, and Grand River and Devil's Lake in Dakota Territory.

41. Prucha, *The Churches and the Indian Schools*, 39, 166.

42. *The Indian Helper*, 16 September 1898.

43. Ibid., 14 October 1898.

44. Ibid., 28 October 1898.

45. Ibid., 23 September 1898.

46. Ibid., 2 December 1898.

47. Ibid., 16 December 1898.

48. Ibid., 7 October 1898.

49. Ibid., 14 October 1898.

50. Ibid., 9 December 1898.

51. *The Salt Lake Tribune*, 29 July 2001.

52. Radding, *Wandering Peoples*, 250.

53. Ball, *Indeh*, 151.

54. Ibid., 290.

55. Schultz, *The Seminole Baptist Churches of Oklahoma*, 5–6.

CHAPTER 6

1. Reaching this agreement was tedious and complicated. Turcheneske, Jr., has described the process in detail throughout his book *The Chiricahua Apache Prisoners of War*.

2. Harper, "Missionary Work," 329. Soldiers blocked the missionaries' access to the Apaches, but one pious young enlisted man, racked with guilt, finally permitted entry to the villages. See also Stockel, *Survival of the Spirit*, 221.

3. Arthur Capell, interview, 24 June 1991. Four carloads of the Apaches' property, including clothing, burned. Published accounts stated that the loss occurred through the negligence of the railroad. See also Stockel, *Survival of the Spirit*, 199.

4. Capell, interview, 24 June 1991.

5. Stockel, *Survival of the Spirit*, 201.

6. Ibid., 210.

7. 1904 was the first year they could purchase their needed farm equipment. See Stockel, *Survival of the Spirit*, 220.

8. Stockel, *Survival of the Spirit*, 220.

9. Ibid., 204. Before statehood in 1907, many Catholic- and Protestant-run schools were teaching Oklahoma youngsters. The government schools taught Indian children.

10. DeJong, *The Dutch Reformed Church in the American Colonies*, 149.

11. Turcheneske, Jr. *The Chiricahua Apache Prisoners of War*, 71.

12. Ruey Darrow, conversation with author, 9 January 2002.

13. Radding, *Wandering Peoples*, 264.

14. Ibid., 250.

15. University of Oklahoma, Western History Collections [hereafter UOWHC]. Jason Betzinez Papers, Box 35-Minor, pp. 126–30.

16. Turcheneske, *The Chiricahua Apache Prisoners of War*, 71–72.

17. This is an original conclusion.

18. Coppersmith, "Cultural Survival," 126.

19. Western Theological Seminary of the Joint Archives of Holland, Holland, Michigan [hereafter JAH]. *Report of the Women's Executive Committee* (June 1903), 67.

20. This is an original conclusion.

21. See the interview with Ruth Spearman, whose mother went from Illinois to Oklahoma as a result of an announcement from the pulpit of her Illinois Dutch Reformed Church. Betzinez lauds several of the female "missionaries" whose descriptions indicate that they were workers, rather than church officials, who were empowered to preach. Along with Maud Adkisson, Anna Heersma (who became Betzinez's wife), Martha Prince, and Mary Ewing were initially the most influential in working with the Indian children.

22. Kathleen Kanseah, conversation with author, 4 July 1999.

23. Jason Betzinez had attended the Carlisle School and Carlos Keanie had attended the Chilocco Indian School in Oklahoma, an off-reservation boarding school also intended to assimilate indigenous students into mainstream American life. Ruth Spearman, Keanie's daughter, doesn't know how he was selected or why he attended this school and not Carlisle.

24. Various conversations between Ruth Spearman and the author.

25. This is an original conclusion.

26. Coppersmith, "Cultural Survival," 120–23.

27. Only a minority of the tribe participated in Reformed Church activities on a regular basis. Most of those who chose to participate represented, according to Euro-American standards, the best educated. Lists have been reproduced verbatim, so spelling varies, dependent on the recorder's ability.

28. Ball, *Indeh*, 56.

29. Debo, *Geronimo*, 431.

30. This is an original conclusion.

31. The Executive Committee had met and appointed the following committees: Prayer Meeting, Lookout, Social, and Sunday School.

32. UOWHC, Chaat, Secretary's Book, 90–91, 106–7, 126–28. Amy Imach, born at Mount Vernon in 1890, was the daughter of interpreter George Wratten and his Chiricahua Apache wife, Annie. Amy married Warm Springs Chiricahua Apache

Richard Imach, a former Carlisle student. One daughter was born to the marriage, Mildred Imach Cleghorn. Amy was the full sister of Blossom, who married Sam Haozous. In 1908 Amy would have been eighteen years old.

33. JAH, *Reports of the Women's Executive Committee of the Board of Domestic Missions.*
34. Ibid. (1899), 28.
35. This quote supports my assertion regarding the students' identifying more with the missionaries than with their families.
36. An original conclusion.
37. JAH, *Reports of the Women's Executive Committee of the Board of Domestic Missions* (1901), 19.
38. Stockel, *Survival of the Spirit*, 265.
39. JAH, *Reports of the Women's Executive Committee of the Board of Domestic Missions* (June 1902), 63.
40. Geronimo may have remembered that he was denied baptism in Alabama and, for the very important reason of saving face, did not want to try again right then.
41. JAH, *Reports of the Women's Executive Committee of the Board of Domestic Missions* (January 1903), 338. Bergen was an RCA minister visiting from Holland, Michigan.
42. *The Lawton Constitution*, 18 February 1909.
43. JAH, *Reports of the Women's Executive Committee of the Board of Domestic Missions* (July 1903), 105.
44. Ibid.
45. Ibid. (September 1903), 176.
46. Ibid. (October 1903), 214.
47. Ibid. (August 1904), 155.
48. Murphy, *So Lingers Memory*, 106.
49. JAH, *Reports of the Women's Executive Committee of the Board of Domestic Missions* (January 1905), 346.
50. Ibid. (February 1905), 366.
51. Ibid. (April 1905), 454.
52. Ibid., 454–55.
53. A side comment made by Raymond Loco.
54. JAH, *Reports of the Women's Executive Committee of the Board of Domestic Missions* (May 1905), 27.
55. Stockel, *Women of the Apache Nation*, 65, 68.
56. JAH, *The Missionary Leaflet*, 5–8.
57. Ibid. (June 1906), 5–8. Maurice died at Mescalero soon after the released prisoners of war settled there in 1913.
58. Ibid. I could find no further information on David Reno.
59. Ibid. When released from imprisonment and given land, Harry sold the property and used the money for an education at the Chilocco Indian School, where he was taught a printer's trade. Debo reported that he "began working for the *Arkansas City (Kansas) Traveler,* and for many years until his . . . retirement he served as foreman of its commercial printing department (*Geronimo,* 453).
60. JAH, *Report of the Committee on Indian Work* (1907), 29–30, 33–34.

61. JAH, *The Day Star,* February 1900–March 1909.
62. Ibid., February 1900.
63. JAH, *The Day Star,* June 1900.
64. Bruce died of tuberculosis in 1910, age twenty, while still a prisoner at Fort Sill.
65. Debo reports that upon release from incarceration in 1914, Arthur and his wife remained in Oklahoma and lived for a time on their farm. "Then they sold it, and he took a position in the civil service. They made their home in Lawton. Throughout his long life—he died in 1967—he was an important source of information regarding the life of Geronimo" (*Geronimo,* 453).
66. Uncas was the son of the scout Noche, but no further information is available.
67. JAH, *The Day Star,* March 1901.
68. Ibid., May 1901.
69. Vincent Binday died at Fort Sill in 1909.
70. JAH, *The Day Star,* July 1906.
71. Ibid., September 1906.
72. Ibid., March 1909.
73. Coppersmith, "Cultural Survival," 124.

CHAPTER 7

1. This process is expertly documented in Turcheneske, *The Chiricahua Apache Prisoners of War,* 105–87, and in an article written by Brenda Haes titled "Fort Sill, the Chiricahua Apaches, and the Government's Promise of Permanent Residence," *Chronicles of Oklahoma* 78, no. 1 (spring 2000): 28–43.
2. Ball, "St. Joseph's Mission at Mescalero," 45. Note the similarity here with the Spanish colonial frontier priests traveling from cabeceras to visitas.
3. Emerson, *Among the Mescalero Apaches,* 75.
4. Numbers have always varied.
5. For a detailed description of the church's early organization and activities, see the interview with former prisoner of war Benedict Johze, Jr., in the next chapter.
6. FNAM, "Record of Proceedings of Conference with Apache Indians," 2–3.
7. Turcheneske, Jr., "Disaster at White Tail," 130, n. 36.
8. Ibid., 121.
9. Ibid.
10. Ove and Stockel, *Geronimo's Kids,* xii, and Stockel, *Women of the Apache Nation,* 68.
11. Dorlie Kazhe, interview with Stallings, 5 July 1993.
12. Information in author's files collected over the years.
13. Ove and Stockel, *Geronimo's Kids,* 88. He was referring to unscrupulous reservation agents.
14. Ibid., 140, n. 12. This story has many versions among Indian tribes.
15. Sister Juanita Little, conversation with the author, August 1993.
16. Coppersmith, "Cultural Survival," 185. I disagree.
17. A personal observation based on two decades of participating in the Oklahoma festivities.
18. Turcheneske, Jr., "Disaster at Whitetail," 125.

19. Carlos Keanie and his missionary-worker wife, Martha Prince, returned to Oklahoma, where their daughter, Ruth Spearman, was born.
20. Farrer and Second, "Coming of Age," 56, 58.
21. Ove and Stockel, *Geronimo's Kids*, 106–7.
22. Mildred Cleghorn, interview, 8 August 1989.
23. Coppersmith, "Cultural Survival," 184. The 1994 ceremony, according to Coppersmith, was "full of political and cultural complexities" (194).
24. Stockel, *Women of the Apache Nation*, 138, and *Chiricahua Apache Women and Children*, 93.

CHAPTER 8

1. Sweeney, *Cochise*, 339.
2. Taza died of pneumonia while in Washington, D.C., and is buried in the Congressional Cemetery.
3. Roe, "The Mission Field XXIV," 7–11 September 1911. Naiche had been a Christian for nine years when he made these remarks.
4. Naiche, interview with ?, 9 March 1915. Copy in author's collection.
5. Page, *In Camp and Tepee*, 241.
6. Debo, *Geronimo*, 432–33.
7. Ibid., 431.
8. Ball, *Indeh*, 56–59. Daklugie returned from Carlisle steeped in the Protestant faith. Here he gives the impression that he has attended a Catholic church, St. Joseph's Mission on the reservation, because of his affection for the Franciscan priest, Father Albert Braun.
9. Roe, "The Mission Field XXIV," 7–11 September 1911. I thank Miriam Perret in Wales for sending me this copy of "The Mission Field."
10. Darrow, "Notes from Tribal Historian," 2.
11. Mildred Cleghorn, interview, 8 August 1989.
12. Griswold, "The Fort Sill Apaches," 68–69.
13. This reference is to the mother-in-law-avoidance taboo.
14. Benedict Johze, Jr., interview, 17 September 1993.
15. Ruth Spearman, interview, 23 April 1994.
16. The late Mildred I. Cleghorn and the late Ruey H. Darrow.
17. Spearman, interview, 11 March 2000.
18. Stockel, *Women of the Apache Nation*, 153–54. The "distance" Ruey Darrow mentioned is emotional, not physical.
19. Darrow, "Notes from Tribal Historian," 2.
20. Hospers, "The Mission Field XXIII," June 1910.
21. Father Charles Polzer, interview, 27 January 1999.
22. Father Kieran McCarty, interviews, 5 January 1999, 12 January 1999, 26 January 1999.
23. Father Paul Botenhagen, conversation with author, 24 March 2000.
24. Reverend Robert Schut, interview, 21 March 1989.
25. Ove and Stockel, *Geronimo's Kids*, xviii.

26. Reverend Robert Ove, e-mails, 12 June 1999, 16 June 1999, 17 June 1999, 18 June 1999.
27. Treat, ed., *Native and Christian*, 209–18.

CHAPTER 9

1. Axtell, "Some Thoughts on the Ethnohistory of Missions," 39.
2. Griffen, *Apaches at War and Peace*, 65, n. 11.

BIBLIOGRAPHY

PRIMARY SOURCES

Manuscript Materials, Unpublished Documents, Collections

Darrow, Leland Michael. "Notes from Tribal Historian." Typescript, n.d.

Frisco Native American Museum, Frisco, N.C., Chiricahua Apache Collection.

Griswold, Gillett. "The Fort Sill Apaches: Their Vital Statistics, Tribal Origins, Antecedents." U.S. Army and Missile Center Museum Archives. Fort Sill, Okla., 1970. Unpublished.

Joint Archives of Holland Collection. Western Theological Seminary, Holland, Mich.

Murphy, Polly. *So Lingers Memory—Inventories of Fort Sill, OK, Cemeteries: Main Post, Apache Indian, Old Fort Reno, Comanche Indian and Comanche Mission Cemeteries, 1869–1985.* Typescript, 1985.

Naiche. Interview with ? Unpublished. Author's collection.

Searcy Hospital, Mount Vernon, Ala. Chiricahua Apache Collection.

Shapard, John. Unpublished manuscript.

United States Army Field Artillery and Fort Sill Museum, Fort Sill, Okla. Chiricahua Apache Collection.

University of Arizona, Arizona State Museum. Documentary Relations of the Southwest. Collection.

University of Oklahoma. Western History Collections. Jason Betzinez Papers.

Yale University. Beinecke Library. Richard Henry Pratt Papers.

Books

Adams, David Wallace. *Education for Extinction: American Indians and the Boarding School Experience, 1875–1928.* Lawrence: University of Kansas Press, 1991.

Anderson, Gary Clayton. *The Indian Southwest 1580–1830: Ethnogenesis and Reinvention.* Norman: University of Oklahoma Press, 1999.

Ball, Eve. *Indeh: An Apache Odyssey.* Provo, Utah: Brigham Young University Press, 1980.

———. *In the Days of Victorio: Recollections of a Warm Springs Apache.* Tucson: University of Arizona Press, 1981.

Barrett, S. M., ed. *Geronimo: His Own Story.* New York: Ballantine Books, 1970.

Bearss, Edwin C. *Historical Structure Report: Fort Pickens. Historical Data Section, 1821–1895. Gulf Islands National Seashore, Florida-Mississippi.* Washington, D.C.: U.S. Department of the Interior, Historical Preservation Division, Denver Service Center, National Park Service, n.d.

Betzinez, Jason, with Wilbur Sturtevant Nye. *I Fought with Geronimo.* Lincoln: University of Nebraska Press, 1987. Reprinted by arrangement with Stackpole Books.

Bourke, John G. *The Medicine Men of the Apache.* Ninth Annual Report of the Bureau of Ethnology to the Secretary of the Smithsonian Institution, 1887–1888. Washington, D.C.: U.S. Government Printing Office, 1892.

———. *On the Border with Crook.* Lincoln: University of Nebraska Press, 1971.

———. *Apache Medicine Men.* New York: Dover Publications, 1993. (An unabridged replication of an accompanying paper, "The Medicine Men of the Apache" [original pp. 443–603] in the *Ninth Annual Report of the Bureau of Ethnology to the Secretary of the Smithsonian Institution, 1887–88,* as originally published by the U.S. Government Printing Office, Washington, D.C., in 1892.

———. "Notes upon the Religion of the Apache Indians." In *Apache Medicine Men.* New York: Dover Publications, 1993. (An unabridged replication of an accompanying paper, "The Medicine-Men of the Apache" [original pp. 443–603] in the *Ninth Annual Report of the Bureau of Ethnology to the Secretary of the Smithsonian Institution, 1887–88,* as originally published by the U.S. Government Printing Office, Washington, D.C., in 1892.)

Boyer, L. Bryce. "Folk Psychiatry of the Apaches of the Mescalero Indian Reservation." In *Magic, Faith, and Healing: Studies in Primitive Psychiatry Today.* Edited by Ari Kiev. New York: Free Press, 1964.

Chilton, Bruce. *Rabbi Jesus: An Intimate Biography.* New York: Doubleday, 2000.

Clendinnen, Inga. *Ambivalent Conquests: Maya and Spaniard in Yucatan, 1517–1570.* London: Cambridge University Press, 1987.

Cole, D. C. *The Chiricahua Apache, 1846–1876: From War to Reservation.* Albuquerque: University of New Mexico Press, 1988.

Cortés, José. *Views from the Apache Frontier: Report on the Northern Provinces of New Spain.* Edited by Elizabeth A. H. John, translated by John Wheat. Norman: University of Oklahoma Press, 1989.

Crossen, John Dominic. *Jesus: A Revolutionary Biography.* San Francisco: Harper San Francisco, 1994.

Cruikshank, Julia. "Oral History, Narrative Strategies, and Native American Historiography." In *Clearing a Path: Theorizing the Past in Native American Studies.* Edited by Nancy Shoemaker. New York: Routledge, 2002, 1–27.

Crumrine, N. Ross and Phil C. Weigand, ed. *Ejidos and Regions of Refuge in Northwestern Mexico.* Tucson: Anthropological Papers of the University of Arizona, no. 46, 85–94, 1987.

Cutter, Donald C., and Iris Engstrand. *Quest for Empire: Spanish Settlement in the Southwest.* Golden, Colo.: Fulcrum Publishing, 1996.

Debo, Angie. *Geronimo: The Man, His Time, His Place.* Norman: University of Oklahoma Press, 1976.

Deeds, Susan M. "Indigenous Responses to Mission Settlement in Nueva Vizcaya." In *Jesuit Encounters in the New World: Jesuit Chroniclers, Geographers, Educators and Missionaries in the Americas, 1549–1767.* Edited by Joseph A. Gagliano and Charles E. Ronan, S.J. Rome: Institutum Historicum S.I., 1997.

DeJong, Gerald F. *The Dutch Reformed Church in the American Colonies.* Grand Rapids, Mich.: Wm. B. Eerdmans Publishing Co., 1978.

Emerson, Dorothy. *Among the Mescalero Apaches: The Story of Father Albert Braun, O.F.M.* Tucson: University of Arizona Press, 1973.

Farrer, Claire R. *Living Life's Circle: Mescalero Apache Cosmovision.* Albuquerque: University of New Mexico Press, 1991.

———. *Thunder Rides a Black Horse: Mescalero Apaches and the Mythic Present.* Prospect Heights, Ill.: Waveland Press, 1994.

Faulk, Odie B. "The Presidio: Fortress or Farce?" In *New Spain's Far Northern Frontier: Essays on Spain in the American West 1540–1821.* Edited by David J. Weber. Albuquerque: University of New Mexico Press, 1979.

Favata, Martin A., and José B. Fernandez. *The Account: Álvar Núñez Cabeza de Vaca's Relación.* Houston, Tex.: Arte Público Press, 1993.

Forbes, Jack D. *Apache, Navaho and Spaniard.* Norman: University of Oklahoma Press, 1960.

Fritz, Dr. Henry E. *The Movement for Indian Assimilation, 1860–1890.* Philadelphia: University of Pennsylvania Press, 1963.

Gagliano, Joseph A., and Charles E. Ronan, S.J., eds. *Jesuit Encounters in the New World: Jesuit Chroniclers, Geographers, Educators and Missionaries in the Americas, 1549–1767.* Rome: Institutum Historicum S.I., 1997.

Griffen, William B. *Indian Assimilation in the Franciscan Area of Nueva Vizcaya.* Tucson: University of Arizona Press, 1979.

———. *Apaches at War and Peace: The Janos Presidio, 1750–1858.* Albuquerque: University of New Mexico Press, 1988.

Griffiths, Nicholas. Introduction to *Spiritual Encounters: Interactions Between Christianity and Native Religions in Colonial America.* Edited by Nicholas Griffiths and Fernando Cervantes. Birmingham, U.K.: University of Birmingham Press, 1999.

———, and Fernando Cervantes, eds. *Spiritual Encounters: Interactions Between Christianity and Native Religions in Colonial America.* Birmingham, U.K.: University of Birmingham Press, 1999.

Gutiérrez, Ramón A. *When Jesus Came the Corn Mothers Went Away: Marriage, Sexuality, and Power in New Mexico, 1500–1846.* Stanford, Calif.: Stanford University Press, 1991.

Guy, Donna J., and Thomas E. Sheridan. *Contested Ground: Comparative Frontiers on the Northern and Southern Edges of the Spanish Empire.* Tucson: University of Arizona Press, 1998.

Hall, Thomas D. *Social Change in the Southwest, 1350–1880.* Lawrence: University of Kansas Press, 1989.

Hatfield, Shelly Bowen. *Chasing Shadows: Apaches and Yaquis Along the United States–Mexico Border, 1876–1911.* Albuquerque: University of New Mexico Press, 1998.

Hefner, Robert W., ed. *Conversion to Christianity: Historical and Anthropological Perspectives on a Great Transformation.* Berkeley: University of California Press, 1993.

Hoijer, Harry. *Chiricahua and Mescalero Apache Texts.* With ethnological notes by Morris E. Opler. University of Chicago Publications in Anthropology. Chicago: University of Chicago Press, 1938.

Jackson, Robert H. *Indian Population Decline: The Missions of Northwestern New Spain, 1687–1840.* Albuquerque: University of New Mexico Press, 1994.

Jacobs, Adrian. "The Meeting of the Two Ways." In *Native and Christian: Indigenous Voices on Religious Identity in the United States and Canada.* Edited by James Treat. New York: Routledge, 1996.

John, Elizabeth A. H. *Storms Brewed in Other Men's Worlds: The Confrontation of Indians, Spanish, and French in the Southwest, 1540–1795.* Lincoln: University of Nebraska Press, 1975.

Kessell, John L. *Friars, Soldiers, and Reformers: Hispanic Arizona and the Sonora Mission Frontier, 1767–1856.* Tucson: University of Arizona Press, 1976.

———. Spain in the Southwest: A Narrative History of Colonial New Mexico, Arizona, Texas, and California. Norman: University of Oklahoma Press, 2002.

Kidwell, Clara Sue. *Choctaws and Missionaries in Mississippi, 1818–1918.* Norman: University of Oklahoma Press, 1995.

———, Homer Noley, and George E. "Tink" Tinker. *A Native American Theology.* Maryknoll, New York: Orbis Books, 2001.

Kiev, Ari. *Magic, Faith, and Healing: Studies in Primitive Psychiatry Today.* New York: Free Press, 1964.

Kluckholn, Clyde, and Dorothea Leighton. *The Navajo.* Garden City, N.Y.: Doubleday & Company, 1962.

Little, Sister Juanita, O.S.F. "The Story and Faith Journey of a Native Catechist." In *Native and Christian: Indigenous Voices on Religious Identity in the United States and Canada.* Edited by James Treat. New York: Routledge, 1996.

McCarty, Kieran, O.F.M. *Desert Documentary: The Spanish Years, 1767–1821*. Tucson: Arizona Historical Society, 1976.

———. *A Frontier Documentary: Sonora and Tucson, 1821–1848*. Tucson: University of Arizona Press, 1997.

———. *A Spanish Frontier in the Enlightened Age: Franciscan Beginnings in Sonora and Arizona, 1767–1770*. Washington, D.C.: Academy of American Franciscan History, 1981.

McDermott, John D. *A Guide to the Indian Wars of the West*. Lincoln: University of Nebraska Press, 1998.

Manje, Juan Mateo. *Luz de Tierra Incognita: Unknown Arizona and Sonora 1693–1701*. Translated by Harry J. Karns. Tucson: Arizona Silhouettes, 1954.

Matson, Daniel S., and Bernard L. Fontana, trans. and ed. *Friar Bringas Reports to the King: Methods of Indoctrination on the Frontier of New Spain, 1796–97*. By Diego Miguel Bringas de Manzaneda y Encinas. Tucson: University of Arizona Press, 1977.

Memorials and Affidavits Showing Outrages Perpetrated by the Apache Indians in the Territory of Arizona during the Years 1869 and 1870. San Francisco: Francis & Valentine, 1871.

Moorhead, Max. *The Apache Frontier: Jacobo Ugarte and Spanish-Indian Relations in Northern New Spain, 1769–91*. Norman: University of Oklahoma Press, 1968.

Murray, David. "Spreading the Word: Missionaries, Conversion, and Circulation in the Northeast." In *Spiritual Encounters: Interactions between Christianity and Native Religions in Colonial America*. Edited by Nicholas Griffiths and Fernando Cervantes. Birmingham, UK: University of Birmingham Press, 1999.

Nentvig, Juan, S.J. *Rudo Ensayo: A Description of Sonora and Arizona in 1764*. Translated by Alberto Francisco Pradeau and Robert R. Rasmussen. Tucson: University of Arizona Press, 1980.

Och, Joseph, S.J. *Missionary in Sonora: The Travel Reports of Joseph Och, S.J., 1755–1767*. Translated by Theodore Treutlein. San Francisco: California Historical Society, 1965.

Officer, James. *Hispanic Arizona, 1536–1856*. Tucson: University of Arizona Press, 1987.

Opler, Morris. "Chiricahua Social Organization." In *Social Anthropology of North American Tribes*. Edited by Fred Eggan. Chicago: University of Chicago Press, 1937.

———. *Myths and Tales of the Chiricahua Apache Indians*. Lincoln: University of Nebraska Press, 1994.

———. *An Apache Life-way: The Economic, Social, & Religious Institutions of the Chiricahua Indians*. Lincoln: University of Nebraska Press, 1996.

Ove, Reverend Robert S., and H. Henrietta Stockel. *Geronimo's Kids: A Teacher's Lessons on the Apache Reservation*. College Station: Texas A&M University Press, 1997.

Page, Elizabeth M. *In Camp and Tepee: An Indian Mission Story*. New York: Board of Publication and Bible-School Work of the Reformed Church in America, 1915.

Perez de Ribas, Andres. *History of the Triumphs of Our Holy Faith Amongst the Most Barbarous and Fierce Peoples of the New World.* English trans. based on the 1645 original by Daniel T. Reff, Maureen Ahearn, and Richard K. Danford. Annotated and with a critical introduction by Daniel T. Reff. Tucson: University of Arizona Press, 1999.

Pfefferkorn, Ignaz. *Sonora: A Description of the Province.* Translated by Theodore E. Treutlein. Tucson: University of Arizona Press, 1989.

Polzer, Charles W., S.J. *Rules and Precepts of the Jesuit Missions of Northwestern New Spain.* Tucson: University of Arizona Press, 1976.

Pratt, Richard Henry. *Battlefield and Classroom: Four Decades with the American Indian, 1867–1904.* Lincoln: University of Nebraska Press, 1987.

Prucha, Francis Paul, S.J. *American Indian Policy in Crisis: Christian Reformers and the Indian, 1865–1900.* Norman: University of Oklahoma Press, 1976.

———. *The Churches and the Indian Schools, 1888–1912.* Lincoln: University of Nebraska, 1979.

———, ed. "Assignment of Indian Agencies to Religious Societies." In *Documents of United States Indian Policy,* 2nd ed., expanded. Lincoln: University of Nebraska Press, 1996.

———, ed. *Documents of United States Indian Policy,* 2nd ed., expanded. Lincoln: University of Nebraska Press, 1996.

———. "Indian Citizenship Act." In *Documents of United States Indian Policy,* 2nd ed., expanded. Lincoln: University of Nebraska Press, 1996.

Radding, Cynthia. *Wandering Peoples: Colonialism, Ethnic Spaces, and Ecological Frontiers in Northwestern Mexico, 1700–1850.* Durham, N.C.: Duke University Press, 1997.

———. "Cultural Boundaries Between Adaptation and Defiance: The Mission Communities of Northwestern New Spain." In *Spiritual Encounters: Interactions between Christianity and Native Religions in Colonial America.* Edited by Nicholas Griffiths and Fernando Cervantes. Birmingham, U.K.: University of Birmingham Press, 1999.

Reff, Daniel T. *Disease, Depopulation, and Culture Change in Northwestern New Spain, 1518–1764.* Salt Lake City: University of Utah Press, 1991.

———. "Old World Diseases and the Dynamics of Indian and Jesuit Relations in Northwestern New Spain, 1520–1660." In *Ejidos and Regions of Refuge in Northwestern Mexico.* Edited by N. Ross Crumrine. Tucson: Anthropological Papers of the University of Arizona, no. 46, 85–94, 1987.

———. Critical introduction to *History of the Triumphs of Our Holy Faith Amongst the Most Barbarous and Fierce Peoples of the New World,* Andres Perez de Ribas. English translation based on the 1645 original by Daniel T. Reff, Maureen Ahearn, and Richard K. Danford. Annotated by Daniel T. Reff. Tucson: University of Arizona Press, 1999.

Ricard, Robert. *The Spiritual Conquest of Mexico: An Essay on the Apostolate and the Evangelizing Methods of the Mendicant Orders in New Spain: 1523–1572.* Translated by Lesley Byrd Simpson. Berkeley: University of California Press, 1966.

Schultz, Jack. *The Seminole Baptist Churches of Oklahoma: Maintaining a Traditional Community.* Norman: University of Oklahoma Press, 1999.

Shoemaker, Nancy, ed. *Clearing a Path: Theorizing the Past in Native American Studies.* New York: Routledge, 2002.

Skinner, Woodward B. *The Apache Rock Crumbles: The Captivity of Geronimo's People.* Pensacola, Fla.: Skinner Publcations, 1987.

Spicer, Edward H. *Cycles of Conquest: The Impact of Spain, Mexico, and the United States on the Indians of the Southwest, 1533–1960.* Tucson: University of Arizona Press, 1962.

Stockel, H. Henrietta. *Women of the Apache Nation: Voices of Truth.* Reno: University of Nevada Press, 1991.

———. *Survival of the Spirit: Chiricahua Apaches in Captivity.* Reno: University of Nevada Press, 1993.

———. *Chiricahua Apache Women and Children: Safekeepers of the Heritage.* College Station: Texas A&M University Press, 2000.

Sweeney, Edwin R. *Cochise: Chiricahua Apache Chief.* Norman: University of Oklahoma Press, 1991.

Tatum, Lawrie. *Our Red Brothers and the Peace Policy of President Ulysses S. Grant.* Lincoln: University of Nebraska Press, 1970.

Thrapp, Dan L. *The Conquest of Apacheria.* Norman: University of Oklahoma Press, 1967.

———. *Victorio and the Mimbres Apaches.* Norman: University of Oklahoma Press, 1974.

———. *Encyclopedia of Frontier Biography.* Vols. I and II. Lincoln: University of Nebraska Press in association with The Arthur H. Clark Company, 1988.

Tinker, George. "Jesus, Corn Mother, and Conquest: Christology and Colonialism." In *Unforgotten Gods: Native American Religious Identity.* Edited by Jace Weaver. Orbis Books: Maryknoll, N.Y., 1998, 137.

Todorov, Tzvetan. *The Conquest of America: The Question of the Other.* Translated by Richard Howard. Norman: University of Oklahoma Press, 1999.

Treat, James, ed. *Native and Christian: Indigenous Voices on Religious History in the United States and Canada.* New York: Routledge, 1996.

Turcheneske, John Anthony, Jr. *The Chiricahua Apache Prisoners of War: Fort Sill 1894–1914.* Niwot: University Press of Colorado, 1997.

Utley, Robert, ed. *Encyclopedia of the American West.* New York: Wings Books, 1997.

Weaver, Jace, ed. *Unforgotten Gods: Native American Religious Identity.* Maryknoll, N.Y.: Orbis Books, 1998.

Weber, David J. *The Spanish Frontier in North America.* New Haven, Conn.: Yale University Press, 1992.

———. *The Mexican Frontier 1821–1846: The American Southwest Under Mexico.* Albuquerque: University of New Mexico Press, 1997.

———, ed. *New Spain's Far Northern Frontier: Essays on Spain in the American West 1540–1821.* Albuquerque: University of New Mexico Press, 1979.

Articles

Arbelaez, Maria Soledad. "The Sonoran Missions and Indian Raids of the Eighteenth Century." *Journal of the Southwest* 33, no. 3 (autumn 1991): 366–85.

Archer, Christon I. "The Deportation of Barbarian Indians from the Internal Provinces of New Spain, 1789–1810." *The Americas* (January 1973): 376–85.

Axtell, James. "Some Thoughts on the Ethnohistory of the Missions." *Ethnohistory* 29, no. 1 (1982): 35–41.

Ball, Eve. "St. Joseph's Mission at Mescalero." *New Mexico Magazine* (February 1981): 45–50.

Basso, Keith H. "The Gift of Changing Woman." Smithsonian Institution Anthropological Papers, no. 76. *Bureau of American Ethnology Bulletin* 196 (1966): 119–72.

Bolton, Herbert E. "The Black Robes of New Spain." *Catholic Historical Review* 21 (1935): 257–82.

Bourke, John G. "Notes on Apache Mythology." *Journal of the American Folklore Society* 3 (April–June 1890): 209–12.

Boyer, L. Bryce. "Further Remarks Concerning Shamans and Shamanism." *The Israel Annals of Psychiatry and Related Disciplines* 2, no. 2 (October 1964): 235–57.

Caywood, Louis. "The Spanish Missions of Northwestern New Spain: Jesuit Period— 1687–1767." *The Kiva* 5, no. 2 (November 1939): 5–8.

Clendinnen, Inga. "Disciplining the Indians: Franciscan Ideology and Missionary Violence in Sixteenth-Century Yucatan." *Past and Present* 94 (1982): 27–48.

Davis, Anne Pence. "Apache Debs." *New Mexico Magazine* (April 1937): 10–11, 40.

Farrer, Claire R., and Bernard Second. "Coming of Age: Mescalero Maidens Graduate to Womanhood." *New Mexico Magazine* (July 1989): 50–59.

Fontana, Bernard. "Biography of a Desert Church: The Story of Mission San Xavier del Bac." *The Smoke Signal* (spring 1996): 1–68.

Griffen, William B. "Problems in the Study of Apaches and Other Indians in Chihuahua and Southern New Mexico during the Spanish and Mexican Periods." *The Kiva* 50, nos. 2–3 (1985): 139–51.

Harper, Richard H. "The Missionary Work of the Reformed (Dutch) Church in America, in Oklahoma. Part II: Comanches and Apaches." *Chronicles of Oklahoma* 18, no. 4 (December 1940): 383–47.

Illick, Joseph E. "Some of Our Best Indians Are Friends . . . Quaker Attitudes and Actions Regarding the Western Indians During the Grant Administration." *Western Historical Quarterly* 2 (July 1971): 283–94.

Keller, Robert. "Christian Indian Missions and the American Frontier." *American Indian Journal* 5 (April 1979): 19–29.

———. "Church Joins State to Civilize Indians, 1776–1869." *American Indian Journal* 5 (July 1979): 7–16.

Kessell, John. "Anza Damns the Missions: A Spanish Soldier's Criticism of Indian Policy." *Journal of Arizona History* 13 (1972): 53–63.

———. "Friars versus Bureaucrats: The Mission as a Threatened Institution on the

Arizona-Sonora Frontier, 1767–1842." *Western Historical Quarterly* (April 1974): 151–62.

Liss, Peggy K. "Jesuit Contributions to the Ideology of Spanish Empire in Mexico: Part I: The Spanish Imperial Ideology and the Establishment of the Jesuits within Mexican Society." *The Americas* (January 1973): 314–33.

Matson, Daniel S., and Albert H. Schroeder, eds. "Cordero's Description of the Apache—1796." *New Mexico Historical Review* 32 (October 1957): 335–37.

Nicholas, Dan. "Mescalero Apache Girls' Puberty Ceremony." *El Palacio* 46, no. 9 (September 1939): 194–204.

Opler, Morris. "The Concept of Supernatural Power among the Chiricahua and Mescalero Apaches." *American Anthropologist* 37, no. 1 (January–March 1935): 65–70.

———. "Chiricahua Apache Material Relating to Sorcery." *Primitive Man* 19 (1946): 81–92.

———. "Reaction to Death Among the Mescalero Apache." *Southwest Journal of Anthropology* 2, no. 4 (1946): 454–67.

———. "Western Apache and Kiowa Apache Materials Relating to Ceremonial Payment." *Ethnology* 8, no. 1 (January 1969): 22–24.

Park, Joseph F. "Spanish Indian Policy in Northern Mexico, 1765–1810." *Plains Anthropologist* 25, no. 90 (1980): 325–44.

Radding de Murrieta, Cynthia. "The Function of the Market in Changing Economic Structures in the Mission Communities of Pimeria Alta, 1768–1821." *The Americas* 34 (1977): 155–69.

Sauer, Carl. "A Spanish Expedition into the Arizona *Apacheria*, 1784." *Arizona Historical Review* 6, no. 1 (1935): 3–13.

Shepard, Sophie. *Lend a Hand.* January (1890): 3742, March (1890): 163–66, May (1890): 333–37.

Stevens, Robert C. "The Apache Menace in Sonora, 1831–1849." *Arizona and the West* 6 (autumn 1964): 211–22.

Stockel, H. Henrietta. "A Good Day to Die: Historical Burial Customs of Western American Natives." *Old West* (summer 1999): 36–41.

Terry, Frank. "Naming the Indians." *American Monthly Review of Reviews* 15 (March 1897): 301–7. Electronic Text Center, University of Virginia Library, 1995.

Trennert, Robert A. "Educating Indian Girls at Nonreservation Boarding Schools, 1878–1920." *Western Historical Quarterly* 13, no. 3 (July 1982): 271–90.

———. "From Carlisle to Phoenix: The Rise and Fall of the Indian Outing System, 1878–1930." *Pacific Historical Review* 52, no. 3 (August 1983): 267–91.

Treutlein, Theodore E. "Jesuit Travel to New Spain, 1678–1756." *Mid-America* (April 1937): 104–23.

———. "The Jesuit Missionary in the Role of Physician." *Mid-America* (April 1940): 120–41.

Turcheneske, John Anthony, Jr. "The United States Congress and the Release of the Apache Prisoners of War at Fort Sill." *Chronicles of Oklahoma* 54 (summer 1976): 199–226.

———. "Disaster at White Tail: The Fort Sill Apaches' First Ten Years at Mescalero, 1913–1923." *New Mexico Historical Review* 53, no. 2 (April 1978): 109–32.

Wheatley, Richard. "The Caged Tigers of Santa Rosa." *Cosmopolitan Magazine*, August 1889.

Whiting, Alfred F., ed. "The Tumacacori Census of 1796." *The Kiva* 19 (1953): 1–12.

Interviews and Conversations

Albert, Sister Mary. Telephone conversation with author, St. Augustine, Fla., 5 July 1991.

Anonymous. Interview with Teresa Pijoan, October 1989.

Botenhagen, Fr. Paul. Conversation with author at St. Joseph's Mission Church, Mescalero Apache Reservation, 24 March 2000.

Capell, Arthur. Interview with author at Searcy Hospital, Mount Vernon, Ala., 24 June 1991.

Cleghorn, Mildred Imach. Interview with author at Cleghorn's home in Apache, Oklahoma, 8 August 1989 and conversation with author in Apache, Oklahoma, September 1993.

Darrow, Ruey. Conversations with author in Phoenix, Ariz., May 1991, and at author's home on 8 January 2002.

Haozous, Blossom. Interview with Pat O'Brien, 22 July 1976.

Howley, Patric. Telephone conversation with author, 27 August 1999.

Jones, Belinda. Interview with author at Searcy Hospital, Mount Vernon, Ala., 24 June 1991.

Johze, Benedict, Jr. Interview with author at Fort Sill Chiricahua/Warm Springs Apache Tribal Complex in Apache, Oklahoma, 17 September 1993.

Kanseah, Berle. Interview with author on the Mescalero Apache Reservation, 19 November 1991.

Kanseah, Kathleen. Conversation with author on the Mescalero Apache Reservation, 4 July 1999.

Kazhe, Dorcie. Interview with Dianne Stallings of *Ruidoso News*, 5 July 1993.

Landis, Barbara. E-mail communication with author, 17 June 1998.

Little, Sister Juanita. Conversation with author at St. Joseph's Mission, Mescalero Apache Reservation, August 1993.

McCarty, Kieran, O.F.M. Interviews with author at San Xavier del Bac Mission, 5 January 1999, 12 January 1999, 26 January 1999.

Ortega, Paul. Interviews with author at the University of New Mexico Health Sciences Center Library, 19 July 1994, 18 October 1994, and 16 January 1995.

Ove, Reverend Robert S. E-mail communications, 12 June 1999, 16 June 1999, 17 June 1999, 18 June 1999.

Polzer, Charles, S.J. Interview with author, Arizona State Museum, Tucson, 27 January 1999, and telephone conversation 10 June 2000.

Schut, Reverend Robert. Interview with author, 21 March 1989.

Skinner, Woodward B. Conversation with author, Gulf Breeze, Fla., 21 June 1991.

Spearman, Ruth Keanie. Interviews with author in Albuquerque, N.Mex., 23 April 1994, and El Paso, Tex., 11 March 2000.

Dissertations

Coppersmith, Clifford Patrick. "Cultural Survival and a Native American Community: The Chiricahua and Warm Springs Apaches in Oklahoma, 1913–1996." Ph.D. diss., Oklahoma State University, 1996.
Deeds, Susan. "Rendering Unto Caesar: The Secularization of Jesuit Missions in Mid-Eighteenth Century Durango." Ph.D. diss., University of Arizona, 1981.
McCarty, Kieran, O.F.M. "Franciscan Beginnings on the Arizona-Sonora Desert, 1767–1770." Ph.D. diss., Catholic University of America, 1973.
Polzer, Charles William, S.J. "The Evolution of the Jesuit Mission System in Northern New Spain, 1600–1767." Ph.D. diss., University of Arizona, 1972.

Newspapers

Albuquerque Journal, 8 October 2001.
Carlisle Arrow, 9 March 1905.
The Indian Helper, 16 September 1898, 23 September 1898, 7 October 1898, 14 October 1898, 28 October 1898, 2 December 1898, 9 December 1898, 16 December 1898.
Pensacola Commercial, 5 April 1887.
The Pensacolian, 11 June 1887.
The Salt Lake Tribune, 29 July 2001.

Miscellaneous

Christmas card, Searcy Hospital, 1989.
Hospers, Hendrina. "The Mission Field XXIII." Report published monthly for the Boards of the Reformed Church in America, June 1910.
Landis, Barbara. "Carlisle Indian Industrial School History." Electronic publication at http://home.epix.net/~landis/histry.html.
News release on tree ring data, University of Arkansas, 7 February 2000.
Polzer, Charles, S.J. "Kino in Mexico." Lecture at Sierra Lutheran Church, Sierra Vista, Ariz., 14 February 2001.
Roe, Walter. "The Mission Field XXIV." Report published monthly for the Boards of the Reformed Church in America, 7–11 September 1911.
Skinner, Woodward B. *Geronimo at Fort Pickens*. Brochure, 1981.
Stevenson, Michael. www.southwestfrontiers.org. Site on the early history of the American Southwest and northern Mexico.

SECONDARY SOURCES

Manuscript Materials, Unpublished Documents, Collections

Arizona Historical Society. Gatewood Collection.
Ferg, Alan. "An Introduction to Chiricahua and Mescalero Apache Pottery." Unpublished. Author's collection.
Merrill, William L. "The Political Economy of Raiding: Nueva Vizcaya in the Late Colonial Period," n.d. Unpublished. Author's collection.
Oklahoma Historical Society, Oklahoma City, Okla. Indian-Pioneer Histories Collection.

Books

Bolton, Herbert E. *Rim of Christendom: A Biography of Eusebio Francisco Kino.* Tucson: University of Arizona Press, 1984.
Broderick, Robert C., and Virginia Broderick (illustrator). *Catholic Encyclopedia.* Nashville, Tenn.: Thomas Nelson Publishers, 1990.
Dawson, Christopher, ed. *Mission to Asia: Narratives and Letters of the Franciscan Missionaries in Mongolia and China in the Thirteenth and Fourteenth Centuries.* New York: Harper and Row, 1966.
DeLoria, Vine, Jr. *Spirit and Reason: A Vine DeLoria, Jr., Reader.* Golden, Colo.: Fulcrum Publishing, 1999.
Griffen, William B. *Indian Assimilation in the Franciscan Area of Nueva Vizcaya.* Anthropological Papers of the University of Arizona, Number 33. Tucson: University of Arizona Press, 1979.
———. "Apache Indians and the Northern Mexican Peace Establishments." In *Southwestern Culture History: Collected Papers of Albert H. Schroeder,* 183–95. Edited by Charles H. Lange. Papers of the Archeological Society of New Mexico 10. Santa Fe, N.Mex.: Ancient City Press, 1985.
Gunnerson, James H. "Southern Athapaskan Archeology." In *Handbook of North American Indians,* vol. 9. Washington, D.C.: Smithsonian Institution Press, 1979.
Hefner, Robert W. "Introduction: World Building and the Rationality of Conversion." In *Conversion to Christianity: Historical and Anthropological Perspectives on a Great Transformation.* Edited by Robert W. Hefner. Berkeley: University of California Press, 1993.
Hirschfelder, Arlene, and Paulette Molin. *The Encyclopedia of Native American Religions: An Introduction.* New York: Facts on File, 1962.
Hultkrantz, Ake. *The Religions of the American Indians.* Translated by Monica Setterwall. Berkeley: University of California Press, 1979.
———. *Native Religions of North America: The Power of Visions and Fertility.* San Francisco: HarperCollins, 1987.

Jones, Kristine L. "Comparative Raiding Economies: North and South." In *Contested Ground: Comparative Frontiers on the Northern and Southern Edges of the Spanish Empire*. Edited by Donna J. Guy and Thomas E. Sheridan. Tucson: University of Arizona Press, 1998.

Kessell, John L. *Mission of Sorrows; Jesuit Guevavi and the Pimas 1691–1767*. Tucson: University of Arizona Press, 1970.

Lamar, Howard, ed. *The New Encyclopedia of the American West*. New Haven, Conn.: Yale University Press, 1998.

Marks, Geoffrey, and William K. Beatty. *Epidemics*. New York: Charles Scribner's Sons, 1976.

Merrill, William L. "Cultural Creativity and Raiding Bands." In *Violence, Resistance, and Survival in the Americas: Native Americans and the Legacy of Conquest*. Edited by William B. Taylor and Franklin Pease G. Y. Washington, D.C.: Smithsonian Institution Press, 1994.

Nye, Colonel W. S. *Carbine & Lance: The Story of Old Fort Sill*. Norman: University of Oklahoma Press, 1988.

Officer, James, Mardith Schuetz-Miller, and Bernard L. Fontana, eds. *The Pimeria Alta: Missions & More*. Tucson, Ariz.: Southwestern Mission Research Center, 1996.

Parsons, Francis B. *Early 17th Century Missions of the Southwest*. Tucson, Ariz.: D. S. King, 1975.

Pease G. Y., Franklin. "Spanish and Andean Perceptions of the Other in the Conquest of the Andes." In *Violence, Resistance, and Survival in the Americas: Native Americans and the Legacy of Conquest*. Edited by William B. Taylor and Franklin Pease G. Y. Washington, D.C.: Smithsonian Institution Press, 1994.

Perry, Richard J. *Apache Reservation: Indigenous Peoples & the American State*. Austin: University of Texas Press, 1993.

Polzer, Charles, S.J. *Kino Guide II*. Tucson: Southwestern Mission Research Center, 1988.

———. *Kino: A Legacy*. Tucson: Jesuit Fathers of Southern Arizona, 1998.

Rand, Jacki Thompson. "Primary Sources: Indian Goods and the History of American Colonialism and the 19th Century Reservation." In *Clearing a Path: Theorizing the Past in Native American Studies*. Edited by Nancy Shoemaker. New York: Routledge, 2002.

Salpointe, Most Rev. J. B., D.D. *Soldiers of the Cross: Notes on the Ecclesiastical History of New Mexico, Arizona and Colorado*. Banning, Calif.: St. Boniface's Industrial School, 1898.

Sweet, David. "The Ibero-American Frontier Mission in Native American History." In *The New Latin American Mission History*. Edited by Erick Langer and Robert H. Jackson. Lincoln: University of Nebraska Press, 1995.

Taylor, William B., and Franklin Pease G. Y., eds. *Violence, Resistance, and Survival in the Americas: Native Americans and the Legacy of Conquest*. Washington, D.C.: Smithsonian Institution Press, 1994.

Turner, Frederick. *Beyond Geography: The Western Spirit Against the Wilderness*. New Brunswick, N.J.: Rutgers University Press, 1983.

Articles

Brinckerhoff, Sidney B. "The Last Days of Spanish Arizona 1786–1821." *Arizona and the West* 9, no. 1 (1967): 5–20.

Caywood, Louis. "The Spanish Missions of Northwestern New Spain: Franciscan Period, 1768–1836." *The Kiva* 6, no. 4 (January 1941): 13–16.

Denker, Debra. "Apache Renaissance Man Taps Deep-Rooted Wisdom." *New Mexico Magazine* (August 1997): 38–43.

Eckhart, George B. "A Guide to the History of the Missions of Sonora, 1614–1826." *Arizona and the West* 2 (1960): 165–83.

Farris, Nancy. "Nucleation and Dispersal in Colonial Yucatan." *Hispanic-American Historical Review* 58 (May 1978): 187–216.

Forbes, Jack D. "Unknown Athapaskans: The Identification of the Jano, Jocome, Jumano, Manso, Suma, and Other Indian Tribes of the Southwest." *Ethnohistory* 6, no. 2 (spring 1959): 97–159.

Freeman, John F. "The Indian Convert: Theme and Variation." *Ethnohistory* 12 (1965): 113–28.

Goodwin, Grenville, and Charles Kaut. "A Native Religious Movement among the White Mountain and Cibecue Apache." *Southwest Journal of Anthropology* 10 (1954): 385–404.

Griffen, William B. "Problems in the Study of Apaches and Other Indians in Chihuahua and Southern New Mexico during the Spanish and Mexican Periods." *The Kiva* 50, nos. 2–3 (1985): 139–51.

———. "The Chiricahua Apache Population Resident at the Janos Presidio, 1792–1858." *Journal of the Southwest* 33 (summer 1991): 151–99.

Haes, Brenda. "Fort Sill, the Chiricahua Apaches and the Government's Promise of Permanent Residence." *Chronicles of Oklahoma* 78, no. 1 (spring 2000): 28–43.

Haozous, Blossom. "A Quarrel between Thunder and Wind." Notes and Documents. *Chronicles of Oklahoma* 41, no. 4 (winter 1963–64): 453.

John, Elizabeth A. H., ed., and John Wheat, trans. "Views from a Desk in Chihuahua: Manuel Merino's Report on Apaches and Neighboring Nations, ca. 1804." *Southwestern Historical Quarterly* 5, no. 2 (1991): 139–75.

LeGrand, James B. "The Changing 'Jesus Road': Protestants Reappraise the American Indian Missions in the 1920s and 1930s." *The Western Historical Quarterly* 27, no. 4 (winter 1996): 479–504.

Martinez, Robert D. "True Witch Tales of Abiquiu." *Tradicion Revista Magazine* excerpt. Online http://www.nmsantos.com, 11 August 2000.

Perry, Richard J. "The Apachean Transition from the Subarctic to the Southwest." *Plains Anthropologist* 25, no. 90 (1980): 279–96.

Pradeau, Alberto Francisco. "Nentuig's 'Description of Sonora.'" *Mid-America* (April 1953): 81–90.

Roe, Walter C. "Apache Prisoners of War." *Southern Workman* (April 1912): 3–12.

Sheridan, Thomas E. "Kino's Unforeseen Legacy: The Material Consequences of Missionization." *The Smoke Signal*. Tucson: Tucson Corral of the Westerners (spring and fall 1988): 151–67.

Treutlein, Theodore E. "The Economic Regime of the Jesuit Missions in the 18th Century." *Pacific Historical Review* 8 (1939): 289–300.
Yellowbird, Michael. "What We Want to Be Called." *American Indian Quarterly* 23, no. 2 (spring 1999): 1–21.

Newspapers

Ruidoso News, 5 July 1993.

Miscellaneous

Carlisle Indian School Catalog, 1912.
"Catholic Encyclopedia online." http://www.newadvent.org.
"History of the Franciscan Movement (4)." http://www.christusrex.org.
Radko, Tom. Personal correspondence with author, 25 April 1991.

INDEX

Note: Page numbers for figures appear in italics.

285n. 13
Ha-o-zinne, *18*, 194
Haozous, Blossom Wratten, 44–45, 185, *185*, 204
Haozous, Sam, 204
Harper, Richard, 207
Hatfield, Shelly, 103–4
hats, religious, 40
Havana, Cuba, 91–93, 281n. 41
Haytennae, *17*
headmen, 58–59, 83, 169, 278n. 29. *See also* leaders
healing, 37, 47–48, 114, 116, 221, 274n. 48
heaven, 34
Heersma, Anna (Mrs. Jason Betzinez), 154, 173, 179, *187*, 249, 252
"The Helper" (West), 159–60
hoddentin, xiv, 27–28, 30–32, 139–40, 273n. 36
Hoijer, Harry, 239, 273n. 36, 274n. 48, 275n. 66
Holy Communion, xiv, 80–81
Holy Spirit, 20
holy water, xiv
homeland. *See* Apacheria
horsemeat, 89
Hospers, Hendrina, 178, *180*, 203–4, 207, 209, 254–55
Howley, Patric, 130
Hugar, Elbys Naiche, 34, 217
humans, status in nature, 13, 19, 30

I Fought with Geronimo (Betzinez), 286n. 33
Ignatius of Loyola, Saint, 53
Imach, Amy Wratten, 185, *185*, 204, 241, 288–89n. 32
Imach, Richard, 241
impregnation by nonmale, nonhuman sources, xiv, 20
incarceration of indigenes, 7; Fort Marion, Fla., 110,

114, 116, 142–43; Fort Pickens, Fla., 119, 123–26; Fort Sill, Okla., 167–71, 209; Mount Vernon, Ala., 126, 128–36, 284n. 43, 286–87nn. 35
inculturation, 270n. 7
Indian agents, 106, 108, 282n. 17
Indian Bureau, 105, 107
The Indian Helper, 157–63
Indian Rights Association, 126, 132–33
Indian Ring, 106
indigenes, definition, xviii
individualization, 144–45
individuals, 3, 52
indoctrination, xix–xx, 7, 49, 74–75, 94, 178–81, 254
infantilization of indigenes, 57
instruction. *See* indoctrination
Instructions of 1786, 79
integration, xx
intermarriage, 83, 179, 210, 222, 224
In the Days of Victorio (Ball), 244
"Into Civilization and Citizenship," 158
Iriarte, Francisco, 97

James, Jewell Praying Wolf, xiii
Jane Francis, Sister, 117
Janos, Chihuahua, 88–96, 98
Jesuits, expulsion from northern Mexico, 70, 85; missions/missionaries, 49, 52–66, 69, *71*–73, 74–75, 255–59, 277–78n. 27; as witches, 4, 64–65
Johze, Benedict, Jr., 173, 204, 242–46
Johze, Mabel, 204
Jones, Belinda, 128–29

Ka-a-ht-eny, Bruce F., 201
Kanseah, Berle, 1, 151
Kanseah, Jasper, Sr., 217
Kanseah, Kathleen, 178
Kaywaykla, Dorothy Naiche, 204, 223
Kaywaykla, James, 118, 150, 152, 204, 210, 286n. 27
Kazhe, Belle, 219
Kazhe, Dorcie, 217
Keanie, Carlos, 179, 204, 247, 250
Kellogg, W. H., 134–35
Ketchum, William H., 213
Kidwell, Clara Sue, xv, xvii–xviii, xxi, 4, 81, 84, 265
Killer-of-Enemies, 27
Kino, Eusebio Francisco, 56–58, 57, 189, 277n. 21
kinship, 70, 93, 267
Kuni. *See* Coonie

labor, forced, 60–61, 84
land, appropriation of, 59, 103–5, 107, 176; fencing of, 169
Landis, Barbara, 158
Langdon, Loomis, 114, 124
language, Chiricahua Apache tongue, 11, 81–82, 109–10, 220–21, 224, 226, 267; Nahuatl, 54; Spanish, 54, 90; translation, 255
laws from Ussen, 10
leaders, 204–5, 217–18. *See also* headmen
life, eternal, 12
lifestyle, return to traditional ways, 169, 176
Lightning, 21
liquor, and indigenes, 84, 162
Little, Sister Juanita, 219, 262–64
Loco, John, *171*, 196
Louisiana Territory, 95
loyalty, compromised, 83, 93

protection from harm, 29–30, 35

Protestantism, 205, 246–53, 267; missionaries, 147, 172. *See also* Dutch Reformed Church; Presbyterians; Quakers

puberty ceremonies, xiv, 40–45, 193–94, 220–21, 253, 267; not held, 224, 226

punishment, of children, 141, 285n. 10; corporal, 52, 59–60, 85, 279n. 1

Putting on Moccasins ceremony, 140

Quakers, 108

Radding, Cynthia, 164, 173

raids, 63–66, 78, 88–89, 98, 102–4, 109

Ramon, 114

rations, 83, 91, 93, 96–97

Raven, Harry, 149

reducción/congregación, 58–59, 169, 181

Reed, Walter, 133, *136*

Reff, Daniel T., 55, 67–69

Reformed Church in America. *See* Dutch Reformed Church

Regimini bull, 53

Reglamento de Presidios, 1772, 69, 86

reincarnation, 12

religion, ancestral. *See* beliefs, traditional

Reno, David, 197

repartimiento, 61

Requerimiento, 55

reservations, 104–5; Mescalero Apache Reservation, 207, 209–11, 267; San Carlos Apache Reservation, 108

resistance. *See* accommodation/resistance

resistant adaptation, 164, 173

rituals, 31. *See also* puberty ceremonies

Roe, Mabel, 178

Roe, Walter C., 175, 178, 195, 209–10

Romero, Oscar, 259–60

Rubi, Marquis de, 69–70

Rubios, Palacios, 55

Russell, Henry E., 210

sage, 29, 35

San Carlos Apache Reservation, 108

sanitation, 5, 92, 190–92, 216, 270n. 12, 271n. 13

San José de Matapé, Sonora, 70

Santa Claus, 134–35

Schut, Robert, 260–61

Scott, Hugh L., 210

Scott, Winfield, 103

Second, Bernard, 220–21

settlement patterns, 5, 53, 88

shamans, 19, 58. *See also* medicine men/women

Shepard, Margaret, 128–29

Shepard, Sophie, 128–29, 133, 135

Sheridan, Philip, 119

Shoemaker, Nancy, xviii

Simmons, Vernon, *214*, 222–23

sin, 81–82, 148–49

Sisters of St. Joseph, 117

slaves, repatriation of, 90. *See also* enslavement

Sluyter, Henry, 207

smallpox, 91, 95

snakes, xiv, 6; taboo against, 19, 125–26

Someruelos, Marques de, 92

"Souls are Houses," 160

Spaniards, cultural domination of, 2, 5–6, 48–49, 53, 55, 95–97, 266

Spanish Expulsion, Decree of, 97, 102

Spanish language, 54, 90

Spearman, Ruth Keanie, 174, 246–53, 247–*48*

spinsterhood, 181

spirituality, xv, 11, 186

St. Joseph's Catholic Mission, *208*, 219, 222, 268

St. Thomas Church, 130

staffs, presented to indigenes, 56

state and church, combined, 107, 117, 123–24

Stephens, Marion E., 132–33

Stevens, Robert, 98

stories, 9; blind man regaining vision, 46; of creation, 9–10, 12–13; crow/cattle, 27–28; giant killers, 20–21; great floods, xiv, 29, 203–4; invented by missionaries, 11–12; lame man walking, 46; man carrying a Bible, 218–19; testing a son, 21; of White Painted Woman, 12–13, 21, 271–72n. 9

"The Story of Water" (Binday), 202–3

submission, pragmatic, 266–67

subsistence, agriculture, 53, 169; hunter-gatherers with a raiding complex, xix, 4, 53. *See also* raids; ranching, 169, 213

sun, symbolism of, 21

surrender, 1886, 7

syncretism, of Christianity and traditional beliefs, 10, 27, 31, 32, 63; dangers of, 271n. 1; definition, xx

table manners, 161–62

taboos against, bears, 125; contact with snakes, 19, 125–26; eating fish, 114; against mentioning the dead, 33–35; owls, 125

tax-paying citizens, creation of, xiv, 5, 49, 73, 91, 98, 101

teaching. *See* indoctrination
Ten Commandments, 10
Ten Haken, Bernice, 219
Ten Haken, Reuben, 218
"The Best We Have,"
    160–61
Thrapp, Dan L., 7
thunder and lightning,
    29–30
Thunder people, 29–30
Tinker, George E., xv,
    xvii–xviii, xxi, 4, 84, 265
Tissnolthos, Wheeler, 217
Tlingits, 99
Toclanny, Siki, *15*
Todorov, Tzvetan, 68
tolerance, religious, 3–4
Toos-Day-Zay, *231*
trade in stolen goods, 88–91
traders, 106
Treaty of Guadalupe
    Hidalgo, 103
Trennert, Robert A., 153
trickery, 87
Trist, Nicholas, 103
Tubac presidio, 78
tuberculosis, 114, 133, 179;
    death from, 151, 154–55,
    161, 169, 176
Turcheneske, John Anthony,
    Jr., 172, 212

Ugarte y Loyola, Jacobo, 85
United States, policy toward

indigenes, 103–5
Ures, Sonora, 54
U.S. War Department, 172
Ussen, homeland selection,
    1, 230–31; laws from,
    10–11; parallels with God,
    xiv, 13, 231, 269(author's
    note)n. 1, 270n. 4;
    personal connection with,
    7, 39; on status of humans
    in nature, 19

visitas, 58
vocational training, 152

warfare, 85, 104, 109
warpath language, 109–10
water, 29
weather as an omen, 30, 53
Weaver, Jace, 3
Weber, David, 5–6, 53, 61,
    102
Wells, Fargo & Company,
    107
West, James H., "The
    Helper," 159–60
Wheatley, Richard, 124–25
White Painted Woman,
    parallels with the Virgin
    Mary, xiv, 20, 205–6; on
    puberty ceremonies, 40;
    stories of, 12–13, 21,
    271–72n. 9; symbolism of,

272n. 10
Whitetail, N. Mex., Dutch
    Reformed Church
    activities, 217–19;
    housing, 211–12, 214–16;
    life at, 219–23
Whitetail Day School,
    students, *213*
Whiting, Alfred, 82
wickiups, *3*, *23*
witchcraft, 35–36, 93–94;
    priests as witches, 4,
    64–65
work ethic, 145
work habits, 87
worship, xxi
Wratten, Amy. *See* Imach,
    Amy Wratten
Wratten, Annie, 134
Wratten, Blossom. *See*
    Haozous, Blossom
    Wratten
Wratten, George, 119, 123,
    127, 133, 135, 156–57
Wright, Frank Hall, 172,
    174–75, 178, 188–89, *189*,
    192, 194

Yastasitasitan-tan-ne, 10–13

Zieh, Viola, 163